MAGENNIS VC

MAGENNIS VC

*The story of Northern Ireland's
only winner of the Victoria Cross*

George Fleming

History
IRELAND

Published by History Ireland Ltd.
PO Box 695, Dublin 8, Ireland

© George Fleming 1998

A catalogue record for this title is available
from the British Library

ISBN 0-9533018-0-X pbk
ISBN 0-9533018-1-8 hbk

Typeset by History Ireland Ltd
Printed in Ireland by ColourBooks, Dublin

Dedication

As with all wars sadness, death and the constant thought of missing loved ones overcomes glory and as one who only served on a submarine in peacetime I would like to begin with a dedication to the brave officers and ratings who lost their lives while serving in submarines during World War II. On 19 January, 1945 Lt.Cdr. H.B. Turner was on his second patrol, laying mines off Penang in the old minelaying submarine *Porpoise*. She was reported missing. Although no official report was given, it was presumed she had been sunk by being bombed by Japanese aircraft. *Porpoise* was the last British submarine lost in World War II. My admiration and deep respect goes to the thirty-nine officers and ratings who lost their lives in X-craft and Chariots 'Special Service'. The officers and ratings who died in our allied American, French, Dutch, Greek, Norwegian, Polish and Russian submarines and finally to over 3,000 officers and ratings who died in the following submarines:(courtesy of the Submarine Museum, Gosport)

H31, H49, Salmon, Seahorse, Shark, Snapper, Spearfish, Starfish, Starlet, Swordfish, Syrtis, Tarpon, Thistle, Umpire, Unbeaten, Undine, Unique, Unity, Untamed, Vandal, Narwhal, Seal, Oxley, Thames, P514, P615, Odin, Grampus, Orpheus, Phoenix, Oswald, Rainbow, Triad, Regulus, Usk, Undaunted, Triton, Catchalot, Union, P32, P33, Tetrarch, Perseus, Triumph, Tempest, P36, P38, P39, Pandora, Upholder, Urge, Olympus, Thorn, Talisman, Utmost, Traveller, P222, P311, P48, Tigris, Thunderbolt, Turbulent, Sahib, Splendid, Regent, Parthian, Saracen, Usurper, Trooper, Simon, Sickle, Stonehenge, Stratagem, Porpoise.

FOR THOSE IN PERIL
by
Bill McGinnes

On through the darkness misty and grey she steams,
Her bridge and sides with keen salt crystals sprayed;
And endless aeons have passed astern it seems
Since she sheltered port her anchor weighed,
To probe with echoes deep beneath the ocean
In ever widening rings, in endless motion.

And dark and sinister shape it lurks unseen
At fifteen fathoms, murky, dank, and chill;
Sent from its lair to wander, vent its spleen
On foe above, to hunt, to maim, to kill;
And now it lies in silent meditiation,
On former triumphs, on future desecration.

But this faint news descending through the gloom?
Oh hated sound! The dread destroyer's screw!
Is this to be their grave? A steel-cased tomb?
These gruesome thoughts assail the hapless crew;
And fear, old ugly tyrant of emotion
Seeks undisputed sway beneath the ocean.

And cunningly arrests the eager pace
Of time, making the fettered moment falter, stare
With hollowed eyes and bloodless tortured face,
As if to mock those matelots, waiting there
With ear-drums tensed to feel the thundrous roar
Of depth charge, challenging the ocean floor.

Come then destruction, bring your swift release;
Depose gaunt fear and set up chaos to reign;
What care they now whose manhood knew no peace
As pressure hull is split and cruel sea gains
Long lusted entry, then with acid mating,
Brings violent birth, the deathly gas creating.

Downward, darkward, silent the sad descent
Through sea, who now triumphant, cares no more;
While high atop recedes in pale lament
The face of light, beneath looms relic-laden shore;
Here in the slime 'twill rest with craft primeval,
Till comes the shock of future great upheaval.

But look! To the sun! How buoyantly she steams,
Her bridge and sides in morning light arrayed;
And happy songs commingle with the dreams
Of home, of sheltered port, of cheerful spread;
While far astern 'neath some bleak shaft of ocean
Is neither dream nor song, just endless motion.

CONTENTS

The Author

George Fleming was born in Bloomfield, East Belfast in 1941. He attended Strandtown
and later Cregagh primary and Holywood Technical College. He left school at fourteen
in 1956 to work in the Belfast shipyard Harland and Wolff to wait until apprenticeship
age of sixteen. His desire to go to sea made him join the Navy at fifteen where he first
attended the Training establishment *Ganges* at Shotley in Suffolk. After finishing one
year training he spent the next ten years serving as an engine room mechanic, at home
and overseas, on board the following: frigates *Llandaff, Yarmouth* and *Lincoln*; the submarines *Sentinel* and *Tabard*; the destroyer *Wakeful*, the survey-ship *Hecla* and
minesweeper *Upton*. In 1969 George left the Royal Navy and went to live in Denmark.
Having worked as a film extra and spending one year as a student at Norgaards Hojskole
(college) in Hadsten, Jutland, he joined the Merchant Navy in 1972. After working over
twenty years at sea, the latter as a second engineer on ships both deep sea, middle and
home trade, George finally came ashore in 1980. He was accepted as a mature student at
the University of Ulster in 1985. He graduated four years later with an honours degree
in fine art and a post graduate diploma in applied art the following year at the age of fifty.

George Fleming is a member of both the Baha'i faith and the Northern Ireland
Inter-Faith Forum. He now lives and works as an artist in Belfast. His first one-person
visual art exhibition 'Echoes' toured Ireland for two and a half years. His next exhibition
launched in January 1996 'All Gods Children' has just finished touring Ireland and
Scotland. This is his first attempt at writing and the research uncovered, he hopes, may
be the catalyst towards a visual art display sometime in the future.

George believes very much in cultural diversity, pluralism, and the equality of sex,
religion and race. These beliefs motivated this study and previous art projects. He
believes his research is artistically and spiritually based. What began as a biography, soon
evolved into a campaign, which changed words into a piece of social sculpture, a memorial to commemorate the last Irishman to be decorated with the highest British award for
valour, the Victoria Cross.

ACKNOWLEDGEMENTS

For information, advice, support and photographs, my thanks to:

Carl Jackson, Chairman HMS *Ganges* Association.

Tony Canavan, formerly editor of *Causeway*,

Patrick McParland, formerly marketing manager, ibid.

Signalman Gus Britton MBE; As a researcher for the Royal Navy Submarine Museum his help was invaluable. He crossed the bar on 21 July '97.

George Malcolmson, Submarine Museum.

Engine Room Artificer Vernon (Ginger) Coles DSM (RN), XE4 Operation Struggle 'cutting cables of Saigon' July 1945, and X24 Operation Guidance 'sinking the *Barnfels Bergen*' April 1944. Shipmate of James Magennis in X-craft.

Lt. Cdr. Ian Fraser VC. DSC. (RNR), XE3, CO Operation Struggle.

Engine Room Artificer Charlie Reed CGM, XE3, Operation Struggle.

Petty Officer William (Nat) Gould VC, HM/SM *Thrasher*, H/SM *Truculent*, Operation Source, Mother boat to X6.

Petty Officer Telegrapher Harold Diggings DSM, MID, (*Ganges* 1932), HM/SM *Regent*, *Takao* and *Ulster*.

Leading Seaman Jim James DSM, gunlayer, HM/SM *Unswerving*.

Stoker Davy Snowball, X25, HMS *Varbell*.

Able Seaman John Clarke (HO), HMS *Bonaventure*.

Chief Stoker Jim Daly, HMS *Cumberland*.

PO SBA JA Smith, HMS *Orion*.

PO William Byres, HMS *Defiance*.

Torpedo Operator Bernard Warwick, HMS *Defiance*, HM/SM *Telemacus*.

Able Seaman Gunner Mick Carroll (*Ganges* 1937), HMS *Kandahar*.

Signalman Stan (Blondie) Millard (*Ganges* 1938), HMS *Kandahar*, crossed the bar 3 July 1997.

Signalman John (Tancy) Lee (*Ganges* 1935), HMS *Kandahar*, HM/SM *Ultor*.

Leading Torpedo Operator Ervine Fleming, HMS *Kandahar*.

Bill McGinnes, brother.

Paul Magennis, son.

Norman Wilson, West Yorkshire HMS *Ganges* Association.

Andy Broadfoot, *Yorkshire Observer*

Tommy Topham MBE, member of Submarine Old Comrades Association, West Riding Branch.

Michael Brooks, No. 12 Irish Area RNA

Dick Lloyd, publishing editor, HMS *Ganges* Association Gazette.

Dave Fletcher, curator Submarine Museum..

George Athroll, curator, Museum, ibid.

John Murphy, former neighbour, Belfast.

Jack Chambers, ibid.

James McIntyre, ibid.

Maureen Bradshaw, ibid.

Stanley McAlinden, ibid.

Robert Morrow, ibid.

Gerry Oates, former pupil of St Finian's School.

Jimmy Webb, ibid.

Robert Taylor, military historian.

Basil McLaughlin, editor, *Andersonstown News*.

Eddie Mc Ilwaine, journalist, *Belfast Telegraph*.

Pamela Mitchell, Gosport.

Colin Burran, Leeds.

Kenneth Anderson, photographer. Newtownabbey, Co. Antrim.

Karen Kenny and other friends for kindly correcting and transcribing all my scribbled notes into this book.

All friends of the Magennis Family: thanks to them all for their letters and support.

Staff and members of the following: The Submarine Old Comrades Association The HMS *Ganges* Association Imperial War Museum Ulster Folk and Transport Museum Royal Navy Submarine Research Museum, Gosport, Hampshire Belfast Central Library Linen Hall Library Belfast

Introduction

James Magennis's story could simply have been told as one of derring-do; undoubtedly his bravery was exceptional. George Fleming has rightly taken on the much more challenging task of telling us the whole story from Magennis's beginnings in the poverty-stricken streets of West Belfast of the 1920s and '30s, his escape to that other world of the Navy–naval life in the late 30s, wartime and the immediate post-war period is vividly portrayed and set against a broader history of the war at sea.

At the centre is Magennis, finding his sea legs, becoming a key operative in the perilous world of midget submarines and emerging, all too briefly, into the limelight as a wartime hero.

It is a tale all the more telling because Fleming, quite apart from making good use of documentary sources, has also used oral recollections extensively. His account has the authenticity given by the men who were there.

Nor does Fleming evade the difficult questions, questions of betrayal. In the post-war era Magennis fell foul of the social prejudices of a new peacetime officer class, and the unbending authoritarianism of the naval system. At home he was doomed by prejudice–the prejudice of a nationalist community that did not want a British war hero in its midst and the prejudice of unionists unprepared to honour a Roman Catholic VC. He died in England in relative poverty and obscurity.

George Fleming has well and truly made the case for remembering him now.

John Gray,
Librarian,
Linen Hall Library, Belfast.

Prologue

The first Royal Navy Victoria Cross to be auctioned by public sale was sold to an anonymous buyer for £31,900 at Sotheby's of London on 3 July 1986. The prized award 'for valour' attracted £10,000 more than the reserve price. A Sotheby's spokesman said at the time, 'it made a good deal more than expected, but estimates are always difficult in a case of something so unique and with such a story'.

James J. Magennis VC was born in Belfast on 27 October 1919. His story is one of poverty, adventure, bravery tinged with sadness and a suspicion of political and religious intrigue. James joined the Royal Navy in 1935 during the Great Depression. He started his career at the famous training establishment for boys entering the Royal Navy, HMS *Ganges* at Shotley, Suffolk. Later he served aboard a post World War I battleship and two cruisers.

The first two years of the World War II saw him serving aboard HMS *Kandahar*, one of the destroyers in the flotilla known as the 'Fighting Fifth' under the command of Lord Louis Mountbatten, commanding the legendary HMS *Kelly*. Early in 1940, *Kelly* was damaged, narrowly avoiding being sunk, during an attack by a German 'E' boat. *Kandahar* towed her sister ship to safety. At the Battle of Crete, HMS *Kelly* was not so lucky and was sunk together with many other ships with great loss of life. On 19 December 1941 HMS *Kandahar* struck a mine and sank off Tripoli. Sixty-seven officers and men lost their lives.

Magennis survived and shortly after being drafted to the submarine service where he later volunteered for the special service X-craft midget submarines. He was one of a successful team of officers and men involved in 'Operation Source' which disabled the German battleship *Tirpitz*, sister ship to the *Bismarck*. Two Victoria Crosses were won that day amongst a number of other awards. Magennis was mentioned in dispatches.

At the end of the European war, Magennis was to become involved in another covert mission directed against the Japanese in the continuing Pacific theatre of war under the command of Admiral Fife, United States Navy. 'Operation Struggle' was another hazardous X-craft mission. XE3 attacked the 10,000 ton heavy Japanese cruiser *Takao* in Singapore harbour on 30th July 1945. Decorations awarded for this attack included the VC for both the commanding officer Lt. Fraser and the diver, Leading Seaman Magennis, the DSO for Lt. Smith and the CGM for ERA Reed.

No fewer than nine VCs were awarded to submarine officers and men in World War II. Magennis worked with three of them.

On his return to Belfast in December 1945 Magennis was treated as a hero. The people of Northern Ireland collected £3,066 as a gift. While other VC winners were to become admirals, Magennis ended his submarine service with twenty-one days detention in the notorious Pompey Detention Quarters in Victoria Barracks, Portsmouth. After leaving the navy in 1949 his return to Belfast was not so joyful. He became a little guy caught in a strange religious and political mind-trap. His son, David, was killed in a road accident in 1952 and shortly afterwards he sold his precious award for just £75 to a local Belfast dealer. The press that some seven years previously had applauded him, now disparaged him. He left Northern Ireland in 1955 to live in a little mining village in Yorkshire called Rossington, where he found employment as an electrician down the local coal mine. Later he moved to Bradford where he lived the rest of his life. He died in Halifax Infirmary on 12 February 1986 aged sixty-six. Shortly after he crossed the bar (died), Bradford City Council and the West Yorkshire Branch of the Submarine Old Comrades Association, erected a memorial plaque inside Bradford Cathedral, to the memory of the last Irishman to win the Victoria Cross.

My inspiration to research a biography of James J. Magennis VC came after I wrote an article 'The Forgotten Hero from West Belfast' in the winter edition 1995 of the cultural traditions' journal, *Causeway*. I followed this with another article 'Ganges personality' in VJ year winter edition 1995 of the *Ganges Association Gazette*. I received a letter of appreciation from Bill McGinnes, his brother:

'When I first read the article I was indeed impressed, not only by the manner in which you put it together but also by the wealth of detail, much of which I was unaware, it contained. So many thanks, George. It is worthy of inclusion in the *Ganges* Mag. Regards, Bill McGinnes.'

I therefore decided Bill's brother James deserved more written about his life and his wartime experiences. So beginning with my own naval history as a boy at HMS *Ganges*, and later service on surface ships and the submarine service, together with having lived most of my life in Belfast, I proceeded to research further. Most of what is in this book has been based on museum references, newspaper cuttings, personal letters, private and public photographs, naval documents, previously published books, and private correspondence between friends and shipmates of the late James Magennis. Some other ex-*Ganges* boys', ex-submariners' and friends experiences have been included to add colour and authenticity to the VC's biography.

There have been numerous historical naval and military books written about World War II. I therefore would request the reader to look more upon this book as a modern social historical biography on James Magennis' life. The story has the unusual politico-religious conjugation, which is part and parcel of the endless conflict and confrontation of Ireland's history.

I commend this book to James Magennis, his brother Bill and his three sons Paul, James and Michael; to the submarine service, and finally to all 200,000 boys and 'hostilities' who were recruits at the shore establishment HMS *Ganges* between the years 1905 - 1976.

Author's note

James was called Jim by his family and friends. In the navy his name was Mick, as it is with many Irishmen who join HM Forces. However when he joined the navy his surname was spelt Magennis. This was unlike his older brother William (Willie or Bill) who joined the Royal Navy in 1934 and was registered in his original surname. There may have been a mistake made on James's entry form and he did not see any reason to change it. The name Magennis is registered for the Victoria Cross, whereas on his birth certificate it is spelt McGinnes. I have therefore used his family name only in the first chapter, and thereafter his better known name, Magennis. Jim's brother was called Willie by his family. Others knew him as Bill, which I intend to use in the book. As chapter one is based on interviews with the author, certain names have been altered out of respect for the feelings of family members still living.

ONE

1919-35
Majorca Street West Belfast

In 1919 William and Mary McGinnes lived at number 4 Majorca Street, a tiny side street running parallel to the main Grosvenor Road. The street was only a few hundred yards from a ten foot high bronze statue of Queen Victoria which still sits at the entrance of the Royal Victoria Hospital. Many of the streets in the area of the Falls and Grosvenor Road had been named after famous battles in the Crimean War; Sevastopol, Inkerman and Balaclava. Lord Raglan even had the honour of a street being named after him. The huge Mulhouse flax mill with its Victorian barrack-like buildings gave its name to Mulhouse Street and dominated these little streets like lord and master. Most of these tiny dwellings had been owned by the mill, and were built to house the workers in the nineteenth century. The Royal Victoria Hospital (named after Queen Victoria) was built at the turn of the century; the mill and surrounding houses being built shortly after the Irish Famine of 1845 to 1849. The old Belfast and district lunatic asylum was situated on the site of the present day hospital.

The crossroads between the Falls Road and the Springfield Road was the centre of activity of West Belfast. The Royal Victoria Hospital was on one corner, Dunville Park on another with St Paul's, the local parish church, facing the hospital across the Falls Road. The Grosvenor Road from the hospital down to the city centre was less than a mile and there were a number of streets and side streets running off the main road. The trams ran up from the city centre on both these main roads. Majorca Street and Mulhouse Street were close to the hospital on the left hand side of the Grosvenor Road going out of town. Beyond the Springfield and Grosvenor Road junctions the future middle and upper Falls and upper Springfield were very much rural in character into the 1930s.

It was 27 October 1919, Mary McGinnes was pregnant. She already had two children. William, (Bill) the older, had been born in Scotland. In four days time it would be his fourth birthday and his tiny sister Peggy who was a weak child was two years old. William, Mary's husband who came from Scotland, was called 'Scotch' by family and friends. Mary's maiden name was Murphy. She originally came from Enniskillen in County Fermanagh, and her friends called her Maisy. When she first married Scotch they lived with his parents in Hamilton, near Glasgow, then moved to Majorca Street, Belfast just after the Great War finished in 1918. Scotch was a musician and at times played his fiddle in the local music halls as well as working part time as a packer in some of the mills. Scotch, as they say in Belfast, 'made the odd bob or two' but it was not enough to keep a wife and two children and another on the way. So the McGinnes family did not have it easy, but then neither did many other people in Majorca Street or the surrounding area. It was one of the poorest parts of town.

It was a cold drizzly Belfast morning, not unusual for that time of year. Around midday Maisy's labour pains came on rapidly and Scotch, who was a bundle of nerves, ran round the corner to fetch the midwife, Miss Glasgow. She lived at number 299, one of the posh houses on the front of the Grosvenor Road. She was a short, plump spinster who delivered all the children in the area and was one of the best loved ladies in the neighbourhood. She could handle most of the problems of childbirth; a doctor was seldom required, if only because of the expense involved. Scotch banged the brass door knocker.

'Oh Miss Glasgow I think Mary's having the wee bairn. Will ye come quickly.'

Miss Glasgow opened the door.

'Will ye calm yerself man dear. Anyone who heard ye would think it was you was having the baby.'

After calming Scotch down, she threw a black shawl over her head and shoulders, lifted the midwife's bag she always kept ready under the stairs and both Scotch and Miss Glasgow hurried round to Majorca Street. Molly McIntyre lived beside Maisy at number eight and was already boiling water and filling the family's tin bath with warm water. She seemed to have a sixth sense that the child was definitely coming this time. It was overdue; four days before there had been a false alarm and with all the fuss and women's talk Scotch's nerves could take no more. He ran out the back door, up the entry, round by the back of the police station, across Roden Street and before you could say 'Jack Robinson' he entered Sally Hannigan's pub in Granville Street.

'A large glass of Red Biddy, Sally dear', Scotch ordered!

He returned home after midnight having settled his nerves with the only medicine he knew could do the trick. He then give his usual manly excuse to his wife.

'A bairn being born is a lassie's job and outside the limitation of my worldly knowledge I only ken how ye put the ball in the back of the net, de ye ken Maisy dear'

Molly had been right, as Mrs Glasgow delivered the child it slipped from her hands and fell into the tin bath of warm water. Miss Glasgow picked him up, laid him on the table, washed him and dried him.

'There isn't as much as a whimper out of him. That boy's going to be a quiet one Maisy dear', said the midwife.

By this time Molly had made Maisy and Scotch a cup of tea, although Scotch would have preferred something stronger. Annie Ferron and some of Maisy's friends from the neighbourhood all came to congratulate the McGinnis's on having their third child.

Paddy McIntyre, Molly's husband, had run up to St Paul's to tell the parish priest, Father Dan Murphy about the birth of Maisy's wee boy. He arrived back to tell them all Father Murphy was on his way. Maisy had the boy in her arms when the priest arrived. He congratulated the McGinnes's and after a cup of tea himself brought out his little book he kept for christenings.

'Well Maisy dear have you decided what you would like to call the boy?'.

'Father, James Joseph–that's what we will call him; don't you agree, Scotch?'

'Sure ye ken rightly; Maisy dear; I always agree with yee.'

'Aye, only when Father Murphy is here, or when you have a few bob to visit Sally Hannigan's, do ye turn the charm on. What do you think Father?'

'Aaah; what two lovely names, straight from the most holy of books; surely with names like that he's famous already.'

THE CHRISTENING AND CELEBRATION

The parish church on the Falls Road, St Paul's, was full of people the Sunday Scotch and Maisy brought their new born son to be christened. But the crowd was not there on the McGinnes family's behalf, as there were four christenings. A couple from the Springfield Road had twin girls who caught all the attention. The first ceremony was the McGinnes's. Scotch was glad, because all the fuss made him nervous and when he was

DUNVILLE PARK AND ROYAL VICTORIA HOSPITAL FALLS RD. BELFAST.

WAG 370

like that, a drink was required; Sally Hannigan's pub was on his mind. Father Daniel Murphy was from the South of Ireland, a plumpish man in his fifties. He had a smile on his face when he intoned, 'In the name of the Father and in the name of the Son and the Holy Ghost, I name this child James Joseph.' There were many candles lit by friends of the family and quickly they left the chapel so that the next ceremony could take place.

That night the family had a small party. After a few stout, a couple of glasses of Red Biddy, Scotch started playing some Scottish and Irish reels on his fiddle. He played better the more he drank. He rolled off a jig or two, saving the hornpipes for later, as he knew his good friend Paddy was fond of sea shanties and the like. Paddy, and a few of Scotch's pals arrived at the celebration with a few bottles of wine and a dozen stout. Molly McIntyre had baked a cake and made some sandwiches, and Annie Ferron from Theodore Street had knitted the wee boy his first navy blue suit with a sailor's collar attached. Paddy had a few jars on him earlier in the day, so he was in a jovial mood and it was not long before he was singing along with Scotch's fiddle tunes and some of his favourite sailor songs.

'This wee lad is going to be a sailor, don't you think so Paddy?'

'Aye! Yer right there Scotch. By the time I'm finished singing he'll either want to go to sea or either he'll be sea sick. Play me my favourite, Scotch, "Over the Sea to Sky". Ye know I loved Bonny Prince Charlie.'

EARLY CHILDHOOD AND PRE-SCHOOL DAYS

In the next couple of years James (Jim as he was called) was to have another sister Rosemary, and brother Anthony who was to be the last of the family. Jimmy McIntyre lives today in Arundel House not far from where the old Majorca Street was. His family lived beside the McGinnes family and he remembers all of them very well:

> There was six or seven years between Bill the oldest and Anthony the youngest. They all grew up very close to one another and most families in the area were large. There were seven in my own family. Times were hard in the 1920s and 30s. Our family was on 'outdoor relief'. My father received twenty-one shillings in chits or coupons to buy food to feed seven of us.

The neighbourhood in West Belfast where Jim and his brothers and sisters were reared, played and attended school was deprived but like children in all back street areas money was not an obstacle to enjoying oneself. They would swing around lampposts, singing local songs such as:

> My Aunt Jane she called me in
> She gave me tea out of her wee tin
> Half a bap with sugar on the top
> And three brandy balls out of her wee shop.

Poverty was endemic throughout Belfast. In 1926, for example, a newspaper reported an application for Outdoor Relief from a man, 'his wife and child [who] were living in one room with seven other persons –men, women and children...Outdoor Relief was refused, but the committee offered infirmary treatment in the Union'.

Playing in Dunville Park across the Grosvenor Road and in the streets and entries adjoining did not require money. Maureen McIntyre and Jim's sisters Peggy and Rosemary played games such as Hop Scotch, Piggy and ball games called Rounders and Queenio; most of the ball games were played off the entry walls. Jim McGinnes, and other boys on the street preferred more adventurous games such as Kick the Bucket, played with an old empty tin, marbles and Blowsies played with cigarette cards which all the boys collected and which was played on window sills.

Mr Robert Morrow, formerly from Symons Street, remembers as a boy

> Chasing the horse-drawn water carts, which was another pastime to while away many a summer's day. The streets became very dusty and the Corporation water carts would go along spraying the streets with water.

It was not until the early 1930s that the cobble streets were covered with cement and flagstones laid on the footpaths. Then new street games arrived: roller skating, cycling, 'Hoop and Cheek' and 'Pirie and Whip'. With the onset of winter the children were able to experience the 'thrills and spills' of sliding on ice. The concreting of roads led to a new fad, 'guiders'. Jim and his brothers built their own from a flat piece of wood, four old pram wheels and a couple of axles. Add a rope for steering and you were in business, racing up and down Majorca Street, taking turns with your pusher to try and beat all comers in good-natured races.

As dusk approached the children on the street would have another happening take place. Robert Morrow remembers:

All the children would follow the Corporation lamp lighters up and down the side streets running off Roden Street. We all wondered how he lit the gas lamps with the long pole he carried. Once the gas mantles became bright we carried on playing games.

HALLOWE'EN AND LOCAL CHARACTERS

The McGinnes's lived in an area where the coal man, rag-and-bone man and the fish man were heard three or four streets away yelling 'Herrings, olay!'. They enjoyed the festivities of Hallowe'en and other holidays such as Easter and Christmas even with very little money. Jimmy McIntyre's older sister Maureen remembers Hallowe'en:

> Bill McGinnes and I had the same birthday 31st October, although I was two years younger and his brother Jim's birthday was the 27th October, so Hallowe'en was a combined birthday party between our two families. We had home baked cakes and ducked for apples and made funny face masks out of cardboard.

Jimmy McIntyre also remembered some of the people who lived in Majorca Street:

> We lived in number eight, the McGinnes's in number four and Mrs Murray the money-lender lived at the bottom in number twenty-four. She had a parrot that used to hang in a cage by the window and her daughter Molly was bedridden. Next door in number twenty-two lived Bulldog Beattie who was one of the area's tough men and Mrs Murray's minder. Mary and Johnny Cunningham lived in number fourteen. Theirs was a mixed marriage. He had been in the army and lost an eye during the Great War at the Battle of the Somme. Mary had four children of her own, but she loved spoiling the kids on the street as well, buying them sweets, gobstoppers and ha'penny lollipops. When she ran out of money she pawned Johnny's glass eye in Welles' pawnshop in Arundel Street on a Monday for half a crown. Johnny's pension came through on Thursday and she retrieved it so he had his glass eye back for the weekend to go to Kelly's, the pub in Granville Street owned by Sally Hannigan.

Jim's two sisters Peggy and Rosemary and Maureen McIntyre (now Mrs Bradshaw living in Blackpool) attended St Vincent's Girls School at Dunlewley Street off the Falls Road. They also attended Sunday School at St Paul's. Father Murphy took the children in the afternoon for Benediction. Maureen remembers all the girls singing, 'We are little Catholic girls and we come from West Belfast; We all go to Benediction and the wind blows up our ass.'

Some of the street traders and local characters brought colour and humour to Majorca Street and the neighbourhood with their eccentric ways. Jimmy Webb remembers Orny Boke dressed up in a long coat and in the company of Blind Dan knocked the doors, begging for coppers. 'Rapper Up' was a woman who rapped windows to get people out of bed in the early hours: for this service she received 3d a week. The rag men, fish sellers, coal men and newspaper boys all had their distinctive calls. One woman who sold wool and thread from a hand cart shouted, 'We're giving them away, with the price never up yet'. The ice cream woman drew attention by banging the tin lid of her wafer box and blowing a little tin horn. One other character whose visit to Majorca Street was always welcome was Maggie Marley. Maggie arrived pushing her well-decorated hand cart on which she had a colourful display of balloons and coloured paper hand streamers which she would give out in exchange for old rags, jam pots or bottles.

Maureen remembers a number of people in the area. Mr McFarlane the coal man and Mr Stewart who came up and down the streets with a donkey and cart selling fire wood and Jody Maginn who sold fish from her cart on Fridays.

> I remember Mary Crawford who lived at number one and then there was Granny Magee who lived at number fifteen. Their family were all pigeon lovers and had a pigeon loft at the back of the house. The rent for all the houses in Majorca Street was five shillings a week whereas in Mulhouse Street which had parlour houses it was seven shillings. We later moved to a house in Mulhouse Street. My mother sold the key for half a crown for number eight Majorca Street. That's what was done in those days.

The houses in both streets had two bedrooms and a small sitting room and the parlour houses in Mulhouse Street had a small porch. A tiny back room at the back was known as a scullery. Toilet facilities were an outside WC. There was no electricity and one water tap. Jimmy Webb, formerly of Raglan Street and a school pal of Jim McGinnes recalls:

> Cooking was done in the front room using an open fire range grate supplemented by a gas ring. Lighting was provided by candles. My

The five McGinnes children in the late 1920s.
(Back row) Bill and Rosemary. *(Front row)* James, Anthony and Peggy

mother and father had ten children, five boys and five girls. One of the boys died of meningitis leaving eleven of us to exist in a tiny home the same size as Jim McGinnes's family in Majorca Street.

The 1920s was a time of great unemployment. There were no social services then and it was quite a task for parents to feed, clothe and rear their families with money so hard to come by. Cotton flour bags sewn together were used as sheets and pillowcases. On top of the bed were multicoloured patchwork quilts made from scraps of material brought home from the mills and clothing factories. In the winter many old coats were piled on the bed for warmth.

FIRST DAY AT ST. FINIAN'S

Jimmy McIntyre's two brothers Eddie and Joci, along with John Murphy and Jim McGinnes and his brothers started attending St Finian's on the Falls Road when they came of school age. It was an all-boys school run by the De La Salle Brothers near Dunville Park. Jimmy started school the same day as Jim McGinnes and remembers it well:

> We first met at what was the first day at school for both of us in 1925 when we were five years old. For the first week we were given sealing wax and sand to play with and after five days of getting used to the place, we started into the serious work of ABCs. Jim and I sat side by side in the classroom and he stood out because he wasn't a chatterbox like the rest of us.

The head teacher was called Brother Joseph and other Brothers were called Wilfred, Cassian, and Dominic. The lay teacher Johnny Blake took the boys for swimming in the Falls Road swimming baths. In his early years Jim started to go to the Falls Road swimming baths after school. He eventually came under the wing of one of the instructors, who saw great potential in his swimming ability. Jimmy Webb remembers:

> Jim never joined us in playing Gaelic football or hurling for the school team and even in the playground while the rest of us were cutting our knees and scraping our elbows, he would stand apart from the boyish pranks and usual rough and tumble that most boys of our age would be involved in. It would not be fair to say however that Jim wasn't sport minded for he practically lived in the swimming baths. He was a tremendous swimmer and perhaps it was because he felt so comfortable in the water that he became a frogman in the navy.

All of the boys were confirmed in St Paul's by Father Murphy when they became eleven. Jimmy Webb recalls: 'We made our first communion and confirmation together. Jim got the name of being a loner but I knew it was just his way.'

SCOTCH LEAVES HOME

Many men from West Belfast travelled to Scotland or England to work. Jim's father (Scotch) had gone to Scotland shortly after Anthony was born. His brother Bill recalls:

> I was about seven when my Dad took me over to live with my grand parents in Hamilton near Glasgow. I stayed for about six months and then my mother came and brought me home. We never heard from

my father again. Like Bonnie Prince Charlie he had done a disappearing act.

In the 1920s and 30s work was scarce all over. Mackie's Textile Machinery Company on the Springfield Road, the docks or going to sea was all that was on offer. In the east of the city the shipyard and the aircraft factory were the two biggest companies but they mostly employed Protestant people who lived on that side of town.

In September 1920, 8,000 Catholic shipyard workers suffered expulsion due to the religious division set up by partition and the new Government of Ireland Act recently passed by the British Government. (*Irish News* 4 Oct.1996)

There was plenty of women's work in Belfast though, mostly in the linen mills as 'doffers', but it was poorly paid. The local saying went, 'You would always know a doffer with her pickers hanging down'. Since 1888 when Belfast was granted a charter as a city vast spinning mills sprang up between the Falls and the Shankill: the Northern Spinning and Weaving Company, the Ulster Spinning Company, T. & T. M. Greeves, the Clonard Print Works and the Falls Spinning Company. This concentration of mills created thousands of jobs, principally for women and children. In the early part of the twentieth century young girls were called 'half-timers'. They attended school for half the week and spent the other half working in the mills.

JIM'S SISTER PEGGY DIES

Like many women in West Belfast, Maisy was left with the job of bringing up five children on her own. With no money coming from Scotch, her husband, who had since gone to Scotland, she took on many part time jobs and brought work home from the factory, sewing and making up men's shirt collars and cuffs, into the early hours of the morning to make ends meet. However, at times no money came in at all. Maureen Bradshaw remembers Maisy's hard times:

Mrs McGinnes at one time had to put four of her children into temporary care in Nazareth House orphanage on the Ormeau Road. She kept Bill and when work picked up, she brought them out again, because she missed them so much.

The end for some was the workhouse, still with its Victorian routine, beside the City Infirmary on the Lisburn Road. Many people had to suffer the humiliation of letting their loved one be buried in a pauper's grave. Although the graveyard was consecrated ground they had a special plot for people who had no money to pay the funeral and grave diggers' expenses. Young people dying was common. Maureen Bradshaw recalls:

> Peggy McGinnes died just after her 15th birthday. She had just started work in the Monarch laundry on the Donegall Road in 1932. She had a blood disorder and her death was so sudden, both our families were shocked, but all the children in the area had to fight their way through the well known diseases of measles, whooping cough, diphtheria and chicken pox. The most feared of all was the dreaded tuberculosis. The people silently whispered to each other. 'I heard so and so's got *it*'. Being infectious, patients were taken away across town to Purdysburn Fever Hospital into an isolation ward. Some never came out except to pass on to the next world like our own beloved Peggy.

HALF-TIMERS AND OUTDOOR RELIEF

Many children started their working life as 'Half-Timers' at the age of twelve. Jimmy Webb remembers:

> My older sisters Sarah and Lily only attended school on Mondays, Wednesdays and Fridays, with Tuesdays, Thursdays and Saturdays being mill days. The girls worked at the same job as adults for the same long hours, from 6.30 am to 6 pm. For this they were paid three shillings and sixpence a week. Both my sisters were allowed to keep only a penny for pocket money and the rest went to help the family's budget.

There was no National Health Service nor any Social Security or Child Benefits. It was a period of great deprivation. Many families had to go hungry, or without medical care, because they had fallen behind in the payment of bills. Joe Devlin, a well-known local MP was responsible for bringing the Victorian work system of 'Half-Timers' to an end, before he died in 1934. In 1928 the 'Outdoor Relief' Scheme started. The purpose of this was two-fold; to relieve chronic unemployment and improve the condition of the road surfaces. In 1932 there were riots with workmen from both sides of the religious divide fighting the police. The riots started in Raglan Street where Jimmy Webb lived. The dispute was over the Outdoor Relief men being given food chits, instead of a cash payment for their work. Sadly two men were shot dead by the police, Sammy Baxter from the Shankill and Johnny Keenan from the Falls.

Bill remembers his brother Jim in the 1932 riots:

> The riots started and Jim was only about ten years old. He ran into a gang of wreckers in the Falls Road area breaking up shops and pubs and battling with the police. The police fired on them. He seemed to be in the middle of it all. He was so scared he rushed into a house and hid under the stairs. The woman nearly fainted when she went to fill her coal bucket and up popped Jim. Black as a boot he was.

On a much lighter note all the boys began to support their local football team, Belfast Celtic. Their ground was called Paradise, situated on the Upper Donegall Road facing Celtic Park, the local greyhound track. In Belfast, or for that matter in the Northern Ireland Football League, Belfast Celtic and Linfield were the top teams and were always neck and neck when it came to the end of the season. Robert Morrow remembers the football matches, and the famous Joe Barnbrack who played for Linfield (the 'wee Blues'):

> Joe Barnbrack scored two hat tricks in an international match. The saying was in those days 'head, heel or toe, slip the ball to Joe'. But of course Belfast Celtic had their own famous players in the '20s and '30s. There was Tom Mullholland, Mike Hamill and their goalkeeper Elisha Scott.

Not unlike the football teams Glasgow Rangers and Celtic in Scotland, players and support came from either sides of the religious divide. At most matches there were punch-ups, and now and again some people were carted off by the police.

POLITICS, RELIGION, HUMOUR

Belfast in the 1920s and 1930s, was going through great political, religious and sectarian agitation. The 1914-18 Great War was over, but Ireland was still in a state of turmoil. The elections after the war led to an Anglo-Irish war from 1919-21. The Government of Ireland Act in 1920 and the Anglo-Irish Treaty in 1922 divided the country into a six county Northern

Ireland and a twenty-six county Irish Free State (later, Republic). 'Partition' as it was called, created a Northern Ireland Government headed by Sir James Craig. The new parliament initially held its meetings in the Presbyterian College behind Queen's University before moving to the Robing Room in the Belfast City Hall. Victory in the Civil War left the pro-Treaty party in control of the Free State. However, Belfast at this time was a hotbed of sectarian tension; there were many riots and disturbances in which a number of people from both sides died.

Michael Collins wrote on 6 March 1922 to Winston Churchill:

> The total death toll from 11th Feb amounted to 48 and 198 wounded while total casualties once the Orange pogrom began in July 1920 numbered 257. The forces doing the work should be at least impartial and attention paid to the haunts of Orange gunmen and aggressors. (quoted *Irish News*, 4 Oct. 1996).

A report was also sent to Churchill from Sir James Craig on 11 March 1922:

> The total death toll in Belfast from July 1st 1929 till March 8, 1922 is 123 Catholics's and 112 Protestants. There had been peace for a considerable period in Belfast before the original murders by Sinn Féin gunmen took place.

Despite all this, in predominantly Catholic places like Majorca Street, Mulhouse Street and the surrounding area, a number of Protestants lived and got on very well with their neighbours. In between periods of unrest their differences would be seen with humour. Many local writers, actors and artists would bring this out in a creative form in books and on the stage. Their ideas came from everyday life. Belfast people developed a form of black humour without which they would have been unable to survive in such a religiously and politically divided environment. This humour would have emerged among the people who frequented many of Belfast's pubs and bars, especially in working-class areas like west Belfast.

There were four pubs, three bookies, two pawnshops, three fish'n'chip shops and a number of corner shops in this little area of Belfast. The favourite pub was Kelly's in Granville Street. Mr Jack Chambers who lived in Majorca Street in the 1930s recalls others:

> There was Lynch's Bar in Distillery Street and Boden's pub in Leeson Street. Then across the Grosvenor Road there still is the Oak Inn fac-

ing the hospital. It's a social club now. It was called Larry Marron's in the 1920/30s and Kevin O'Kane was the owner. With most people having little money only stout and wine were drunk. Whisky you would only have seen at Christmas time or at a wedding or some other special occasion. Red biddy was the cheapest. The wine was called 'Kingstinio' or 'Drawbridge' at one shilling a bottle, and a better wine called 'Opal' was two pence dearer. Nowadays it's the in thing to drink wine. Half of West Belfast drank it in the 1920s and 1930s!

SATURDAY NIGHT AT KELLY'S WITH RED BIDDY

The pub in any area is usually the centre of entertainment and Kelly's was just that. It was also the centre of local knowledge and a general gossip shop. Stories about the people were the chit chat of the customers who were a mixture of local characters. On many a Saturday night with rumour, red biddy, poteen and bottles of stout, coupled with a Belfast vernacular, sanity found it hard to survive.

One Saturday night Kelly's was packed. Bruiser Mallon and Paddy McIntyre were in their usual seats in company with a few locals. They were in the best of form, as Paddy had 'touched for a treble' (won money on three horses). He collected his winnings of thirty-seven shillings, from Blinks the bookie at the corner of Abbot Street. There had been a funeral in the morning and the wake had carried over into the pub which often happened in West Belfast. An excuse was never needed to have a drink at Sally Hannigan's bar, but if one was needed, a wake was as good an excuse as any. If you had no money, Sally would set you up a few drinks 'on tick' (this meant you paid later). Failing that it entailed a trip round to number 24 Majorca Street to Mrs Murray, the money lender, to borrow five bob, with six bob to be paid back at the end of the week. Bruiser and Paddy would not be her customers today.

Jimmy McIntyre, Paddy's son, recalls Kelly's:

Sally only sold wine and stout but she kept the odd bottle of poteen hidden under the counter. She had a pleasant jovial wit about her that even Sergeant Fitzpatrick and the constables from Roden Street police barracks liked. They knew she was supplied with this illegal strong spirit made from potatoes from a still in the Sperrin mountains, but they never booked her as most of them liked a jar themselves. Especially after a wake, Sally would always set them up a glass of poteen free. It kept the peace, at least for that day anyway.

Romeo Regan was the nickname the locals gave him. He was standing on his own drinking at the bar when they all came back from the funeral. He was celebrating his first day of freedom. Drink wasn't Romeo's problem, women were. He was always falling in love and paying a heavy price for it. Romeo Regan had just been released from his last stint at His Majesty's Pleasure in Crumlin Road prison. Regan had been caught many times for bigamy. They overlooked his first offences because he was over sixty-five years old. His good wife, who was ever so forgiving, always took him back as his romantic flings were with Protestant late middle aged spinsters from the Shankill Road. She was convinced, as the ceremonies all took place in Gospel Halls, he was really being lead astray and the women were trying to convert him and take him away from his one and only good Catholic wife.

Johnny Cunningham from number fourteen Majorca Street was in his best suit, with his wig on and his glass eye in. He never knew for a number of years how Mary his wife pawned his glass eye for half a crown in the pawn shop in Arundel Street. She always managed to retrieve it (with Johnny's pension) before the weekend, when Johnny's Saturday night in Kelly's was a ritual. He and two of his old ex army friends, Peg Leg Patton and Lucky Gordon, were sitting in their usual corner in the snug Sally kept for Great War veterans. They spent hours living past memories squeamishly talking about how many of their friends had died, and how many that had lost some part of their anatomy at the Battle of the Somme in the Great War. Lucky Gordon had been burnt badly by mustard gas and had many skin grafts. His face was left with a permanent grin, which the medical profession tried to make resemble a face. He never complained about anything and told most people he was one of the lucky ones. Peg Leg had been given a brand new shiny metal leg with the compliments of the War Office, but had pawned it for 7/6d over a year ago in Tuckers pawn shop. Every time he had enough money to retrieve it he got drunk again. He was telling Tommy and Lucky Gordon, that the week previous, when he wished to retrieve his leg that Tucker had sold it to a man from Sandy Row, (a Protestant area of the town). The man had his own false leg stolen and he wanted to march on the Twelfth of July. Tommy told Peg Leg it couldn't have gone to a better man. 'Just think, Peg Leg, it will be marching for King Billy and Ulster' and looking round the bar whispered in Peg Leg's ear, 'It could have gone to the other side.' Peg Leg agreed with him and got up to buy another round of drinks, forgetting that he had already bought the last round, completely satisfied his leg was at least going to a good cause. Peg

Outside No.4 Majorca Street, 1930.
Peggy, Rosemary and James with his dog Prince.

Leg considered himself a good Orangeman but he had been thrown out of his Orange Lodge for not paying his dues.

Hero Harry, another local character with a nickname, was in their company wearing all his medals from the last and previous wars, some before he was born. Harry had joined some six different regiments during the war, deserted them all and pawned the uniforms for money to drink. It was when he tried to join the navy, he was nicked for a string of petty offences and cheating His Majesty's Government. Harry spent most of the war years in His Majesty's Prison, Wormwood Scrubs. Apparently he found the medals in some bin when he got out of jail. His crack was mighty and his knowledge of military history which he learned in prison, was always good for a laugh, although he would get his years mixed up. Many people bought him drink but never took him seriously.

Most of the early conversation that night in Kelly's was about the funeral at St Paul's, earlier in the day and then on to the paupers' plot at Milltown cemetery where most attended, except the ex-army boys and Romeo Regan. Pat Reid had previously lived in Mulhouse Street before he died. His wife had run away to England with an Italian sailor, who had jumped ship in Belfast. The women in the area who had seen the good-looking Italian said he looked 'just *gorgeous*, like Rudolf Valentino'. The incident had happened six years before but the month after she left, Pat sold every stick of furniture in the house and drank the money. The Black Maria was forever carting him off, to either Roden Street or Townhall Street police barracks, for yelling obscenities at women in the street. The poor man ended up in and out of Purdysburn Asylum, at least twenty times in five years. On Thursday last, the bin man found poor old Pat lying dead in his back yard. In a drunken stupor, he had apparently drank bleach which was in a coloured wine bottle. Pat had two sisters who hadn't spoken to each other for over twenty-five years. One went to the funeral and on her return, she caught her other sister removing Pat's last bit of coal from the coal hole. 'My God!' says she, 'his body's not even cold yet and you're stealing his coal'. Her sister replied in usual black Belfast humour, 'He won't be needing it, where he's gone to, he'll be as warm as toast'. The word of this had got round to the pub and everyone was having a good laugh.

Wino Willie and his two boozing pals lived on the street in the summer and the boarding house in Carrick Hill in the winter. They had been Pat Reid's last drinking companions and were at the funeral. They called into Kelly's and after having a few free drinks, Sally Hannigan sent them on their mourning way with a few bottles of Kingstinio wine.

St Finian's de la Salle hurling team 1934.
Contemporaries of James Magennis.

They headed off to the tram shelter beside Dunville Park where the down-and-outs did their drinking.

'Hard-man' Jo Jo McCabe was also in the bar that night. He had just finished his three months as a pioneer that morning. In the Catholic church one can stop drinking by taking a pledge. This is followed by wearing a pioneer pin to state the wearer is not a drinker. He was lowering the glasses of red biddy, as if his stomach was an empty hole, making up for lost time as he knew his time was short. His good wife would give him a week or ten days. Into the pub she would come one night and like a roaring lion, grab Jo Jo by the ear, yank him out of the pub's door, yelling nasty remarks at the other drinking occupants, accusing them of leading her good husband astray. Jo Jo's nickname 'Hard-man' was given because he was henpecked by his wife. Early the next morning she would take him to see Father Murphy, insisting he take the pioneer pin for another three months. She always got her way in the end, but tonight and this weekend, he was safe; because his wife and all the family were away to Lough Derg on pilgrimage with some other women and three nuns from Clonard Monastery. Father Murphy had told everyone in the chapel the week before, that Mrs McCabe was a great pillar of strength and a fine walking example of what a good Catholic wife and mother should be.

Maggie Mullan and Sean the coalman, came into the bar half an hour before closing. Maggie told everybody Sean was her brother, but they all knew he was her 'fancy man'. Her husband was working in England. Religion was no barrier to romance between Sean and Maggie. Sean was really John, a Protestant from the Newtownards Road in East Belfast and he worked for Kelly's Coal Merchant. The coal dust on him was an excellent disguise, all you could see was his eyes. Maggie always had a full coal hole and if you wanted to borrow a bucket of coal, Maggie was your woman. She told most of the women who failed to return the kind gesture not to worry there was plenty more where that came from, the whole dockside at Queen's Quay where Kelly's Coal Merchant was.

Maggie never went to mass, but the women all told Father Murphy how kind she was and many a cold night they were so glad of her generosity. Father Murphy, who had a good sense of humour, knew about everything that was going on in the area. He told the women the good Lord would take that into consideration on the Day of Judgment, but if John had been really called Sean, she might get off with a lighter sentence, when she went to meet her maker.

By the time the evening ended, the subject of conversation had flowed backwards and forwards from Pat Reid's funeral to Romeo Regan's love life and the usual debates on the previous Great War, Partition and the Anglo-Irish and Civil War. By the time they were all due to head home, most of them had forgotten everything they had been talking about, whether it had been true, false, or make believe. Another Saturday night out in Kelly's was over. Most of the men leaving the bar hadn't too far to go, they all lived in the area. Some of them ended the evening, by paying a visit to the fish and chip shop in McDonald Street. Like a true Belfastman and loving husband, Paddy McIntyre brought his wife a peace offering of a bag of steaming hot chips from Fusco's fish'n'chip shop, paid for out of the remainder of his winnings.

ENTERTAINMENT

Picture houses in the early 1920s were great places of entertainment. The silent movies with Charlie Chaplin, Buster Keaton and others helped bring laughter to many in difficult times. Jimmy Webb remembers visiting one such place:

I visited the Arcadian, or Johnny Donnelly's as we called it, after the coal merchant who owned it. When silent films were shown the dialogue was written across the screen. The older people could not read, so we used to shout the words out loud. If a priest appeared in the film, everyone would cheer and clap. At these noisy times Mick Kavanagh the manager would soon restore order, by threatening to split a few heads with his flashlight. With the coming of the 'talkies' the era of everyone taking an active part in the film sadly came to an end.

The McGinnes brothers, McIntyre brothers, along with John Murray, Louie Mullan and Francie Ferron from Mulhouse Street all went to the penny matinee on a Saturday at the Diamond near Cupar Street and Clonard Street. Flash Gordon, Buck Rodgers and other new 'talkies' were beginning to appear. The Diamond, the Colosseum on the Grosvenor Road and the Arcadian in Albert Street were the cheapest at a penny for an afternoon matinee. The Clonard picture house facing Sebastopol Street on the Falls Road was two pence. It was much more up-market and this is where the older boys brought their girlfriends at night.

When the boys came out of the pictures they all headed for Fusco's fish'n'chip shop. His Italian ice cream was known as the best in the area. Ned's chip shop was beside the Colosseum. Although Ned never made ice cream his hot peas were what was needed on a cold winter's day.

John Murphy who lived at number two Mulhouse Street remembers the fish'n'chip shops:

Fish and chips cost three pence and hot peas a ha'penny. Fusco's and Ned's were the closest, which we all used, but now and again if we wanted a treat we would go to Long's in Durham Street, renowned as the best although they cost more. Looking back we lived on fish and chips. Now and again my mother would have made a feed of Irish stew if she could get the meat cheap. There was also the herring man who sold five fish for sixpence around the doors. I remember also the 'tick man', he was a wee Jewish man who sold 'everything and anything' out of a suitcase. All the women disappeared to mass, when he came round to collect his money. When the bread man came up the street, we all used to swing around the lamppost singing: 'Barney Hughes bread it lies in your belly like lead; no wonder you fart like thunder–Barney Hughes bread.

The shop Pattons and Bar at the corner of Mulhouse Street and the Grosvenor Road, was used by the people in the neighbourhood. Most families including the McGinneses used its credit facilities. 'Strap' allowed customers to have groceries on credit, until the end of the week. Pattons and Bar was a haberdashery, hardware, grocery shop, that sold anything from tin baths and christening gowns to Ballynahinch eggs. It supplied nearly everything, except second hand goods, required by any local family.

Food was in constant demand by the growing McGinnes children. Jim went to school, as did many of his classmates, with no breakfast, maybe on better days a bowl of porridge, or a glass of buttermilk. At times, like other children, he had to make do with a slice of bread with treacle on top. Jimmy Webb remembers:

> At dinner-time we usually had champ [mashed potatoes and scallions]. Sometimes there was stew, potatoes, or tripe and on Fridays ling or herrings. Most weekday meals would be potatoes alone. Supper was always tea, bread and treacle. On a Sunday we might get meat which had always been boiled first, as stock for soup. Some Sundays we were lucky and got an egg for breakfast.

Most of the women baked soda bread on the griddle on the fire. The milkman, Barney Caulfield from Hannahstown, delivered both sweetmilk and buttermilk. He had five gallon cans on his cart and the women came to the doors holding their jugs. Both Barney Hughes and Kennedy's bakeries supplied a shilling worth of yesterday's bread, which could be collected in pillowcases. Jimmy Webb recalls:

> If you asked for a shilling worth of smalls, you would get a selection of exotic sounding items such as 'Donkey's Noses', or 'Sore Heads', which were large buns with lumps of sugar scattered on top, 'Fly's Graveyards (currant squares), Paris buns, baps and 'Peelers Batons' (like Vienna rolls), barnbracks and potato bread.

Welles' pawnshop in Arundel Street and Tucker's in Roden Street, did a roaring trade, not only from Tommy Cunningham's glass eye, but from every other item known to man that was saleable, false teeth, wigs, legs, musical instruments, clocks, watches, and more. Most women went to what they called their 'uncle's', to pawn their husband's Sunday suit; which, like Tommy Cunningham's glass eye, they would redeem at the end of the week. Jimmy Webb recalls:

In our house it was Dad's suit which went in and out of 'uncle's' every week. By the time it had reached the end of its pawnable life, the weekly interest paid on it over the years would have bought half a dozen suits.

Smithfield market, at the bottom of the Falls Road, was well known for second hand shops. It was frequented by mostly working class people, looking for a second hand bargain, or who had an item to sell. Then there were the local bookies in the area. Blink's, at the corner of Abbot Street and Herbert McDonald, who was a threepenny bookie in Gibson Street, and McAleavey's, facing the Grosvenor Hall near the town centre, was where the money men went. On Tuesday and Thursday evening, the doggie men punters (gamblers), with over five bob in their pocket, headed up to Celtic Park the greyhound track facing the football ground, Paradise, on the upper Donegall Road.

The police barracks in Roden Street was only a stone's throw away, its red brick back wall faced the bottom end of Majorca Street. After Partition in 1921 the new Royal Ulster Constabulary (RUC) was formed. Many of the men from the disbanded Royal Irish Constabulary (RIC) transferred from one force to the other. Jack Chambers remembers some of the policemen well:

There was Sergeant Fitzpatrick whom all the neighbourhood liked because where there was any trouble (fights, brawls, etc.) he used to take off his jacket and have a go himself. He preferred his own form of judgment rather than bringing them to court. Another constable from Springfield Road barracks, who just loved fighting, was called Pig Meneelly. The other constables Parker and Patterson were quieter types and then Detective Kerningham who seen to any serious crimes. But looking back, they were all a pretty tough bunch; they had to be; they were stationed in a rough area. I remember one occasion Pig Meneelly fought for over an hour with local tough man 'Bruiser Mallon' in Majorca Street. Even the bookies had come round to lay the odds on who would win. They ended up deciding it was a draw and all went round to Kellys for a drink.

Of all the policemen who were famous Pig Meneelly was the one most remembered in West Belfast. His nickname came about from an incident when some local wit left a bucket of skins (potato peelings) at Springfield barracks, requesting that they be given to Constable Meneelly. People gave skins to the skinman to feed the pigs and once it was realised that Constable Meneelly kept pigs the nickname stuck with him until he died in the 1980s at well over eighty years of age.

The Bog Meadows was a favourite meeting place for the working class people of Belfast at weekends. The geographical layout with the Black Mountain, the Castlereagh Hills and the River Lagan and smaller rivers created this large wild life sanctuary. In former times the Bog Meadows had been used as a hunting ground for game and wild fowl by the gentry. In the 1930's it was only one fifth its original size as with the growth of Belfast land had been reclaimed. But nevertheless it, provided an area where the lower classes, would meet, play pitch and toss, have cock fights and the odd dog fight was known to have taken place. All these forms of entertainment were gambling-related and prohibited by law. Lookouts had to keep their eyes open for the police. If they were spotted, the Bog had many escape routes to accommodate those who were breaking the law.

Local tough men, such as Barney Ross and Silver McKee from the Markets area, Stormy Weather and Buck Alec, from the Shankill and Dock area of the City, earned their living as scrap metal merchants, cattle herders, minders, bouncers and dock hands. They helped and assisted, with the gambling and made sure any rules were not broken. No one paid any attention to the official law anyway, except Sergeant Fitzpatrick and Pig Meneelly. To add to all these goings on Buck Alec had a pet lion with no teeth. He had legal documentation to own this cat which was fearsome looking until it opened its mouth. Buck would carry on an act, much to all the children's enjoyment, of sticking his head in between its jaws. Anyone who could pay gave a ha'penny, which went to help feed the lion. He also gave the children a ride on its back for the same price. Buck also travelled round all the working class areas through the week performing the same act.

Bill McGinnes remembers the boys from the street going to the Bog Meadows and up the Cave Hill:

Some of the lads from the neighbourhood would have visited the Bog Meadows to pass a long Sunday afternoon. Most of us, went as spectators in the 1930s, as no one had any money except the odd fly by night. Some weekends in the summer we would climb up the Black Mountain and walk over to the top of the Cave Hill. Jim would have brought his dog Prince with us. It was a Kerry Blue and boy could he fight.

ENLISTING IN THE NAVY

Belfast is a city and port situated at the mouth of the River Lagan. It is surrounded by hills. To the north west lies Cave Hill and to the south east the Castlereagh Hills. The River Lagan meanders through the miles of the Lagan Valley before entering Belfast Lough. At the top of Cave Hill which dominates the city from the north one can look right out to sea, or catch sight of the great gantries of the shipyard of Harland and Wolff where the handiwork of the shipyard men has slipped into the River Lagan and sailed over the oceans of the world. The river opens out into Belfast Lough, the twenty mile stretch of water that leads out into the Irish Sea.

The boys had a tremendous view over the whole city and could look down Belfast Lough right out to sea. They could see the ships coming and going, out of the docks beside the shipyard. Would they have wondered,'where do all these ships come from and go to'? The seed to adventure may have started here. Maybe it was from this point both Jim and his brother decided they wanted to go to sea. In late 1934 Jim's brother Bill joined the Royal Navy. Jim was only fourteen so he had to wait until the following year. Bill McGinnes recalls:

I was the first to join up. My cousin Bert Pollock who lived in Lincoln Street joined the Navy a few months later and Jim the following year.

Jim remembered those early years before joining the Navy:

I was still in the fifth class at St Finian's on the Falls Road when I left at fourteen to work in a wine store. Next I sold ice cream in a fish and chip shop until the boss complained, 'You are giving my profit away.' He sacked me for being too generous.

In 1935 Jim McGinnes was to follow Bill and join the navy. Later his younger brother Anthony would do likewise. Far away in continental Europe, unknown to the children still playing in Majorca Street, the dark clouds of conflict were beginning to stir. Within a few years, these lads from this West Belfast area would be in the thick of another world war. Stanley McAlinden remembers the day Jim joined up:

Jim McGinnes and I went to Clifton Street navy recruitment office. Jim was accepted as a boy recruit and paid three and nine pence. I was told to come back in six months as I was too young.

John Murphy also recalls boys joining up:

Jim and Bill joined up before the war. Myself and Eddie McIntyre and Jim's younger brother Tony joined later, when the war started. Jim of course was the influence for such activities, as on his first leave his smart Naval uniform made such an impression on his pals, that we decided to join up. Remembering the fifteen shillings in his pocket was a great incentive at that time. There was also Louie and his brother Dick Mullan and Francie Ferron from Theodore Street. Altogether in the three streets I think a dozen or so boys joined the navy before and during the war. I joined the RAF and others joined the army.

Later, Jim was to tell a *Daily Mail* reporter:

I wanted to be a soldier but the army turned me down. 'Your education is not good enough,' said the Belfast recruiting officer. So I joined the navy. I was just fifteen, a pale faced city lad when I was introduced to the tough life of HMS *Ganges*, the boy's training establishment at Shotley, Suffolk.

In the Great War, only two decades previously, the Irish Divisions, both North and South, had fought side by side in the Trenches of France, Belgium and Turkey. Their proud heroes were welcomed back to Ireland. Now these two families and a number of lads from a small area of West Belfast were about to serve in another war which was to last six years. Maisy McGinnes had done well rearing her children in the hungry 1930s on her own, in such arduous conditions. She and Rosemary were later to go to England to help in the war effort and find work in a munitions factory. Her three sons were to bring her great credit by all serving throughout World War II in the Royal Navy.

TWO

HMS *Ganges*

The metamorphosis of James McGinnes
into Boy Seaman Magennis

JOURNEY TO ENGLAND

In the early evening of 4 June 1935, Jim's mum, his brother and sister
waved their goodbyes at the gangway leading up to The *Duke of Lancaster*,
the ferry that sailed overnight between Belfast and Liverpool.

Jim's mum and his sister Rosemary had tears in their eyes. They knew
it was only a matter of time before Anthony would leave home too. There
was no permanent work for the teenage lads in Belfast. It was a hard time
for all during the depression years. People throughout Europe and
America were out of work. Great Britain and Northern Ireland could not
avoid the dark clouds of unemployment and the dole queues which result-

ed. The Belfast shipyard and the aircraft factory on the east side of the
river barely managed to keep going. Many of the work force were laid off.
There was little chance of work for many of the men from West Belfast.
Maisy found some comfort knowing Jim was 'going to a job with three
square meals a day'. Her tears, shed in private, were tears of emotion. She
did not want the boys to see her like that. Young men do not understand
or feel the way a woman does. Tony was full of excitement and like Jim his
thoughts were only on adventure.

The ferry sailed overnight to Liverpool. Jim was going to miss his
dog Prince. Anthony had promised to look after him. He sat in the pas-
senger lounge and re-read the letter his brother Bill had sent home
recently. After training he had been drafted to the battle cruiser HMS
Renown, flagship of the home fleet. Jim wondered if when he finished
his training maybe he too would be sent to the same ship as his brother but that was unlikely as there were so many ships in the navy.

The next morning Jim was up on deck as the ferry entered harbour.
He had never been out of Ireland before and noticed the large Liver building as the boat entered the River Mersey. The ferry docked and all the passengers pushed and shoved their way down the gangway. At the bottom
was a naval petty officer. Jim had been instructed to meet this naval man
in his smart blue uniform with gold buttons. The naval petty officer and
Jim headed for the recruiting office in Canning Place where other lads
were waiting. It was here he met John Lee who remembers the meeting
well:

> Myself and a lad called Don Wynne and another boy who was joining
> the marines were in the recruiting office, at Canning Place Liverpool,
> the morning Jim Magennis came off the boat from Belfast. I had come
> from Ellesmere Port in Cheshire and Don Wynne came from Chester.
> We were all escorted to Lime Street railway station and then put on a
> train to London.'

The train came into Euston Station and from there the boys travelled by underground to Liverpool Street station, where the fifteen year
old lads boarded another train to Ipswich. Jim Magennis DJX 144907,
John Lee DJX 144904, and Don Wynne DJX 144905 had all accepted
the 'King's shilling', John and Don in Canning Place recruiting office
and Jim in Clifton Street Belfast. Now they were heading to HMS
Ganges, Shotley, Suffolk, to begin training before going to sea. Other
boys had joined the train in London and during the train journey Jim
was slightly puzzled by their different accents. Never before, had he

heard such dialects, spoken by many of the boys who came from all over the British Isles.

The three new pals were excited about what lay ahead of them, as part of a new recruitment entering the Senior Service. At Ipswich they left the train to board a coach waiting to carry them on the last part of their journey to Shotley. The village stood at the confluence of the rivers Stour and Orwell, overlooking the port of Harwich, with its naval history and tradition and currently base to a continental ferry port. In the earlier part of the century, Harwich had been a Royal Naval base for squadrons of destroyers and submarines.

When the coach arrived from Ipswich train station the boys jumped out to be met by a friendly smiling man in a dark navy blue uniform with gold buttons and a white cap like the man in the recruiting office at Belfast:

Welcome to HMS *Ganges*. My name is Petty Officer Watkins. As most of you have had a long journey, some as far away as Ireland, for the rest of the evening I will show you your sleeping accommodation, where you can leave your bags and then we will all go over to the mess hall to eat. What do you think, lads? Right let's go. Follow me.

Bacon, egg, sausage and a huge plate of chips, four rounds of bread and a big mug of tea–Jim thought of the many school days with no din-ner– 'This is some navy. I think I'm going to like this.' After being issued with bedding and turning in at 2130 hours, tired from his jour-ney, Jim could hear a bugler playing the 'last post' somewhere in the distance. Lights out. The boys all fell asleep after a long day's journey to begin a new exciting career the following day.

TIN TOWN, THE ANNEXE

The initial training centre where boy entrant Magennis now found him-self, was Tin Town, the Annexe to HMS *Ganges*, the main establishment. Jim and his new shipmates would spend one month there learning the rudiments of being a boy sailor. All new recruits at Shotley were required to successfully pass through the Annexe, before continuing their extensive training at the main establishment. Boys spent between nine and fifteen months at HMS *Ganges* before qualifying and leaving to join the fleet.

At 0530 hours the lights of the mess flashed on, Jim automatically jumped out of his bed. He could see, in the centre of the mess deck, a pair of 'dustbins' unbelievably burnished and polished to gleam like silver, being banged with sticks held in the horny hands of a Chief Petty Officer. The noise was deafening, that was of course the intention. The Chief yelled, 'Wakey, wakey, rise and shine, the morning's fine, the sun is burning your bleedin' eyeballs out!!'

After this initial shock to the system, the new recruits dressed and quickly made up their beds. Later they would learn the *Ganges* way to make up their 'pit'. The boys were issued with a mug of 'kye' (naval hot chocolate drink) and marched off to be kitted out, with uniform and accessories. In the wooden store room, they passed quickly in single file, in front of a long low counter, behind which stood the SAs, (Stores Assistants) automatons, dishing out the kit. First came the kit bag, the traditional canvas bag in which 'Jack' carried his belongings around the world during his naval service. Next, two of everything: blue serge suits, boots, collars, white fronts, sea jerseys, overalls, duck suits, plus numerous pairs of socks, underwear, three sailor's hats (one white, two black) oilskin, ditty box, and all the other items of uniform and kit necessary to fit out a boy sailor for service in the King's Navy.

Staggering under the weight and bulk of the clothing issue, Jim reached the end of the counter where a 'Jack Dusty' (stores assistant), expertly hurled a heavy blue serge overcoat onto the mountainous pile of clothing, towering over the diminutive figure. As with all the other kit issue, he knew Jim's size, just by looking at him. At least that's what he told him. The rest of the morning would be spent changing from civilian clothes into 'Pussers', white duck suits. The final transition from 'civvy' to sailor came with the parcelling up in brown paper of his civilian clothes to be sent home. Jim knew Maisy would give them to Tony.

The afternoon began with a haircut, then to the parade ground to practise marching in step–'Fall in! Dress off! Ho! By the right! Quick march! Right turn! Left turn! About turn! Ho! Stand at ease! Stand easy!'

Over and over again. Someone was heard to mutter, 'If I wanted all this crap I'd have joined the Irish Guards.'

'So we have a comedian in the ranks,' said the instructor. 'Right Double march. About turn.'

Over and over and over again; for two hours. That night the over tired boy recruits all fell onto their beds and when the last post sounded they were all fast asleep. No one heard it. Jim, John and Don were out for the count.

NOZZERS AND NEEDLEWORK

The first few weeks of training flew by. A top priority during the first few days was the sewing in of individual names onto every item of kit. That included two inch high stitches on the thick service blanket issued to recruits. Everything else sewn in with red silk, chain stitched to be examined by an Instructor Boy (a boy who had completed his training at *Ganges* but was selected to remain to train new recruits. Though only slightly older than the 'nozzers' he was addressed as 'Sir'.) If not to the Instructor Boy's liking, he slashed the offending stitching with a razor blade ordering, 'Not good enough, do it again.'

Jim remembers his early days at Tin Town. He told a *Daily Mail* reporter in 1960:

> Our heads were shaved. My first lesson in needlework was sewing my name in chain-stitch on to my newly issued naval kit with red silk thread.

Jim could never remember having new clothes as he inherited his brother Bill's hand me downs which he later passed on to his younger brother Tony. To have something new, his own, with his name on it, gave him a warm feeling of satisfaction. John Lee recalls:

> I was lucky my name was short. There were other boys like Magennis who had longer names. Clements who later became PO boy and Tomkin, Hanrahan, Bloomfield and Christy all became leading instructor boys when we later transferred over to Benbow Division of the main camp.

The kye with its greasy surface began to taste better each morning before the 0600 hours muster outside the mess, preparatory to 'scrubbing out'. The smells that had been strange to Jim at the outset, soon became familiar including the Pussers 'Ronuk' floor polish on the wooden mess decks, polished by the boys, to a mirror-like gleam. The wearing of footwear on the polished deck by the boys was forbidden. Officers, instructors and badge boys were exempted from that rule. Pussers Hard (blocks of navy soap) was used in the deep sinks to dhobey kit (wash clothing), under the watchful eye of 'Nobby' Clarke, the ex-Royal Marine in charge of the wash house.

Jim, together with the other boys, stripped and donned brief G-string-like bathing trunks. On the direction of Nobby Clarke each recruit dhobied a specific item of clothing. It was then presented to Nobby who accepted it, or rejected it. If accepted, the owner was allowed to rinse the item in a bath of warm water. If rejected, the offending item was rinsed in ice cold water and unceremoniously wrapped round the neck of the boy presenting it. He was then ordered to re-dhobey and re-present it. A couple of visits, clad only in a 'G' string, to that ice cold water bath, soon had its effect and the kit of all the boys was maintained at a very high standard of cleanliness. This was an essential requirement in the making of a sailor. Cleanliness in the confined space of a warship was imperative. Dirt encouraged disease and disease spread like wildfire on a ship. Their beds had to be made up to specific dimensions, blankets stacked precisely at the bed head, name showing, mattress cover pulled taut. On a ship space was limited, it was necessary therefore to train young sailors to be neat, tidy and economic with space. There had to be spit and polish, bulling boots, kit inspection, with kit set out in orderly rows upon the mess deck, rolled and clothes stopped, red silk names gleaming from the spotless uniforms and gear on display. There was frustration, when the inspecting officer indiscriminately 'trashed' the kit, so meticulously set out, requiring it to be rearranged for further inspection. Time was spent preparing clews and lashings for a hammock and learning the mystery of 'slinging a Mick' before lashing and stowing, as one would on board ship. At *Ganges* they slept in single beds rather than hammocks.

Not every boy has good memories of Tin Town. Ed Carrol (*Ganges* 1937) recalls:

> One person who stands out in my memory at Tin Town was an instructor by the name of Haversgill. Under the foot of each bed was a solid round bed chuck. For punishment Haversgill made all our class empty our kit bags and fill them up with these bed chucks. The boys fell in on the parade ground and they were told to put their kit bags on their shoulders and double round the parade ground.

Doug Smith (*Ganges* 1935) had an interesting experience the first week in Tin Town. One 6 am muster, he was booked for talking in the ranks and ordered by the instructor to double around the parade ground, carrying a cannon ball. It was a very cold morning and he dropped the ball on his big toe. Later his toe became swollen and poisoned with the dye from his new pussers sock. He reported to the sick bay and then on to hospital. He recalls:

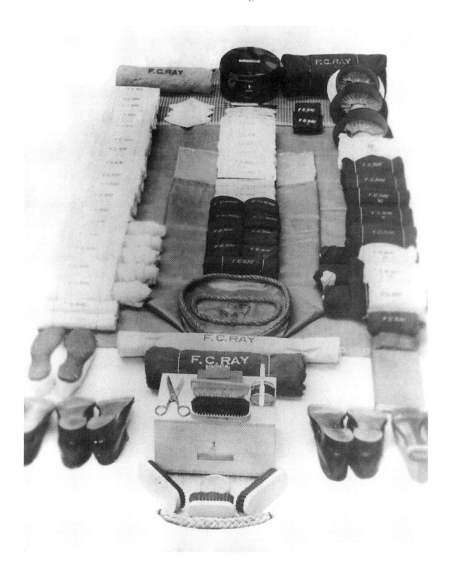

Typical kit lay out. HMS *Ganges* 1935

From Tin Town to heaven, nurses in red cloaks, POs who didn't bash you with broom handles. My toe recovered and three weeks later I joined another class. After leaving *Ganges* they made me a 'Regulating Petty Officer' before invaliding me out; no one was ever put in the rattle by me.

Most afternoons, having completed their 'square-bashing', the boys took part in sport including football, rugby, cricket and cross country running. Every boy was obliged to enter the boxing competitions, for Jim 'no big deal'. He had grown up with his brothers in the rough and tumble of the streets of Belfast. Here there were real boxing gloves and a ring the size of Dunville Park, with its canvas stained with the blood from earlier fighters. Three rounds with an opponent, a PTI (physical training instructor) acting as referee, Jim won his first fight in some style. Euphoria was short lived however, as in his second contest he ended up having seven bells knocked out of him, by a lad from Liverpool. The Scouse went on to win the Annex Championships in his weight, receiving a medal and certificate, indicative of his skills. He would no doubt progress to the boxing team over at 'The Main'.

John Lee recalls: 'I wasn't the best of boxers but I ended up in the boxing team and the cross country team as well.'

THE MAIN ESTABLISHMENT

Suddenly the basic training was over. What had been a ragtag bunch of undisciplined civilians, now presented themselves on final parade at the Annex, as disciplined, well-turned-out recruits, able and ready to continue their training across at 'The Main'. Wearing their best blue serge number one uniforms, seven creases sharply defined in each bell-bottomed trouser leg (representing the seven seas) immaculate navy blue collars edged with three white stripes representing three famous battles of Admiral Nelson. Copenhagen where he 'saw no signal' and where the first HMS *Ganges* won a battle honour, the Nile and Trafalgar where he lost his life. The black square silks, pressed into narrow bands worn around the boys necks and secured at the front of their jumpers with neat bows, was a further traditional reminder of the great Admiral's death. The boys marched out of the Annex, arms shoulder high, to the strains of 'Hearts of Oak' played by the Royal Marine Band at the head of the procession in their smart blue uniform with their white helmets and sparkling musical instruments to match. They marched proudly in

Front Gate HMS *Ganges* 1935.

HMS *Ganges* Boys' Bugle Band 1935.

through the famous *Ganges* main gate, gave a sharp 'eyes right' to the officer of the day standing outside the guard room who responded with a perfectly executed salute.

Was that a cynical smile Jim detected on the officer's lips? He did not have time to contemplate as the order 'eyes front' brought him beneath the shadow of the great mast towering above him, dominating the enormous area of tarmacadamed parade ground, which he and his classmates would soon know intimately. The stony stare of the figure-head of the old sailing ship HMS *Ganges*, 'The Indian Prince,' a silent sentinel at the base of the famous mast must surely have been warning him of what was yet to come. From the time the boys entered the main gate they were moving at 'the double' (running instead of walking). At *Ganges*, the boys doubled everywhere. The new class doubled through the establishment, down the long covered way to number three mess, Collingwood Division. Jim and his classmates looked like matelots, felt like matelots but to the 2,000 boys already under training they were simply 'nozzers', nothing more, nothing less, boys second class, the lowest of the low. Boy second class Magennis was about to begin his training in earnest, preparing him to take his place in the fleet.

John Lee remembers that very day:

Don Wynne, myself and others were doubled right down to the bottom of the long covered way to join Benbow division. I wanted to become a signalman (bunting tosser), my course would be for one year. Don wanted to become a sparker (telegraphist) whereas Jim Magennis joined as a boy seaman and all his class in Collingwood Division would leave *Ganges* after nine months.

SAILING SHIP

From 1866 to 1899 *Ganges* served as a boys' training ship in Falmouth. Many boys died before training was over. Their bodies lie in a small church graveyard in the village of Mylor outside Falmouth. It is said that forty boys committed suicide during this period and they were buried in un-consecrated ground outside the graveyard.

In 1899 *Ganges* left Falmouth to continue as a boys training ship anchored in the River Stour off Harwich. In 1905 technical advances in steam and the decline in sail led to the setting up of a shore establishment at Shotley Gate, Suffolk. That same year the boys left the old wooden wall for the last time, to march from seaward and commission what was to be

Signalman Stan (Blondie) Millard
Ganges 1938. Shipmate of Mick Magennis on HMS *Kandahar*

recognised as the nation's most successful training centre for boys entering the Senior Service. The old sailing ship was subsequently towed away to end her life in the breakers yard. She was replaced by HMS *Boscawen*, later renamed HMS *Ganges II* (nicknamed 'Twicer') where she remained as tender to the boys' establishment until 1922, when she followed her predecessor to the breakers yard.

Timbers from the sailing ship HMS *Ganges* today form part of the magnificent staircase to be seen at the National Maritime Museum, Greenwich. Others can be seen in the form of wooden crosses in Guildford Cathedral and the Chapel of The Royal Hospital School Holbrook, Suffolk. The stern cabin transon of *Ganges* now forms part of a hotel sited on Burgh Island, Bigbury Bay. The training establishment developed rapidly, boasting a hospital, school, Olympic size swimming pool, and mess decks for the 2,000 boys it would eventually house and train to the high standards of professionalism, recognised throughout the fleet. To have been a '*Ganges* boy' was an affirmation of excellence, acknowledged by senior naval officers, non-commissioned officers and ratings serving on board His Majesty's Ships.

GANGES MAST

The famous *Ganges* mast, standing at the head of the parade ground, a distinctive landmark, seen for miles around from land and sea, is the single best known trademark of the establishment. It was brought ashore by the boys in 1906, manhandled to the spot it now commands as a national monument and stepped. It was erected as a compromise to those who could not accept the training of sailors on land and those with the foresight to see the way forward. It was constructed from the masts of HMS *Cordelia* and *Agincourt* and stood 143 feet high. Every boy trained at *Ganges* was obliged to climb the mast. The first ascent was a terrifying ordeal for anyone. For boys of fifteen and sixteen it was to be their baptism of fire upon that great edifice, symbol of the heady days of sail. It was officially intended 'to build character' and in that respect it was successful. Having once assailed the mast's great height, scrambling outwards and upwards on the rope ladders forming the futtock shrouds, known to sailors as 'the devil's elbow' angled at forty-five degrees to bypass the fighting platform, thus depriving the climber of the easier route aloft through the 'lubbers hole', having hauled himself up the ratlings, over the 'half moon' before descending to the deck below, the young sailor knew no fear of heights. He found within himself qualities and strengths that he did not realise he possessed until he was put

Boys up the mast. HMS *Ganges* 1928

to the test. It was part of the *Ganges* process of turning 'boys into men'.
Boy Seaman Magennis in later years would be required to call upon that
inner strength time and time again.

Ronald Bell (*Ganges* 1931) recalls:

> On arrival at Shotley I soon met the challenge of the mast and swiftly
> attained the button! On Saturdays I used to be first up there to settle
> down (or should I say up) for a crafty puff at Players Virginia cigarettes
> sent by my dear old mum in dark jams. Up there I felt a marvellous
> sense of freedom from authority. They could not get me and I was lord
> of all I surveyed.

Bert Hiscox's (*Ganges* 1921) wages were sixpence per week which
would buy a twopenny bar of chocolate, a packet of writing paper and
envelopes and stamps. His class instructor Petty Officer Bill Simmonds
lined up the class at the foot of the mast and in lines of six ordered 'Way
aloft', as Bert recalls:

> The instructor started to offer sixpence each Saturday to the first boy
> over the mast and threepence to the second. I was very nimble and
> found that a short way up the ratlines nobody could pass me. Three
> weeks after getting the sixpence I was banned.

However, one boy fell to his death in 1928. Ted Appleby (*Ganges*
1928) saw it happen.

> I had been in *Ganges* just a few weeks when I actually saw a boy fall
> from the mast to his death. Very little was said at the time of the unfor-
> tunate incident except that he died on his way to hospital. It was not a
> very good start for those of us who had still to climb the mast and pass
> the test.

HMS *Ganges* ashore developed to become self-contained. Living
accommodation for the boys, in orderly rows, opened out onto 'covered
ways'. These were the main arterial routes cutting through the establishment, creating natural boundaries between the Divisions to which the
boys gave their individual loyalty. Each Division carried the name of a
famous senior naval officer. Drake, Benbow, Anson, Collingwood, Hawke,
Grenville, and the like. Interspersed amongst the living accommodation
were the dhobey house (laundry), shower house, heads (toilets) and galley
(kitchen where food was prepared and served to the boys who carried it to

the mess deck for 'dishing out'). Food was very important in the lives of *Ganges* boys. They could never get enough. After all, they were growing boys!

14 DAYS JANKERS

Although most of the nineteenth century brutality was gone, this did not mean *Ganges* was a picnic. The seamen instructors were often GIs, who struck fear into the hearts of their charges. Some, to enforce their authority upon the boys, carried 'stonakies' (small lengths of rope ends), the sight alone of which created fear. *Ganges* was renowned for strict discipline. Breach of the establishment rules attracted sanctions. Even for the most minor infringements boys were punished. Most boys at some time during their training fell foul of the system, generally through ignorance. Talking in the ranks, out of the correct dress of the day, smoking, and numerous other trivial offences which would not be taken seriously in civilian life were viewed as breaches of King's Regulations and, more importantly, *Ganges* regulations. (For the 'Rules for Boys' see Appendix 2.) Magennis recalls the mast and being punished for smoking:

> My fear of heights was to be shortly overcome by acrobatic drill on the high mast and yard arm. My pay was eight shillings and nine pence per week. For becoming a member of the draggers union, stealing a smoke, I got 14 fourteen days jankers, the punishment of marching with a heavy stick above my head during recreation time.

Corporate responsibility was preached at *Ganges*. It was important that sailors worked together as a team, it was an essential ingredient aboard a warship in action. That after all was what the *Ganges* boys were training for. Individuality was not sacrificed however. The system, whilst teaching team spirit, worked to bring out the best in an individual. Second class Boy Seaman Magennis would call upon his *Ganges* training in life and death situations as he carried out his duties in various theatres of war in the years ahead.

SHOTLEY ROUTINE

Punishment was an ingredient in the philosophy of corporate and individual responsibility. When one member of a class or mess broke the rules, invariably the whole group suffered. It was intended to engender a responsibility in the individual to the benefit of the group. To that end, a pun-

Magennis VC

Sunday Divisions and later march past. HMS *Ganges* 1935

ishment to fit the crime involved the whole unit being subjected to a severe regime of physical exertion (on top of that already being practised during normal training) and deprivation of privileges. 'Shotley Routine ' was the name of that game.

• It involved an early morning call by a not happy instructor also caught up in the 'Shotley Routine '. Another lesson to be learned was, do not incur the wrath of the instructor or badge boys.

• Next, early morning bath (shower) either scalding hot or freezing cold. Back to the mess deck, scrub out. Not a particle of dust must be found on inspection. Sanction: re-scrub.

• Before breakfast kit up with full pack, tin helmet, heavy oilskin (foul weather gear) boots, gaiters and .303 rifle. Doubled to the parade square which the mess, under punishment, (including badge boys) circumnavigated in true naval fashion, until, tired, sweating and aching in every limb, the boys were allowed to take breakfast.

The routine continued during the day, afternoon and into the evening but it did not excuse normal training. At the end of a week, the boys had learned a lesson. They did not readily offer themselves as future candidates for 'Shotley Routine'.

Ken Kent who was a boy at *Ganges* in 1936 remembers:

We suffered under the tyranny of the Divisional Officer. I think his name was Lt. Clark. He was obsessed with obstacle cutters and had the 'Hawkes' down on the river at every possible opportunity rowing and sailing in every kind of weather. Hawke Division did more Shotley routine than any other. Imagine the horror experienced by about fifty boys who had joined the battleship *Warspike* (after leaving *Ganges*) when it was revealed that the boys' Divisional Officer was to be none other than the 'Obstacle Cutter King from Shotley, Lt. Clarke himself.

Doubling up and down Laundry Hill or Faith, Hope and Charity (three rows of steps) was common while under Shotley Routine. Some instructors had their own way of punishing individual boys. Ed Carrol (*Ganges* 1937) recalls one instructor's method: 'His cute trick was to make a boy get down on his hunkers on the parade ground. A rifle is passed behind his elbows and behind his knees and he was made to hop round the parade ground.' Yet not everyone has bad memories of Shotley Routine, T. Lane (*Ganges* 1933) recalls his experience:

Strange to say, the best week I spent at *Ganges* was when our mess was on Shotley Routine for a week. It happened when a few lads were caught using Morse keys to light fags (cigarettes) and burnt the wires out. Well, I was detailed to the camp coal lorry, delivering coal with the leading seaman and ABs of the camp. I lived really high with extra food from the officers and boys' galleys and received tips from officers' houses. It was a great week.

CUTS OF THE CANE

The worst punishment of all was the cane (strokes or cuts they were called). This was only given for more serious offences like theft, running away and total disobedience to your instructors or commanding officer. The days of flogging over a cannon, or worse still flogging around the fleet, were over, but cuts were the closest to it. Carried out over a gym horse the offender was held down by a physical training instructor. The Master at Arms called out to the Duty Officer 'one stroke, sir' and so on until six strokes were given by a Jaunty or RPO (Regulating Petty Officer or naval policemen.) The punishment was meted out with a long 'sally wack' cane which left weals and cuts across the buttocks or upper legs. A medical officer was also present to observe and ensure the punishment was not in excess of what was awarded. Most boys could not sit down for a week or ten days and had to sleep face down.

Ed Carrol (*Ganges* 1937) recalls:

I remember one boy in my class, a lad called Hourihane. He was from Liverpool and developed a painful boil on his backside. He was also unfortunate to be caught smoking by the Royal Marine Patrol. Poor Scouse was ordered to suffer six cuts.

One other incident is remembered very well by Nobby Hall who joined *Ganges* two years before Jim:

One day I found a ha'penny green stamp (unused) on the parade ground and put it in my money belt. Later I was charged with stealing by finding and received six cuts and fourteen days jankers (extra work and loss of pay). That's what is called in the navy 'a bloody green rub' if ever there was one.

Jim's upbringing in West Belfast, and just as tough De la Salle Brothers schooling, gave him a good grounding for the time he spent at *Ganges*, after Jim's class (No. 47) had joined another class in Collingwood division. Their instructors were PO Biddlecombe and CPO Jones, PO

Boy Mason, Leading Boys Randall and Try. The Divisional Officer was Lt. Pumphries and Second Divisional Officer was a Mr Clark. The Commanding Officer was Captain H. H. Rodgers.

SUMMER LEAVE

Soon July was over and summer leave was due. Jim and his classmates headed for home. They had lain awake most of the night, waiting for that special bugle call which signalled leave. 'Tiddly Charlie' played in a most unorthodox but skilful manner by a boy bugler from the *Ganges* bugle band. Triple tonguing a plenty, the hundreds of boys going on leave joining in with their own impromptu rendering of 'Charlie'. What it sounded like in the nearby village and across at Harwich can only be speculation. Kit was packed, 'bag meals' containing sandwiches and other light refreshment (not to be consumed before boarding the train at Ipswich) gripped tightly in an eager hand. The duty paymaster attended to hand out cash payments to the boys. Many had never possessed such large sums before. They felt like millionaires. Jim's weekly pay on entry had been eight shillings and nine pence per week. After qualifying as a first class boy, it rose to fifteen shillings. After deductions, and the additional 'rationed ashore' allowance paid by the navy for victualling whilst on leave, Jim Magennis felt quite 'flush'.

Maisy, Rosemary and Tony were delighted to see him home for three weeks. He had no sooner been away and here he was all dressed up like a Jolly Jack Tar back home again. Jim Magennis shared with them his new experiences in the navy and his old school chums from St Finian's came around to Majorca Street most nights to see him. Stanley McAlinden remembers Jim's first leave:

> When Jim came home on his first leave in the summer of 1935 I remember him coming up the street in his smart navy uniform. We were all standing at Patton's and Bar, the grocery shop at the corner of Mulhouse Street and Grosvenor Road. I remember saying 'Jim you just look smashing.' I was never to join the navy as I met Toni, an Italian girl, and later we opened a fish and chip shop in Roden Street. We were as renowned for our Italian home-made ice cream as Fusco's on the Grosvenor Road.

Jim Magennis enjoyed his three weeks leave but was pleased to return to Shotley. He looked forward to the long boat and train journey that lay ahead.

Three Mess, Collingwood Division. James Magennis third from the right hand side, front row.

BACK FROM LEAVE

Back at *Ganges* the training began in earnest. The days were occupied from dawn to dusk. Early morning started with the communal bath (shower). Even this basic human requirement presented a test of skill and initiative. The naked boys scrambled to get through their ordeal as quickly as possible. This was no leisurely, pleasurable, cleansing of the body, but an attempt to provide the appearance of having showered, whilst avoiding either the 'scalding hot' or 'freezing cold' torrents of water streaming from the overhead faucets. Having somehow achieved that miracle, each boy stood in turn, naked, with arms and legs akimbo, before the class instructor who was muffled up in his greatcoat, against the chill morning air and not too pleased at having been obliged to leave his warm 'pit' in the PO's mess at such an unearthly hour, to supervise a 'shower of worthless nozzers'. The boys who passed the inspection raced through to towel themselves dry. The less fortunate were ordered back to renew their ordeal. Jack Waspe (1939) recalls with humour:

> His eyes started at the boy's head, then travelled to his feet and paused unnecessarily in the midship area. 'My God, boy, you didn't have any toys to play with when you were young did you?' The lad replied, 'I did, sir, but the rest of the other kids didn't'. The boy made a dash for the door. Maybe that was when the phrase 'Time for a sharp exit', was coined.

The day began with the usual issue of a mug of kye and a hard ship's biscuit. A variety of tasks awaited their attention. Kit to be dhobied, including scrubbing of white duck suits with a hard deck scrubber. Boat work on the river, in all weathers, gunnery training, seamanship, navigation, educational classes. For communications ratings, Morse training, coding, radio practice and theory, touch typing, radio telephone procedures, and signalling. Sporting activities played a great part in the development of the young sailor. Emphasis again on the corporate spirit as well as encouraging the individual to express himself. The boys were benefiting from their energetic, outdoor lifestyle. Their physiques were improving as well as their confidence and professionalism. Food was very important in this ongoing development. Stan Millard (1938) remembers mealtimes:

> At meal-times the galley in the long covered way was where the cooks of the mess collected the dinner trays while we boys ate on the

mess square. The food generally, whilst not over exciting was whole-some, and not a lot went in the gash bucket.

SWIMMING TEST

Every boy had to be able to swim and pass a swimming test. This was seen as a top priority in their training schedule. The swimming test was not easy to pass. Often good swimmers failed. It was no ordinary test. Examinees were required to wear a canvas duck suit throughout. This was to simulate the wearing of clothing in the sea, when forced to aban-don ship. The test was carried out in the Olympic-sized swimming baths. Boys were required to enter the pool in the deep end from off a high diving board. That in itself was a daunting experience. All air was forced from the heavy canvas duck suit, which quickly absorbed water making the suit a weighty, dragging impediment to progress through the water. The test required that the boy swim a number of lengths of the pool, returning to the deep end, where he was to tread water for three minutes under the watchful eye of PTI's. Armed with long boat hooks, they unceremoniously hauled out boys experiencing difficulty, or pushed back those attempting to leave the pool before completing the test. At least one death resulted during the swimming tests.

To fail the test was to be labelled 'a backward swimmer'. This incurred sanction, and backward swimmers were obliged to attend the swimming baths every morning, where they trained to pass the test. Many boys could not swim at the outset and the training took place before the normal day's routine began. Each backward swimmer was identified, whilst subject to that status, by a bulky cork and canvas lifebelt worn over his outer cloth-ing from awakening each morning, to lights out, as a symbol of his failure. End of term leave was denied to backward swimmers. Boys quickly learned to swim under this carrot and stick system. Many a sailor owed his life in later years to the system which dictated that he would be a swimmer before he joined the fleet.

TIME TO JOIN THE FLEET

Nine months of arduous training was over. First class boy seaman Magennis had qualified, and wearing his new individually tailored 'sea suit' had marched with his class on their final Sunday morning parade. As senior draft class, they proudly marched as leading platoon ahead of the 2,000 other boys on parade. Jim had done well, only being in the rattle (trouble) a few times for small offences. The fifth of March 1936 was the day No. 3 mess Collingwood division were to go on draft. Boy seaman Magennis and his classmates were all issued with hammocks. They were all going their separate ways, some never to see each other again. Having been promoted to First Class Boy Jim's wages had risen to fifteen shillings per week. The Boy Seamen were drafted to HMS *Vernon* or other seamanship courses like the torpedo school at HMS *Defiance,* Plymouth, some straight to ships. Others went to train in gunnery at HMS *Excellent* at Whale Island, Portsmouth. Those who wanted to become signalmen or telegraphists would stay on another three months at *Ganges.*

Out the main gate the coach that brought them in ten months ago took them back to Ipswich station where the train went to London. The boys said their farewells and headed to Chatham, Portsmouth or Devonport. Left behind was Laundry Hill, Faith, Hope and Charity, Shotley Routine and names they would never forget. They all had sailors names now. Jim would shortly be called 'Mick' Magennis. Other boy seamen would have names such as Tancy Lee, Jumper Collins, Slinger Woods, Shiner Wright, Nobby Clarke, Dixey Dean, Buster Brown, Jock, Taff, Jan, Scouse, and Geordie. The boys would learn many more names, that have passed through the matelots' vernacular over the years. Mick would meet PO Watkins his Tin Town class instructor later on in his naval career. But now it was time to join the fleet. Jim, or now with his new sailor's name of Mick, Magennis remembers leaving *Ganges* as he told the *Daily Mail* on 4 April 1960:

> Moderate, that was my efficiency assessment on leaving *Ganges*, with my character marked as very good. I had escaped the most feared of all punishments but my luck was not to hold out as I soon was to receive the worst punishment for a boy, six cuts of the cane, a few months later on board the cruiser HMS *Dauntless.*

THREE

1936-39 General Service

GENERAL SERVICE ON *ROYAL SOVEREIGN, DAUNTLESS, ENTERPRISE, HERMES*

Chatham, Devonport and Portsmouth were the three main naval ports. These three dockyards with barracks attached were called Pembroke, Drake and Victory, and are part of the history of the Royal Navy. The Admirals of the Red, the White and the Blue, were based in these ports. In later times these all came under one flag. The White is where the flag of the Royal Navy comes from, the 'White Ensign'. The 'Red Ensign' (The Red Duster) became the Merchant Navy flag and the 'Blue Ensign' became the flag of the Royal Fleet Auxiliary, the fuel and store ships that serviced the Royal Navy. All three services depended on each other, one to bring the much-needed materials which an isolated group of islands like the British Isles needed to survive, the second to protect both merchant ships and the islands from outside attack and the third to service the Royal Navy. The trade with overseas countries created wealth from the earliest times which in turn brought taxes to pay for this form of protection. So Mick had joined a huge system of sea-going policemen whose one and only job was to protect the interests of Britain and the British colonies overseas and their peoples.

The morning of 6 March 1936 was cold and bleak. First Class Boy Seaman Magennis was to join his first warship, HMS *Royal Sovereign*. The battleship lay in Portsmouth Harbour preparing for sea. She flew an admiral's flag and she and the fleet were to sail on the morning's tide for a shake-down cruise in the Bay of Biscay. Her silhouette with her huge 15 inch guns stood out against the sky more prominently than the much smaller cruisers and destroyers, some of which were to accompany her the next day.

The ship's Liberty Cutter came alongside the jetty and Mick, three other boys and a number of ratings all with kit bags and hammocks boarded her for the short journey across the harbour to join the ship. The cutter taking Mick and the other new drafts across the harbour to join the battleship was to stand off as the admiral's barge came alongside the gangway first. The shrill call of the bosun's pipe could be heard in the still morning air as the ship's side party piped on board the admiral and some other senior officers who had spent the last night ashore with their wives. The cutter shortly manoeuvred alongside the gangway. Boy Seaman Mick Magennis and a number of other naval ratings left the cutter, climbed the gangway with their kit bags and hammocks and joined the warship.

FIRST DAY AT SEA

0300 hours: *Royal Sovereign* slipped her moorings and headed out to sea and the fleet followed her.

0600 hours: Mick heard the bugle calling Charlie (Reveille) down the tannoy system and the words 'Call the hands, call the hands, call the hands, lash up and stow, lash up and stow'. Mick and all the boys who slept in hammocks for the first time jumped out and started to lash their hammocks as they had been taught. They were then stowed in hammock racks at the corners of the mess.

0615 hours: A shrill call of the bosun's pipe called their attention to hear 'Cooks to the galley, cooks to the galley, men under punishment fall in outside the Master-at-Arms office'. While the duty cooks hurried to the galley to collect the breakfast trays, the killick (leading hand) of the mess organised the boys to square off the mess for breakfast when the duty men brought back the food trays.

0630 hours: Guard and steerage men from the middle watch who had brought the ship to sea had an extra half hour's sleep. They now lashed their hammocks.

0800 hours: Bosun's pipe again 'Forenoon watchmen to muster. Day work hands turn to'. The morning watchmen came off watch and had their breakfast. They then scrubbed the mess out and turned to with the rest of the day work hands. Mick was in a boys' mess. Battleships and large ships such as cruisers had boys' messes because they had a large number of boy seamen. On smaller ships the boys would be mixed in with the rest of the crew. That morning Mick and all the new drafts were mustered outside the Master-at-Arms office. They were issued with station cards and given the usual run-down of what they could and could not do. They would later be given a tour of the ship, appointed their killick, PO (Petty Officer), CPO (Chief Petty Officer) and divisional officer and given their duties.

1015 hours: Bosun's pipe, 'Stand easy, stand easy'.

1030 hours: Bosun's pipe, 'Turn to, turn to'.

1100 hours: Bosun's pipe, 'Up spirits, up spirits'. The Duty Officer along with PO, RPO (Regulating Petty Officer) and Duty Jack Dusty would open up the rum store. He measured out the daily rum issue and then mixed the rum ration with water for the junior rates. Each mess rum bosun collected the daily mess issue of rum in a large rum fanny. A whole ceremony went along with this Royal Navy tradition.

1200 hours: Bosun's pipe, 'Hands to the mess for rum, call afternoon watchmen, hands to dinner'. All men over twenty were entitled to a rum ration except men under punishment, or those who preferred temperance. The ratings had water mixed with their rum. Only senior ratings, POs and CPOs were entitled to neat rum. Rum in the navy was better than money and although frowned upon was used for bartering. Most officers turned a blind eye.

1300 hours: Bosun's pipe call, 'Day work men turn to'. During the afternoon except when emergency station exercises were taking place, watch keepers were able to catch up with a couple of hours sleep. All the rest of the crew worked through the day.

1600 hours: Bosun's pipe call, 'Call first dog watch'.

1800 hours: Bosun's pipe call, 'Call the last dog watch'.

2000 hours:. Bosun's pipe call, 'Call the first watch'.

2130 hours: The Duty Officer's rounds to see all messes were ship shape before pipe down.

2200 hours:. Pipe down, a royal marine bugler sounded the Last Post, lights out.

2400 hours and 0400 hours: Middle and morning watchmen called quietly.

This routine would generally be followed on most Royal Navy ships. The smaller ships would not have Royal Marine buglers and all calls were preceded by the bosun's pipe call to attention. Large battleships would sometimes have Royal Marine Bands on board in peace time. When the Flag Ship was visiting foreign countries on the first day in port, the officers, captain and admiral had cocktail parties with music for the local town dignitaries. It was called 'showing the flag'.

And so Mick's first day to gain his sea legs was over. *Royal Sovereign* and the battle cruiser HMS *Renown*, which his brother Bill was on, were two of only twenty-two capital warships the Royal Navy had in commission. In the previous war the *Royal Sovereign* was a modern efficient warship. Now she was getting old. Her main engines, boiler rooms and her mighty 15 inch guns were giving her trouble. She had just had a major refit and this shakedown cruise was to try and improve her efficiency.

BATTLE OF JUTLAND VCs

The old battleship had done her duty in World War I and had a long history with famous officers and men who had served on board. Her vice admiral, Sir Richard Bell Davies, won a Victoria Cross at Ferry Junction, Thrace in November 1915. He was executive officer on the battleship when she was flagship of the Atlantic fleet from 1924-26. At the Battle of Jutland on the 31 May 1916 the Grand Fleet lost fourteen ships with 6,097 killed and 510 wounded. The German High Seas Fleet lost eleven ships with 2,551 men killed and 507 wounded. Captain Edward Bamford (RM) won his award at Zeebrugge in April 1918 and was on board *Royal Sovereign* at the surrender of the German High Seas Fleet in the Firth of Forth in 1918. The German admiral later ordered the fleet to be scuttled in Scapa Flow. Four Victoria Crosses were awarded at Jutland. Boy Seaman Trevor Cornwell was on HMS *Chester* and was just sixteen, when he died in action. He was decorated posthumously with the VC. Cornwell was the youngest and perhaps the most famous boy award winner during World War I. The other three officers were, Major William Harvy (RM) VC on board the light cruiser HMS *Lion*, Cdr. William Jones (RN) VC was commanding officer on board the destroyer HMS *Shark*, and the fourth award that day in 1916 was won by Cdr. (later Rear Admiral RN) Edward Bingham VC (from Bangor, County Down). He was commanding officer on board the destroyer HMS *Nestor* which was subsequently sunk in action with the German High Seas Fleet. (The History of the Victoria Cross–Appendix 1).

HMS *DAUNTLESS* AND HMS *ENTERPRISE*

After three weeks at sea, *Royal Sovereign* anchored off Gibraltar and on 30 March 1936, Boy Seaman Magennis was drafted to another ship. His time on board the battleship was indeed short. He had really only been in transit while the navy decided where to send him and shortly after the battleship dropped her anchor, he found himself in the liberty cutter being rowed across the harbour to join the light cruiser HMS *Dauntless*. The warship (4,850 tons) had been built the year he was born (1919) and was being used as an escort for troop ships going east. She was one of the navy's D class fleet cruisers, armed with six inch guns and one of eight ships built at the end of World War I. There was a demand for the fast light cruisers that effectively scouted at Jutland in the previous war. They went in and made contact with the High Seas Fleet and reported its movements. This type was intended for work in the North Sea. Many years after the war was over, they were deployed for other uses, e.g. troop escorts.

Dauntless sailed in April 1936 and joined the troop ships in the western Mediterranean to escort them east to India. During the journey to India the ship stopped at Malta, where Mick's only run ashore earned him the honour of Kissing the Cannon's Daughter, receiving six cuts of the cane for being a bad boy. After sailing through the Suez Canal and a stop at Aden, the troop ships sailed to Bombay and *Dauntless* joined the other ships in the East India Station at anchor in Trincomalee in Ceylon. Mick was drafted again to join the 7,550 ton cruiser HMS *Enterprise* on 27 June 1936.

Enterprise and her sister ship *Emerald* were built after the Great War in 1926. She had been on patrol in the Indian Ocean with Emerald and other ships belonging to the fourth cruiser squadron. The heavy cruiser had been the first British ship to have a twin 6 inch turret. This innovation proved successful and led to the *Nelson* battleship receiving twin 6 inch guns as a secondary battery. Both *Emerald* and *Enterprise* were fast and their long 'trawler' bows made them very good sea boats.

In October 1937 Mick was promoted to Ordinary Seaman and had an increase in pay to twenty-six shillings a week. But he was really looking forward to his twentieth birthday when he could draw his rum ration. He still had two years to go.

Enterprise was coming to the end of her commission and one morning in January 1938 the warship left the beautiful natural harbour of Trincomalee for the last time. She sailed back to England via the Red Sea, Suez Canal and the Mediterranean Sea, stopping only at Malta and Gibraltar for fuel, water and stores. Bill's ship HMS *Hostile* was in Malta harbour the day *Enterprise* tied up in Selema Creek on her journey home to England. Bill remembers the night his brother and himself spent ashore together. He recalls:

Jim was still under age and not allowed overnight leave. I remember having to sign a statement so he could stay ashore. We stopped in a boarding house called the 'Cock and Bottle' after a good day and night ashore in the sailor's district known as the 'Gut'. The next day the *Enterprise* sailed on to Gibraltar on her way home. The Spanish

HMS *Enterprise* at anchor at Trincomalee, Ceylon 1937

Civil War had started in July 1936 and *Hostile* along with ships from six other nations were constantly on patrol off the Spanish coast. We rescued many refugees from Palma (Majorca) and Barcelona. Once while we were playing football against the German navy in Palma, republican aircraft came over and attacked our ships. Another time I remember we rescued a Madam and a whole troupe of ladies of the night and shipped them back to Malta.

ENTERPRISE ENDS COMMISSION

Mick's short meeting with his brother Bill was over. *Enterprise* sailed to Gibraltar the next day. Bill had given him a few 'rabbits' (presents) to bring home to Belfast for his mum and sister Rosemary. At Gibraltar, on board *Enterprise,* the ship's company changed from their white tropical uniforms into winter blues. Mick later washed his whites and when dry he ironed them as he was taught at HMS *Ganges* and neatly packed them away in his kit-bag for another ship and another day. While the ship was crossing the Bay of Biscay the crew were all excited about heading home. Some had been away for over two years. Mick's last leave had been Christmas 1935. The morning the cruiser entered the Solent it was cold damp and grey. He remembered a similar day twenty-one months back when he joined the battleship *Royal Sovereign* to go to sea for the first time. Now he was coming home after serving on three warships since that day.

Mick and other seamen were on deck making final preparations for entering Portsmouth harbour when the duty signalman hoisted the long thin 'paying-off' pennant, which flew from the main mast in the cold winter's breeze above the quarterdeck flagstaff, which in turn flew the Royal Naval white ensign. The sailors lined up in single file and manned the ship's side dressed in their blue uniforms. They felt the climate bitter and cold; more so that bleak February morning in 1938, as the warship sailed into harbour. Later with the help of a dockyard tug boat *Enterprise* was slowly manoeuvred alongside the naval dockyard jetty.

The ship docked and the Royal Marine band was on the jetty playing 'All the nice girls love a sailor'. The jetty was crowded with wives, families and girlfriends of the officers and men of the *Enterprise* and Mick felt slightly sad that Maisy and Rosemary were not there to greet him. It was only a passing thought as it was a long way from Belfast and anyway the next day he would be off home on well deserved leave. He was a real Jolly Jack Tar now and boy had he some stories to tell them back in Belfast!

HOME FOR LEAVE 1938

Having not been home for two years Belfast was going to be some crack. Maisy and Rosemary were delighted to see their son and brother home. Mick would have had his leave pay and he brought home 'rabbits' (presents) for the family from himself from the Far East and his brother Bill from Malta. He visited Kelly's while on leave. School pals John Murphy and Eddie McIntyre, Sally Hannigan and local character Johnny Cunningham and his ex-army pals Lucky Gordon and Peg Leg Patton, who all frequented the bar gave Mick and his pals a warm welcome. The crack was mighty as many army and sea stories were told. Sally brought out bottles of poteen from under the counter to supplement the usual red biddy and stout. Old and young, Protestant and Catholic, mixed and a good time was had by all.

Sergeant Fitzpatrick and constables from Roden Street police barracks called in to receive their customary peacemaking glass of poteen. The McIntyre family, Francie Ferron and his mother Annie from Theodore Street ended up most nights in each other's houses. Eddie McIntyre told Mick that the Mullan brothers, Francie and Dick, also from Theodore Street, had joined the navy. After Mick told him about

the runs ashore in the Far East, Tony told Mick that he too was thinking of joining up. Earlier in the year Tony and Joci McIntyre had run off
to England. Jimmy McIntyre recalls:

> My brother Joci and Tony McGinnes ran away to England and
> joined the army. They had lied about their ages and Maisy had gone
> over and found out what regiment they were in and brought both of
> them home by the scruff of the neck.'

Poor Tony listening to Mick's sea stories. He could not wait until he
came of age. Anyway his time would come sooner than he expected.
Mick and his school pals all went over to watch Belfast Celtic v Linfield
football match at the Paradise football ground where there was the usual
punch-up. Among many tears and the now getting-used-to farewells,
Mick set out on the journey back to Portsmouth in April 1938 to join
HMS *Enterprise*.

When in Portsmouth Mick would have been able to have a look
around the old historic dockyard. The one ship worth visiting was HMS
Victory, the old wooden ship of the line in which Nelson had fought the
Battle of Trafalgar. She was preserved in a special dry-dock so visitors
could go on board and look around her in peacetime. Mick was struck
by her smallness compared to modern warships. Larger ships like HMS
Hood, a 41,200 ton battle cruiser alongside the harbour wall just behind
it dwarfed it. There was a mixture of warships in the dockyard. Some
were in a state of repair and some like *Enterprise* were just back from
serving overseas. Further to the right lay an aircraft carrier and she was
preparing to go to sea. She had no aeroplanes on board. They would fly
on board after the ship had sailed. Mick was to join an aircraft carrier
HMS *Hermes* at Devonport later, but first he was to spend a short time
time in naval barracks which most sailors often did between drafts when
in home waters.

HMS *HERMES*

After a short spell in Devonport barracks Mick joined the aircraft carrier HMS *Hermes* on 25 May 1938. She too had been built in 1919. He
now had been on three ships that were built the year he was born. The
10,850 ton ship sailed for exercises shortly after he joined her. *Hermes*
was the first ship designed by the admiralty as an aircraft carrier. In
1923 she was commissioned for service with Captain A. Stopford in

command. She joined the Atlantic fleet and later served in the Mediterranean. From 1925 to 1933 *Hermes* saw continual service in the Far East operating with seaplanes on the Shanghai River and in Hong Kong. Flights from *Hermes* included eight sorties in connection with anti-pirate operations against the Chinese pirates attacking and capturing merchant vessels. In 1933 *Hermes* returned to home waters and began a long refit at Devonport. On completion of the £217,740 refit she returned to the China station under command of Captain G. Fraser on 1 November 1934. After two more years service on the China station *Hermes* returned home to join the reserve fleet. When Mick Magennis joined the aircraft carrier she had just returned to service and was being used as a training ship for the fleet air arm. She had a speed of twenty-five knots and a complement of 550 to 650 men.

Three other fleet carriers *Courageous, Glorious* and *Furious* had been built as battle-cruisers after World War 1. They were later converted to fleet carriers in the early 1920s. During 1938 *Hermes* was based with the home fleet.

In October 1938 Mick was promoted again, to able seaman and another pay rise followed. One more year to go until he was entitled to his rum ration. After Mick's Christmas leave at home in Belfast, *Hermes* was deployed for more exercises with the Mediterranean fleet and was later to return to Gibralter as a training ship. However in 1939 the buzz was going around the ship that they would be heading home again as the Reserve Fleet was being called up and that only meant one thing, the threat of war.

BUILD-UP TO WORLD WAR II

Back at sea, while all this preparation for war was going on, the British Royal Navy went about its usual duties preparing for its 1939 annual spring cruise. In January of that year, the home fleet was at anchor in Gibraltar. The capital ships present were *Nelson, Rodney* and Mick's first ship *Royal Sovereign*. Also in harbour were the cruisers *Southampton, Newcastle, Sheffield, Glasgow* and *Aurora*. The fifth destroyer flotilla joined them and in early February the fleet sailed for their spring shakedown cruise. *Hermes* was later to visit Lisbon in Portugal in between exercises. Mick noticed the ship was starting to have more damage control exercises, and there were more exercises for abandoning ship. He felt something was in the wind. After some months of preparation exercises with the fleet, the ship docked and he was sent on leave. He had only arrived home

Vintners Ball Christmas 1938, Falls Road Belfast.
(Standing, on the extreme left) James Magennis with his schoolfriend John Murphy next to him

for one week when he heard that his brother was on HMS *Electra*, one of the E-class destroyers.

On 1 August 1939 Mick was drafted to HMS *Defiance*, the torpedo school, for a torpedo course. On 8 August the King reviewed the home and reserve fleets in Weymouth Bay. One hundred and thirty-three ships took part and 12,000 naval reservists were called up. While Mick was at HMS *Defiance* Britain and France declared war on Germany on 3 September 1939 honouring a promise to protect Poland which they had made in April.

Mick's brother, Bill, on board HMS *Electra*, recalls:

It was Friday, 1 September, and we were listening to the news. When it was announced that Germany had invaded Poland, there was a brief silence, then one bloke suddenly, speaking for all of us, said, 'The bastard's not going to back down!' However the British and French forces in Western Europe were too far away to stop the German invasion. So for the next seven months they did little actual fighting on land. People called it the 'Phoney War'.

FOUR

HMS *Kandahar* 1939-41

The day war was declared the 13,500 ton SS *Athenia* was torpedoed by the German submarine U-30 off the coast of Ireland. One hundred and twenty-eight lives were lost. The ship had sailed from Glasgow on 1 September and called at Liverpool and Belfast to collect passengers before departing for Montreal, Canada. SS *Athenia* was carrying 1,103 passengers, of whom 311 were American citizens, when she was attacked 250 miles off Inishtrahuir. To add to this sad incident on the 10 September the British submarine *Oxley* being out of position was torpedoed and sunk in the North Sea by *Triton* a friendly submarine. Only the commanding officer and one rating from *Oxley* survived. One week later on 17 September HMS *Courageous,* an aircraft carrier, was sunk by U-29, 500 miles off Lands End. Of her crew of 1,202, 515 were lost. Commander Mountbatten and his crew on board the destroyer *Kelly* helped rescue numerous survivors from HMS *Courageous.* Mick's brother Bill recalls the rescue of passengers from SS *Athenia*:

> I was on board the destroyer *Electra* and remember rescuing many survivors from the torpedoed passenger liner SS *Athenia*. We manoeuvred within a mile of her and prepared to receive lifeboats, a number of which were making for us. Sadly, as well as lifeboats there were bodies, old, middle-aged, young, all in pyjamas or in nightwear...When it was thought that all possible survivors had been taken aboard, one last thing was done: a boat was sent to the *Athenia* carrying two of her own officers to confirm that there was no-one left on board. To their amazement they found a woman in the sick bay.

The next month HMS *Royal Oak* was sunk in Scapa Flow by U-47 on 14 October with the loss of 800 lives. There were 424 survivors. Britain's second capital warship had been sunk in World War II. Some of the

Navy's other aircraft carriers were the *Hermes*, the *Formidable*, and more modern ships of 24,000 tons each, the *Indomitable, Victorious, Illustrious, Ark Royal, Eagle* and fleet carriers *Glorious* and *Furious*. On board these ships *Albacores, Seafires*,and *Fairey*, Swordfish torpedo spotter reconnaissance planes and other Fleet Air Arm aircraft were practising taking off and landing and continuous day and night sorties week in week out in preparation for the long war that lay ahead of them.

Early in the war Germany's U-boat offensive mounted an impressive list of shipping casualties before Britain could get the convoy system working. The early success for the navy in late 1939 was the sinking of the German pocket battleship *Graf Spee* in the running sea battle in the South Atlantic and finally the River Plate with the cruisers *Ajax, Achilles* and *Exeter*. The old cruiser *Cumberland* (nicknamed 'One Player and two Willie Woodbines' after her three funnels) had been damaged early in the action. Finally *Graf Spee* was scuttled in the River Plate; afterwards the German captain shot himself. The first major success by a British submarine was in the North Sea in December 1939 when HM/SM *Salmon*, under Lt. Cdr. Bickford DSO and Bar, in three separate attacks torpedoed and damaged the German cruisers *Leipzig* and *Nürnberg* and sank U-36. His crew were awarded three DSCs and seven DSMs. *Salmon* was later sunk by a mine off Norway six months later on 9 July 1940.

After serving on board four ships that had been built during and after World War I, Mick was at last to get a new ship. On 6 October 1939 he was drafted to HMS *Kandahar*. The new crew travelled from Devonport to Dunbarton in Scotland where *Kandahar* had been built. She was one of eight thirty-six knot destroyers. They had two 4.7 inch guns forward and ten twenty one-inch torpedo tubes and was 1,670 tons. Commander Robson was the commanding officer and once the ship was commissioned she sailed for a work-up month. On 27 October 1939 Mick reached twenty years of age and was entitled to his rum ration. His station card was stamped 'grog.' Those days in St Finian's school on the Falls Road seemed so long ago. Now he was on a new warship at war and entitled to have a rum ration.

Leading Torpedo Operator Ervine Fleming from the Shankill Road, Belfast, was one of the advance party who joined *Kandahar* one month before the main crew:

I was one of twenty in the advance party who travelled up from Devonport barracks to join the destroyer *Kandahar* in Scotstown when she was built by Denny Brothers in Dumbarton. When the

LTO Ervine Fleming *(left)* with his Shankill Road friend Acting PO Sam Patterson at Bellvue, Belfast. Sam won a DSM while serving on board the submarine *Satyr* when she sank U-987 off Norway on 15 June 1944.

main crew arrived I first met Mick Magennis. We became shipmates. I found out we both came from Belfast. He came from the Grosvenor Road and I came from the Shankill Road. *Kandahar* sailed and started the ships work-up and sea trials in the Clyde Estuary.

Mick later told the *Daily Mail* :

When war broke out I was on a seaman torpedoman's course in HMS *Defiance* at Devonport. Things were so hectic that I was drafted in the middle of my course to the new destroyer *Kandahar,* one of Lord Louis Mountbatten's fifth flotilla. Already on board was his nephew the Marquis of Milford Haven, David Michael Mountbatten, a twenty-one year old Sub Lt. who was later to put me on commander's report for returning late and without cap after all night leave. The ship's company was later to become very proud to serve with Sub Lt. Mountbatten and other officers on board *Kandahar*, including our commanding officer, Cdr. Robson DSO.

After *Kandahar* had finished her work-up and engine and boiler trials, she sailed for Devonport to take on ammunition. The new destroyer sailed on to Spithead off Portsmouth for gunnery and torpedo trials, and then to Greenock to join the other ships being detached for patrol in the North Sea and Atlantic Ocean. During November/December 1939 and the first few months of 1940 *Kandahar* was continuously at sea, only returning to port to fuel and return on patrol. The frequent action stations and damage control exercises made life on board very uncomfortable for everyone during these early months of the war at sea. Nineteen-forty started sadly for the British Navy, especially the submarine service who lost three boats in four days. The *Undine, Seahorse* and *Starfish* were all sunk by enemy attack near the Heligoland Bight, on 6,7 and 9 January respectively. The German radio gave out the news on 16 January that survivors from *Undine* and *Starfish* had been rescued.

Able Seaman Edmond Carroll, later PO Gunner, joined *Kandahar* along with Mick in October 1939:

I first met Mick Magennis when we joined a brand new destroyer and became shipmates. I, like Mick, came from Belfast where I lived with my mother and stepfather in Northwood Road off the Shore Road before joining *Ganges* as a boy in 1937. Mick was one of four quartermasters on board *Kandahar*. They had their own little mess deck under the bridge which isolated them from the rest of the crew. We did have a few runs ashore together but early in the war we were rarely in port except to fuel the ship and take on board ammunition.

Scapa Flow was the home base for *Kandahar* to return to for fuel and stores. Bill, on board *Electra* remembers:

One day *Kandahar* tied up alongside *Electra* at Scapa Flow. My brother came on board that night and shared supper with myself and a couple of shipmates. It was the last time we would see each other for another two years. Six weeks later *Electra* was in collision with another destroyer, *Vanock* in the North Sea. The ship limped into Troon and went into dry dock for repair. I was drafted to HMS *Vernon* to do my Killicks course before being drafted to HMS *Vanquisher*, a World War I destroyer.

Mick Magennis remembers those early war days when in 1960 he told a *Daily Mail* reporter:

Those early days were spent chasing around the North Sea hunting U-boats, seeking the elusive *Graf Spee* before she headed south to her doom. For months on end we fought rough seas. Once we did a roll of forty-five degrees. I was on the wheel. It spun out of my hands. I crashed against the bulkhead. 'Do you think we will come up again', called George Cook, my mate.

FIRST ENCOUNTER WITH THE ENEMY

In early May 1940 *Kandahar* sailed from Greenock with her sister ship *Kelly* in company with other ships. That evening *Kandahar* reported she had contacted a U-boat. She and *Kelly* were ordered to hunt the contact with depth charge attacks. This proved unsuccessful and with dusk approaching Cdr. Mountbatten on board *Kelly* decided to rejoin the main force which now included the cruiser *Birmingham*. Meanwhile the destroyer *Bulldog* which had lost contact with her own flotilla signalled *Kelly* asking permission to join her. The signal was approved but the *Bulldog* was a long way back. In the falling light the *Kelly* and *Kandahar* steamed on with *Bulldog* following up the rear. Then the explosion came. A torpedo smashed into *Kelly's* plates on the forward boiler-room and burst with a terrifying blast. A great lick of flame roared up into the night, the mast head silhouetted black and stark against its flare. The men lay dead, dying, wounded and stunned. *Kelly* lay over to starboard in a cloud of hissing steam and smoke with a great hole torn in her side from her keel almost to her upper deck. All power was gone. The men on the bridge of the *Kandahar* saw the terrible flash of the torpedo and searched vainly in the pall of the smoke and steam for signs of *Kelly*. They decided that she must have gone down. Mountbatten's nephew, the Marquis of Milford Haven, was officer of the watch on *Kandahar*. At action stations the coxswain was on the wheel, usually the job of a quartermaster, like Mick, who took over the telegraph during action stations. Lt. Clay was the first lieutenant and gunnery officer and Lt. Graham (another marquis) was the navigating officer. Able Seaman Carroll was closed up at his action station on the machine gun under the bridge.

Then a second unusual incident happened. A German E-boat appeared out of the blackness going at forty knots. The whole boat with its screaming crew rode right up onto the canted deck and smashed its way aft. The E-boat disappeared in the darkness astern with her engines still running. German sailors' screams tailed away into silence as she sank.

On 10 May, as dawn approached *Kandahar* put her stern alongside *Kelly* and took off the wounded. Now came the task that everyone on board *Kelly* dreaded. PO Gunner Clark had been ordered to find as many bodies as could be found among the wreckage and sew them up in hammocks so that they could be given a Christian burial. Lord Mountbatten then read a short funeral service and they consigned their mess mates to the deep. These were the sailors' bodies they could find. Another 22, stokers, engine-room staff and other crew were later buried ashore.

Mick Magennis knew fear for the first time in his life. He recalled his feeling many years later in 1969 to David Francis of the *Daily Mail*:

> Fear is a word people never mention to me, as though they don't think I could ever be afraid. But fear came to me when the smoke of battle had died down; when all that lingered was a dawn mist that hung like funeral crepe...and death. The action was over. Enemy E-boats had torpedoed *Kelly*. Her sister ship *Kandahar* was edging alongside to take off the injured. It was the sight of the dead and dying that struck real fear in me for the first time in my life. It made me sick. It paralysed me. I remembered the remedy my old gunners mate gave for everything: 'fight it'.

Aboard *Kelly* they were still fighting for the lives of their shipmates who were still trapped in the wreckage. A tall gaunt figure in a duffel coat

The destroyer, HMS *Kelly* at full speed.

Memorial stone to the twenty-seven men who died on board HMS *Kelly*
in the North Sea in 1940 and to Lord Mountbatten

strode the quarterdeck helping the injured. Lord Louis Mountbatten, then a captain, was in command. 'Steady, easy there, hard away.' His words were as confident as when he had cleared the lower decks on taking command of the destroyer flotilla. That day in harbour he was all tiddled up (seamen's talk for naval smartness); now his face was blackened by smoke. His clothes were dishevelled by hours of action. His crew loved him for it all. No one could say a wrong word about Lord Louis to any of his crew without fear of getting 'filled in' (knocked out). He was as popular as that.

Gunner Edmond Carroll recalls:

> We were steaming just behind *Kelly* along with the destroyer *Bulldog* and we heard this enormous bang. We momentarily switched on our searchlight, but all we could see was a huge cloud of steam and we thought she had gone. At dawn we found her still afloat, our skipper put our stern against *Kelly* and took off most of her crew and somehow (with *Bulldog* towing and *Kandahar* escorting) we managed to get our own battered sister ship back home to the Tyne. What a reception we got from the Geordies. I'll never forget it. The remaining twenty-two dead sailors were buried in Hebburn-on-Tyne. *Kelly* went into dry dock to be repaired. My wife and I still go occasionally to visit the memorial. It still brings tears to my eyes when I go there.

The war on land carried on. France surrendered and the Germans occupied northern and western France and the Channel Islands. The phoney war was over. The Battle of Britain had begun. Winston Churchill had become Prime Minister in May 1940 and since the beginning of 1940 the Royal Navy had been fighting the German Navy for control of the Atlantic Ocean. German U-boats began to sink merchant ships coming from America with food and raw materials much needed for Britain's war effort. British destroyers were out hunting the U-boats which were beginning to hunt in wolf packs.

FIRST THREE NAVAL VICTORIA CROSSES OF WORLD WAR II

In April 1940 Lt. Cdr. Roope was to be awarded the first naval Victoria Cross of World War II. He was captain of the destroyer *Glowworm*, one of the escorting ships to the battle cruiser *Renown* heading north in the Norwegian Sea. On 7 April a man was lost overboard and Roope turned the ship around to try, unsuccessfully, to find him. While doing so the weather deteriorated and he lost contact with the flagship *Renown* and escorting ships.

At first light on 8 April *Glowworm* made contact with a German destroyer *Paul Jakob* and engaged action. Another German destroyer *Bernd von Arnim* and the 10,000 ton heavy cruiser *Admiral Hipper* arrived on the scene. Roope was out gunned by overwhelming opposition and should have retreated but instead he went into action. He was hit several times. The doctor and all the sick bay party were killed by a direct hit on the captain's day cabin. Another shell brought down part of the foremast. After firing her torpedo which missed, *Glowworm* with her steam siren wailing, turned to ram the *Admiral Hipper*. She struck the larger ship amidships tearing away 100 feet of her armour plating and damaging the starboard side torpedo tubes. After drawing clear, Roope ordered 'abandon ship.' He stayed on the bridge smoking a cigarette.

One officer and thirty men survived out of a crew of 149. Captain Helmuth Heye, the *Hipper's* captain, chivalrously stayed back for an hour to pick up survivors. Lt. Cdr. Roope drowned with most of his crew and was awarded the VC. The surviving officer Lt. Ramsey was awarded the DSO and three of the ship's company received the CGM.

Two more Victoria Crosses were awarded in April/May 1940. HMS *Harty*, under Captain Warrington-Lee in Narvik, sank or damaged several merchant ships. Five German destroyers eventually cornered her and he beached the ship to save the crew. The Norwegian people hid the survivors until another British destroyer picked them up. He was gazetted a posthumous Victoria Cross on 7 June 1940.

Also in April/May, Lt. Stannard RNR on the trawler *Arab* won a Victoria Cross at Namsos in Norway. After landing 850 French troops, he had a running battle with German aircraft shooting down a Heinkel bomber. He received his Victoria Cross from the king on the first anniversary of the war in September 1940.

KANDAHAR SAILS EAST

When *Kandahar* returned to Devonport, Mick met his old friend and *Ganges* classmate signalman Tancy Lee. He remembers the day himself as he got, what is called in the navy, a pier head jump:

When I left *Ganges*, like Mick Magennis, I joined *Royal Sovereign*. There we parted company. I was to spend the next three years on the battleship *Rodney* before joining *Royal Oak* which was sunk in Scapa on 14 October 1939. I was lucky, I only lost my kit as I was ashore at the time. Then I was drafted to *Horizon*, a drifter working in Scotland next to Guzz barracks and a pier head jump on to *Kandahar*.

(Left) Signalman 'Tancy' John Lee. HMS *Ganges*1935, HMS *Kandahar* 1940-41,
HM Submarines 1942-45. *(Right)* Signalman 'Blondie' Stan Millard. HMS *Ganges*
1938, HMS *Kandahar*1941, HM Submarines 1942-45.

On 17 May 1940 the four destroyers *Kingston, Khartoum, Kimberley*
and *Kandahar* sailed east at great speed, stopping only for fuel at
Gibraltar, Malta and Alexandria, then through the Suez Canal and into
the Red Sea. The first disaster happened when *Khartoum* was deployed
on patrol off Perim. On 23 June 1940 an air vessel off the starboard torpedo mounting exploded causing an uncontrollable fire, necessitating
beaching the ship and abandonment. The crew were re-drafted home
or to other ships. After arriving in the Red Sea, *Kandahar* was involved
in towing a captured Italian submarine prize into Aden. The submarine
Galileo Galilei surrendered after being hit by gunfire from the trawler
Moonstone. The three inch shell hit the conning tower and killed all her
officers and most of her senior ratings. Her code books were captured
which led to two other submarines being sunk in the Red Sea on 23
June, and the Gulf of Oman on 25 June. Lt. Cdr. Pelost surrendered to
Cdr. Robson on board *Kandahar* after the *Torrecelli* was scuttled.

Ervine Fleming recalls:

> We sank one Italian submarine and captured another. It was during
> those operations Mick Magennis' reputation for bravery first came to
> the fore. He voluntarily dived into shark infested waters to help rescue

The captured Italian submarine *Galileo Galilei* is towed into
port by HMS *Kandahar* June 1940

some Italian submariners from the submarine *Torrecelli* and drag them
to safety. It would be honourable enough to do the same for one's own
shipmates, but Mick was risking his neck for the enemy.

Back in Aden with the honour of war, Cdr. Robson and his officers
dined with the captured Italian submarine commander. Later the local
flag officer met him to convey their naval lordships' congratulations on
a remarkable fight for which the submarine commander was later to be
awarded the Italian equivalent of the Victoria Cross.

Mick Magennis, Tancy Lee, Gunner Carroll and other members of
the ship's company had a run ashore when *Kandahar* returned to Aden.
Gunner Edmond Carroll recalls:

> Some of our shipmates including Mick Magennis, Ervine Fleming and
> myself went ashore to the Royal Engineers Club for a sods opera night
> with the army boys. Aden was very unexciting and Crater City was
> dead compared to Alexandria or Mombasa where we visited later.

Kandahar sailed from Aden shortly afterwards to transfer Indian
troops to Somaliland. After which she and the cruiser *Capetown* called
into Mombasa for a weekend break. While in Mombasa a humorous
incident happened after a night ashore with some members of the crew.
They all missed the last liberty boat. Mick decided to swim back to the
ship, which was anchored half a mile off shore. He dived in and
although a good swimmer his navigation was poor (he was 'Brahms and
Liszt', in slightly high spirits as the upper deck would say). He swam

to the wrong ship HMS *Capetown*, the cruiser anchored near *Kandahar*. He was dragged out and taken back to his own ship with a note from the duty officer. Immediately he was put on a charge and the next morning at the first lieutenant's table he was charged with entering the ship improperly dressed. The punishment was one day's stoppage of leave. Only later did he find out that the Marquis of Milford Haven, the nephew of Mountbatten, thought the whole incident hilariously funny. What was written on the note was, 'Found this floating in the water. If it isn't yours throw it back in again'.

4th AND 5th VC 1940

By the end of 1940, two more Royal Navy men were to be awarded the Victoria Cross for valour. The first junior rate was Leading Seaman Mantle. On 4 July the 5,500 ton armed merchant cruiser *Foylebank* was in Portland harbour when a force of twenty German Stukas attacked. The Battle of Britain was at its peak. Mantle was a gunner and he was manning the starboard twenty millimetre pom-pom. He had already been mentioned in dispatches for being the first naval gunner to bring an enemy plane down while on convoy protection service. On 4 July he was wounded many times. His left leg was shattered yet he refused to leave his action station. The electricity failed yet he went on to operate the gun manually and he fell by the gun he had so valiantly served as had Boy Cornwell at the Battle of Jutland. His VC was presented to his parents by King George VI at the Palace in June 1941. His mother was later to say when she was interviewed:

> Jack didn't seem to be the heroic type. He was so gentle that we all used to say he ought to have changed places with his eldest sister who is the toughest in the family. He was such a quiet, earnest boy. He never was brilliant at school. He had an intense dislike for pain. He was always afraid of the dentist.(John Winton, *The VC at Sea*)

The fifth Victoria Cross, and last in 1940, was won by Captain Edward Fegen in command of the *Jervis Bay*, a converted armed merchant cruiser escorting a convoy. His little ship, although completely out-gunned, openly attacked the pocket battleship *Admiral Scheer*. He knew he was doomed but with guns blazing he went into action. The *Jervis Bay* was sunk. Fegen was awarded the Victoria Cross posthumously on 17 November 1940. Thirty-one ships of the convoy escaped. Fegan had been commander of HMS *Dauntless* in 1936, Mick's old ship.

RAID ON TARANTO:
KANDAHAR JOINS MEDITERRANEAN FLEET.

Before November was over in 1940 the aircraft carriers *Illustrious* and *Eagle* were to prove their worth. On 11 November the attack on Taranto harbour by squadrons of aircraft from these two carriers severely damaged three battleships of the Littorio class, two cruisers and two auxiliaries. Italy had only six capital ships, now only three were left fully operational.

Earlier, on 8 June 1940, the fleet carrier and sister ship of *Courageous*, HMS *Glorious*, had been sunk by the German battleships *Scharnhorst* and *Gneisenau* off northern Norway. The fleet carriers' two escort destroyers were also sunk by the two German warships and more than 1,500 sailors perished. Some 900 had taken to the lifeboats, but only forty-one survived in the Artic waters, being rescued by a Norwegian trawler many days later. The two A-class destroyers *Ardent* and *Acasta* had managed to launch a torpedo attack on the heavier armed German warships before being destroyed themselves by gunfire. *Scharnhorst* received a hit by a torpedo and forty-three sailors died.

In early 1941 *Kandahar, Kingston* and *Kimberly* travelled through Suez to join Admiral Cunningham in the Mediterranean. He was commander-in-chief of the Mediterranean fleet and they were suffering heavy casualties, ships being sunk and damaged by air attack from the Luftwaffe. The enemy had just damaged the fleet's only aircraft carrier, HMS *Formidable*, and the ships, with no air cover, were doing the best they could with their own anti-aircraft fire in addition to the reinforcements. Prior to the battle to come, the fifth flotilla *Kashmir, Kelvin, Kipling* and *Jackal* had arrived at Malta in early May with Lord Mountbatten as commander on board *Kelly*. *Kelly* had just arrived in the Mediterranean after being repaired in England. The Battle of Crete was an air attack by German and Italian forces which was to go down in history as an attack upon warships exceeding anything previously experienced. The British fleet suffered heavily and the experience was to change the whole approach to modern naval warfare. The same was to be experienced at the end of the year in the eastern front against Japan.

Before the battle of Crete, Mick received letters from his mum, and Bill at Alexandria. His brother had been promoted to Killick and after finishing his LTO course at HMS *Vernon* he had been drafted to the *Vanquisher*, an older destroyer built after World War I.

THE BATTLE OF CRETE

May 22 1941 was a warm sunny Mediterranean day but before it was over more than one thousand sailors were to perish at the hands of German bombers.

The Germans had invaded Crete and the British Fleet was there to prevent further reinforcements landing on the island. The destroyer *Greyhound* was dispatched to deal with a vessel ferrying Germans to the island but although successful in her mission she became the sole target of fierce attack and was quickly sunk. Two destroyers, *Kingston* and *Kandahar*, were sent to rescue survivors, and two cruisers, *Gloucester* and *Fiji*, accompanied them to provide anti-aircraft covering fire. *Kandahar* lowered her whalers and under a savage bombing and machine gun-attack picked up a number of officers and ratings including the *Greyhound* CO, Cdr. W. R. Marshall A. Deane DSO DSC. But to stay longer would mean the suicidal destruction of fighting units. They flung their Carley floats among the remainder of the swimming survivors and withdrew; of all the cups men are called upon to drink, there was none more bitter than this. Mick Magennis remembers nearly being left behind as he told the *Daily Mail* nearly twenty years later:

> I was in one of our Whalers returning to the ship with survivors. I was trying to row. Our boat was full. I had to keep pushing down a survivor, oil covered and in a bad way, who kept putting his head up for air and stopping me from rowing. What scared me most was the speed at which *Kandahar* gathered away immediately we got the survivors aboard her. I was last in the boat and had to make a jump for the scrambling net as we left the water behind. It nearly tore my arms out. For a moment I thought I had been left behind. I rejoined my destroyer which was still without a battle scar.

The air attacks intensified, survivors and rescuers alike being continuously bombed and machine-gunned, so that the rescue effort had to be cut short, leaving a large number of *Greyhound's* crew still in the water. Shortly afterwards *Gloucester* was so severely damaged that she had to be abandoned. After several hours of concentrated air attacks, *Fiji* with damaged steering gear, turning helplessly in circles, and listing thirty degrees, was in such bad shape that her crew was also forced to abandon ship.

It was too dangerous for *Kingston* and *Kandahar* to stay but they returned after dark and managed to find a considerable number of men from *Fiji*. After spending two hours searching the vicinity, guided by the flashing torches from the *Fiji's* rafts, Lt. Cdr. Somerville commanding *Kingston* rescued 339 officers and men from the water; The *Kandahar* fished out 184. However they were unable to search for *Gloucester's* crew with the result that only eighty-two of them survived. They were picked up by the Germans and spent the rest of the war as prisoners of war. Many acts of gallantry took place that day, the most notable being those of Marshall A. Derne, *Greyhound's* commanding officer, already rescued by *Kandahar,* and the Revd. Kit Tarner, *Fiji's* padre, both of whom dived repeatedly to save more than thirty of *Fiji's* crew. Both eventually failed to return through exhaustion and both were posthumously awarded the Albert Medal which was later replaced by the George Cross.

Gunner Edmond Carroll remembers it like yesterday:

> We picked so many of them out of the water when their ship was dive bombed and sunk at Crete. Actually we had the survivors of three ships as well as *Fiji*. We also had men from the destroyers *Greyhound* and *Juno* on board. Our lads firmly believed that only the expert ship handling of our skipper Commander Robson saved us from joining them. He was terrific.

The destroyer *Juno* commanded by Cdr. Tyrwhitt was hit by bombs and the after boiler and engine room were blown open to the sea. A third bomb detonated the after magazine. She broke in half and sank within minutes. PO Edwin Lumley was blown over the side from the gun station by the explosion and badly burned; he swam forty yards into the thick layers of floating oil fuel to rescue a shipmate in difficulties. *Kandahar, Nubian* and *Kingston* between them rescued six officers and ninety-one ratings. The attacks were practically incessant. Several bombers were shot down but nobody had time to count them. Ervine Fleming recalls Mick's bravery:

> Unbelievable is the only word I would use to describe Mick's actions. I saw him repeatedly risk his own life to dive into furnace fuel oil and burning diesel to bring other shipwrecked sailors out. I lost count of the times we had to fish him out, and in he would go again. His actions were even more remarkable considering he was in real danger of being left behind. Ships under attack had to speed away and manoeuvre constantly to avoid the Stukas. A lot of allied shipping was sunk by Hitler's elite Stuka dive-bombers and dozens of sailors owed their lives to Magennis and others who jumped into treacherous waters to rescue them.

Their task completed *Kandahar* and *Kingston* made rendezvous with Admiral King's squadron which consisted of the cruisers *Naiad, Perth* and the destroyer *Nubian* on the dawn of 23 May.

THE 6th VC, 1941

The sixth VC and first senior rate to win a naval Victoria Cross was Petty Officer Edward Septon. He was serving on board the old World War I cruiser *Coventry* which had been converted into an anti-aircraft ship. Admiral Cunningham signalled the Mediterranean Fleet: 'We must not let the army down. It takes three years to build a ship and three hundred to uphold a tradition.' The aircraft carrier *Formidable* had been damaged and the hospital ship *Aba* which had Red Crosses on her side was being attacked by the German Luftwaffe. *Coventry's* ten four-inch high-angled guns, oerlikons and pom-poms were being directed onto their targets by the forward director which PO (Petty Officer) Septon, along with Lt. Robb and three other seaman, manned. During the action south of Crete a German Stuka penetrated the barrage and raked the bridge and director towers with machine gun fire. PO Septon was mortally wounded and one bullet passed through his body and injured Able Seaman Fisher sitting behind him. Septon stayed at his action stations until the attack was over. Admiral Cunningham wrote that: 'Septon's action may well have saved Coventry and the hospital ship *Aba*.' His citation read:

> Until his death his valiant and cheerful spirit gave heart to the wounded. His high example inspired his shipmates and will live on in their memory.' (John Winton, *The VC at Sea*)

Two destroyers of the fifth flotilla were lost in the Battle of Crete on 22 May. *Kashmir* sank after aircraft attack off Crete and the next day Mountbatten's *Kelly* met the same fate. She was struck by a 1,000 pound bomb when she was doing thirty knots under full starboard rudder. *Kelly* had previously been mined and once torpedoed, each time she had struggled back to harbour. But this time there was no return for *Kelly*. Cdr. St Clair-Ford in *Kipling* lowered all boats and Carley floats and rescued *Kelly's* crew, all 128 of them. She then rescued *Kashmir's* Captain Cdr. King and 152 officers and men.

Kandahar returned to Alexandria with survivors and the wounded. On 25 May *Kandahar*, *Kelvin* and two other destroyers proceeded to the fishing village of Sitia in Crete to evacuate troops in a rearguard action. The passengers included three women, a Chinese, two children and a dog. The

Shipmates on HMS *Kandahar* working on a torpedo. Alexandria 1941.

imagination tends to wonder in conjecture as to their subsequent story. Anyhow they all reached Alexandria on 25 April.

Kandahar later was involved in Malta convoys, the odd bombardment along the coast of North Africa and Syria, the evacuation and invasion of Greece, taking stores and mail to the soldiers at Tobruk and bringing back more wounded soldiers to Alexandria. All this had to be done at night because of air attacks. *Kandahar* took on the nickname of the 'Tobruk Ferry'. On 14 November 1941 the aircraft carrier, *Ark Royal,* was torpedoed by a U-boat fifteen miles east of Gibraltar, and while being towed home to port she foundered.

On 18 December 1941 Force K, a group which included the cruisers *Neptune, Aurora* and the *Penelope* and the destroyers *Lance, Lively* and *Kandahar,* sailed from Alexandria and Malta to intercept an Italian battle force spotted by RAF aircraft in the area between Benghazi and Tripoli off the Libyan coast. In October, Force K had sunk some 60 per cent of enemy shipping sailing between Italy and the African coast. Hopes were high on board the British ships by early morning on 19 December. The steepness of the seas forced Captain O'Connor, in command of the force, to reduce speed.

KANDAHAR AND *NEPTUNE* MINED

Disaster struck at 1.00 am on 19 December. *Neptune* struck a mine. The ships were in line ahead. *Aurora* too struck a mine. By this time *Neptune* was going full astern in a bid to reverse out of the minefield. Instead she hit a second mine. After another few minutes she hit the third mine which produced a severe list to port. The Italian Navy had laid this minefield in April 1941 after a bombardment of Tripoli by Admiral Cunningham's battleships and cruisers.

On board the third cruiser *Penelope*, Captain A. D. Nicholl first thought *Neptune* and *Aurora* had been torpedoed and he turned the ship to starboard. Captain W. G. Agnew on board *Aurora* gave the command to Cdr. Robson on board *Kandahar* to go alongside *Neptune* and the other destroyers to go alongside *Aurora*. Later he signalled *Penelope*, 'I am damaged and returning to Malta. Do what you can for *Neptune* but keep clear of the minefields. The others are to join me.'

Captain Robson decided to take his ship into the minefield to help *Neptune* and at 3.00 am she herself struck a mine which blew her stern off. She managed to stay afloat. Mick Magennis told the *Daily Mail* nearly twenty years later what happened:

Shipmates on board HMS *Kandahar,* Mediterranean 1940

I was closed up at action stations. I remember arguing with the chief over finding a loose end of electrical cable. Then it happened. We were all thrown flat on deck. The ship shuddered. When I got up I saw a big glow aft. The upper deck plating had been torn up and bent like paper. Water was lapping the port deck. I feared the ship would sink any moment. Lt. Mountbatten (Lord Louis' nephew) told us all the boats had been riddled by shrapnel. Captain Robinson ordered the best be repaired to take the injured. Many had died. My 'oppo' (friend) George Cook, who came from Leeds, could not swim (he had not gone to *Ganges* like me). 'I'm going to get a mess deck stool and float on that.' He gave me a letter in case he did not make it. I rolled it with my money in a sou'wester and tied it round my neck.

Mick's Belfast oppo, Ervine Fleming, was lucky not to die. He explains:

What saved my life was the control cubicle I was in belonging to the after torpedo tubes. The cubical took the impact of the blast and saved my life. Part of the iron deck was blown up all around me.

The other destroyers were ordered out of the minefield and then *Neptune* struck her fourth mine. She turned turtle and sank immediately. All except thirty of her 765 crew went down with her. The thirty survivors managed to climb on board a life raft but all but one of them died through exhaustion. Able Seaman John Walton was picked up by an Italian destroyer and ended up a POW until 1943.

NEPTUNE'S ONLY SURVIVOR

Out of the 765 officers and men drowned on board the 5,220 ton cruiser *Neptune*, 150 of them were New Zealanders. The sadness of this story is increased by the knowledge that *Neptune* was on her way to join the New Zealand navy in May/June 1941. The 150 New Zealand men on board were an advance party before the ship was to be handed over to the New Zealand navy. On her way to New Zealand, Admiralty ordered her to join Cunningham in the Mediterranean campaign because of the heavy losses at the Battle of Crete. *Neptune* was used to cover the losses and as sad as all war is, joined them on the sea bed.

Able Seaman Norman Walton, the only survivor of the *Neptune* recalls his escape from death:

> I climbed down the anchor and dived in from there. Then I swam to a raft some forty yards away. By that time around thirty men had clambered in and around it. It was designed for four. The captain and some officer were on another raft and we lashed them together. Little did I realise I would be clinging to that raft for a total of five and a half days as my shipmates slowly died around me. A few died that night and by first light there were only sixteen of us left. I remember the skipper saying that when the ship hit the mine his position was only four miles from Tripoli. It seemed incredible that we could be so close to land and still see no signs of our rescue.
>
> By the fourth day only four of us were left. The skipper died that night. By Christmas there were only two of us left, myself and a leading seaman. An Italian aircraft spotted us and an Italian destroyer picked us up. The Leading Seaman died and for the first few days in hospital I was blind. My tongue was swollen to twice its size and my left leg was broken, but at least I was alive. All the other 765 men had died.

'ABANDON SHIP!'

Lt. Cdr. Tyrwhitt manoeuvred the destroyer *Jaguar* alongside *Kandahar*. Tancy Lee and a dozen of so of the crew clambered aboard but Tyrwhitt could not hold his ship alongside the yawing helpless *Kandahar* without grave risk to his own ship. He backed clear and signalled that the rest must swim for it and swim they did; eight officers and 170 ratings.

The *Kandahar* captain ordered 'abandon ship' and Mick heard the Marquis of Milford Haven standing on deck, 'Right men follow me'. He dived into the sea and struck out strongly for *Jaguar*. Once again Mick was in the drink. He began to think they were so right back at HMS *Ganges*. The swimming test they had been put through saved many lives. He explained:

It seemed a long way. One moment I could see the destroyer *Jaguar* on the crest of a wave. The next it was gone. When I reached her a big fender hung over her side. Each time I almost reached the scrambling net the fender would crash down and I would have to swim away to avoid being hit. This happened five or six times. I was exhausted. Just as I thought I was going a seaman threw me a line. I had just enough strength to put it around me and be hauled aboard. There to my delight was non-swimmer George. He was a bit burned up. He had taken a calcium flare from a bridge life-jacket, punctured it with his knife and paddled across on his chair with a great flare lighting him up like a beacon.

The following day *Kandahar* had not sunk and *Jaguar* sank her with her own guns before heading back to Alexandria with the survivors. Sixty-seven men had lost their lives. Cdr. Cole remembers that night:

I discovered that the destroyer HMS *Jaguar*, in which I was first lieutenant, rescued Magennis and other crew members from HMS *Kandahar*. What a stormy night it was. It took us three hours to find the *Kandahar*. Later we heard the sad news that *Neptune* had sunk with all hands.

HAPPY SHIP'S COMPANY AND OTHER EXPERIENCES

Cdr. Cole on *Jaguar* took all the *Kandahar* survivors back to HMS *Canopus* in Alexandria where the wounded went into hospital. Mick and other survivors were issued with a steaming kit and without a ship were sent back to Devonport in England on the SS *Orduna*. Mick recalls:

The *Kandahar* had been a happy ship. The crew had been together a long time. So the captain put in a plan for us to stay together. We came home as a ship's crew for survivors leave and Cdr. Robson was awarded the DSO. 'I want you to know it is yours as well as mine. I am only carrying it for us all.

Signalman 'Blondie' Stan Millard (*Ganges* 1938) was a boy signalman on board his first ship the cruiser *Calypso* when she was torpedoed by an Italian submarine in the Mediterranean on 12 June 1940. Thirty-six crew members died and the *Caledon* picked up most of the survivors and brought them safely back to Alexandria. He remembers a *Ganges* boy called Kimber pulling him out of the water and saying 'Hello Blondie, fancy meeting you here'. Stan missed being shipwrecked a second time when he left the *Kandahar* just before she was sunk. He recalls:

I served on *Kandahar* from 7 August 1941 until 6 December 1941 when I left her in Alexandria. The date is vividly inscribed in my memory as thirteen days later (19 December) *Kandahar* was lost. I returned home on the SS *Orduna* and joined HMS *Raleigh* in April 1942 and in July joined the submarine service. I later served on the T-boat *Thorough* in the Far East.

Gunner Edmond Carroll, who left the ship shortly before *Kandahar* sailed from Alexandria, recalls:

I left the ship about a week before she was sunk to go into HMS *Canopus*, the barracks at Alex to take a higher gunnery course, and although I met some of the lads when they came into the barracks to be kitted up after the sinking I didn't bump into Mick. I was extremely upset when I spoke to them and they reeled off all the names of those who had lost their lives, all sixty-seven of them. If I had remained on the ship, I would have been casualty number sixty-eight because the ship was at defence stations, and I would have been on number three gun aft where the mine hit and blew the whole stern off. This was just another instance among many when my mother's prayers were surely answered. I've often asked myself, why me?' One of the lost sailors was Petty Officer Writer William (Billy) Carson from 69 Twaddell Avenue, Belfast. Ervine Fleming was the sailor detailed to contact his parents later and tell them of the terrible tragedy.

Kandahar ship's company photograph taken in Alexandria 1941. Circle (*on the left*) shows Magennis .

When Gunner Edmond Carroll joined his next ship HMS *Naiad*, a Dido class cruiser he was not so lucky because she was torpedoed and sunk in March 1942. He recalls:

> It happened about 9.00 pm. We were down in the mess having a belated supper, having been closed up at the guns all day. The main hatch was shut, but the manhole in the middle of it was open which allowed only one man to go through at a time. When the ship was hit there was an almighty scramble to get through it with the result that blokes were jamming the ladder, and also getting jammed in the manhole. All this time the ship was keeling over more and more, and I had given up all hope of getting out alive when someone had the sense to open the main hatch, allowing us to get through. When I got on deck, all the boats and rafts had gone. I slid down the ship's side miraculously without a scratch from the barnacles and I just swam through the pitch black water, not knowing where the boats or rafts were, and as if guided by some divine hand, I swam straight onto one of the rafts, and was picked up by one of the destroyers.

Once again the strenuous swimming test at *Ganges* was to prove its worth.

THE BATTLECRUISER HMS *HOOD* IS SUNK

1941 was also a year to remember in the Battle of the Atlantic. In the month of May 1941 Germany's largest battleship *Bismarck* and heavy cruiser *Prinz Eugen* had sailed out south of Greenland. Both these warships were being shadowed by the battle cruiser *Hood*, the battleship *Prince of Wales* and the cruisers *Suffolk* and *Norfolk*. What was to happen between two of the world's most mighty warships was to go down in the annals of naval warfare as quite exceptional. Ian Hay (*Ganges* boy 1937) was closed up at action stations in 'A' turret on board the *Prince of Wales* (one of Britain's new King George V class battleships). She was close by *Hood* and her ship's company were closed up at action stations. He recalls:

> Suddenly 'alaaarm.' Both gun loading cages come up in a high hydraulic scream to a thumping stop abreast both gun breeches, like barn doors, shut with a hiss and click, and the hoarse shouts 'Right and left guns ready.' The red lights burn. Now the silence is deafening except the chattering of my range and deflection pointers.

Outside the huge gun barrels and turret turns in short hydraulic grunts and snorts, the barrels silhouetted like snouts sniffing the wind come to rest. Then the drawled out 'broadsides.'The turret fire control gong gives two short rings. Adjusting my anti-flash hood to eye level, I took a deep breath and kept my mouth wide open. It was at this point somewhere near us on the *Hood*, their A turret had reached the same degree in the loading cycle as she was witnessed to get off a broadside seconds before a direct hit in a magazine from the *Bismarck* and *Prinz Eugen*.

Bismarck sank the battle cruiser *Hood* with her first salvo straight into her ammunition and magazine bunkers. The *Hood* just exploded and 1,497 officers, men and boys were incinerated in seconds. There were three survivors which in itself was a miracle. They were Midshipman Bill Dundas, Able Seaman Bob Tilburn and a bunting tosser (signalman) A.E.P. Briggs.

Many *Ganges* boys straight from training 242 class No. 24 mess were on board *Hood* that fateful day 24 April 1941. In *Hood's* magazine bunkers the cordite bags were unprotected unlike the German ones which were in brass cages. A direct hit meant being blown asunder. Arthur Whittle (*Ganges* 1938), who was on board HMS *Suffolk*, remembers encountering the *Bismarck*.

On sighting the *Bismarck* the captain, R.M. Ellis, said on the tannoy, 'This is the captain speaking. The *Bismarck* is dead astern. The alarm will not be sounded, close up quietly as she may not have seen us.' I closed up to my action station in the ADP above the bridge and I relieved AB Sewell who won the DSM. The *Bismarck* was still astern about eight cables length. I could see her forward guns and windows of her bridge but the rest was surrounded in fog. The *Suffolk* fired a broadside which passed over the top of *Bismarck* and landed amidships off the *Prinz Eugen* - that was the only time they were hit. We only left action because we were out of fuel and were ordered to proceed to Conception Bay in Newfoundland where a tanker was waiting. We then left and picked up a convoy in Iceland, P218 for Russia.

THE GERMAN BATTLESHIP *BISMARCK* IS SUNK: 7th VC

Bismarck was to come to her end only one month after the sinking of *Hood*. As she was trying to make her way back to France at 10.00 pm on the evening of 24 May 1941, Lt. Cdr. Esmonde left the aircraft carrier

Victorious with a strike force of nine Swordfish armed with torpedoes to make a 120 mile flight in foul weather and into head-winds to attack *Bismarck*. In spite of having to come down out of the clouds prematurely to sight the US coast cutter *Modoc*, however *Bismarck* herself was also visible only eight miles away with all her gunners alert. *Esmonde's* aircraft scored one hit amidships on the starboard side.

Bismarck had also been torpedoed in her propellers and her rudder had jammed. She could only move in circles and more aircraft from *Victorious* severely damaged her. The cruisers *Norfolk* and *Dorsetshire* finished her off with torpedoes and she joined the mighty *Hood* on the sea bed. Lt. Cdr. Esmonde received the DSO for this action and was at the palace on 11 February 1942 to receive his award. The very next day he and five others left Manston, Kent, in six Swordfish to attack three of the heavy units of the German fleet, the battle cruisers *Scharnhorst* and *Gneisenau*, 32,000 tons each, and the 13,900 ton heavy cruiser *Prinz Eugen*, as these warships made a dash through the English Channel. All six aircraft and their pilots were lost. Esmonde was awarded the Victoria Cross, his four officers the DSO and one rating the CGM. Lt. Cdr. Esmonde received the 7th Victoria Cross to be won by a naval man.

On 25 November 1941 HMS *Barham*, Britain's third capital ship, was torpedoed by U-231 off Sallum, Egypt in the Mediterranean. Richard Laland (*Ganges* 1936), a survivor from the Barham, remembered:

> I received a head wound jumping overboard when I banged the keel. When asked later in hospital how I got off I told this gentleman in a civilian suit, 'I just followed the bloody admiral.' Later the sailor in the next bed told me the man in the civilian suit was the bloody admiral.

On 18 December 1941, the day *Kandahar* and *Neptune* sailed from Alexandria for the last time, the battleships in the harbour, *Queen Elizabeth* and *Valiant*, had been attacked by Italian frogmen on human torpedoes. Both warships were damaged but looked all right above water. In order to confuse Italian spies, Admiral Cunningham on board *Queen Elizabeth* and Captain Morgan (later Vice Admiral) on board *Valiant* ordered crews to carry on their duties as if nothing had happened. Receptions were held, bands played, and steam was kept up so that it looked as if both ships were ready to sail at any moment. Indeed Mussolini's navy missed a fine opportunity there! Both battleships were later repaired in drydock in 1942. The Italian frogmen had been captured and later in 1945 Count Luigi de la Pene was presented with the Italian

'VC', the Medaglio d'Oro by the Crown Prince of Italy for his attack on *Valiant*. Admiral Morgan was present and stepping forward he took the gold medal and pinned it on the breast of the man who had knocked out his own ship three years before.

REPULSE AND PRINCE OF WALES ARE SUNK

The modern battleship *Prince of Wales* and the older battlecruiser *Repulse* were in Singapore the day Pearl Harbour was attacked and these two large warships and four escorting destroyers sailed immediately. The task force was to intercept the Japanese landing troops at Singora on the east coast of Malaya. Both large warships were sunk by torpedo bombers. The four escorting destroyers picked up 2,081 officers and men of the 2,921 on board the two ships. Within a short time Singapore would be captured. Winston Churchill said it was Britain's saddest hour.

Ian Hay has already explained his feelings on board *Prince of Wales* when HMS *Hood* was blown asunder, now he recalls boys from *Ganges* joining one of these mighty warships and the final sinking of *Repulse* and the *Prince of Wales* in the South China Sea:

> We were all volunteers. That, you will recall, meant 'you and you' to join the battle cruiser *Repulse*, the fastest in the fleet and the only one to compare with the *Scharnhorst*. She had six fifteen-inch guns and would give a speed of thirty knots, displacement 32,000 tons. We remember with tremendous bitterness the twelve (repeat twelve) months without going ashore. The appalling weather in patrols and convoys. It was no wonder when at Rosyth on a twenty-four hour emergency dock, the girls marched behind us chanting, 'Who shagged the sheep at Scapa Flow'.

Repulse and *Prince of Wales* had spent the first two years of the war in the North Atlantic. Both ships had been sent out east to help strengthen the Far East fleet towards the end of 1941. Ian Hay recalls that fateful day:

> Somewhere in the South China Seas, *Repulse* was zig-zagging at full speed. The main steam valves were opened up in the engine room for the first time in twenty years, and like some hunted, wounded stag a huge black pall of smoke from her guns trailed astern. She was fighting for her life. She was taking avoiding action from Japanese high level bombers and torpedo carrying aircraft. Already she had

taken four and the fifth was to prove fatal. She sank in four minutes, still under way, her guns still firing.

After explaining the end of *Repulse*, he goes on to tell about the end of the *Prince of Wales* and the death of some *Ganges* boys:

> There was no 'abandon ship' as our guns were still firing and we continued to bring up shells from below to the guns although having a heavy list to port. Suddenly a high savage lurch to port sent the shells spinning from our shoulders and we found ourselves on hands and knees dodging the awning stations stowed overhead, any of which could be fatal. Next the ship's piano cast loose down on us before we eventually came on deck. The list was now greater, and as we gazed upwards to the spotting top, high up in the mast, we knew how easy it would be for the spotters to only take a few steps to clear the ship's side and enter the sea. But instead, we heard a sound like sacks of wet concrete falling. In the spotting top had been a young officer and six boys formally from *Ganges*. The officer dived over the starboard side, the boys followed fearlessly–but too late out from the mast he knew they were all dead.

Singapore fell to the Japanese on 15 February 1942 and two days before a flat bottomed 1,000 ton paddle steamer HMS *Li-Wo* sailed with a mixed crew of Malay, Chinese and British sailors (eighty-four of whom were survivors of *Repulse* and *Prince of Wales*). Also left on board were army and RAF men including one civilian. A real mixed bag if ever there was one. The commanding officer was Lt. Wilkinson (RNR). She sailed into the Java Sea and had already survived Japanese air attacks. They sighted a Japanese convoy, troop ships, store ships and escorting warships (the Japanese invasion fleet for Sumatra). In such a hopeless situation Lt. Wilkinson and his officers decided to attack rather than try to escape.

Li-Wo had only one four-inch old gun, two machine guns and a depth charge thrower. She had twin rudders (for river handling) and with the manoeuvrability, Lt. Wilkinson (RNR) was able to survive long enough to damage a Japanese transport and set it on fire causing it to be abandoned by her crew. She stayed in action for over one hour against a cruiser and when trying to ram another transport she was hit at point blank range and sunk. There were only ten survivors who unfortunately did not all survive captivity. Lt. Wilkinson went down with *Li-Wo* and was awarded the Victoria Cross. The only surviving officer, Lt. Derbridge (RNZNVR) received the DSO and PO Thompson got the CGM. The machine gun crew both received the DSM. Lt. Wilkinson was the navy's eighth VC and his brother William collected his award after the war in 1947.

SURVIVOR'S LEAVE

Back in Alexandria Mick, Tancy Lee and other survivors of *Kandahar* were sent back to England on board the troopship SS *Orduna*. The ship was also carrying Italian POWs. On arrival home most sailors were given fourteen days survivors' leave when possible, a new kit issue to make up for what they did not receive at Alexandria and £5 for personal effects. Mick travelled home to Belfast with Ervine Fleming to visit his mum and sister. Leading Seaman Ervine Fleming remembers the survivor's leave:

> Mick and I proceeded on leave. After the SS *Orduna* docked we travelled over on the Heysham overnight ferry and on arrival in Belfast we shared a taxi, first up the Grosvenor Road to West Belfast. But when it pulled up outside Mick's home his mother nearly fainted because she had been told he was missing presumed dead. I headed over to Brussels Street on the Shankill Road where my Mum and Dad and sisters were delighted I was still alive.

Mick and Ervine Fleming heard what had been happening at home. Attacks by the Luftwaffe on Coventry, Plymouth and other cities in England had heralded the 'blitz', a truly appropriate word, so evocative of sudden, terrifying, deadly aerial bombardment. Mick also heard the news of four Luftwaffe attacks on Belfast on the nights of 7-8 April, 15-16 April, 4-5 May and 5-6 May 1941 lasting ten hours in total. Eleven hundred had died and thousands of homes in the city had been damaged. Majorca Street and Brussels Street were still standing and none of Mick's or Ervine's families had died. Mick also heard news of his two brothers. Anthony had been drafted to a landing craft and Bill had been drafted in August 1941 to the minelayer *Manxman*.

After leave the former shipmates, Mick and Ervine Fleming, reported back to Devonport Barracks. This was their last meeting, as Ervine Fleming remembers:

> I was drafted to the battle cruiser *Revenge* and finally to HMS *Wallflower*. We made arrangements to meet up in Belfast after the war. But whether it was my fault or his, it never happened.

FIVE

The Submarine Service
1942-1945

Devonport naval barracks HMS *Drake* was like a transit camp with sailors returning from ships that were sunk and others waiting in between drafts. Plymouth, like Belfast and Coventry, had been badly bombed by the Luftwaffe so there was just as great a chance for dockyard workers and civilians going to meet their maker in Devonport as at sea. Mick Magennis had never been on a submarine before. He heard there was extra money for hard layers and you got neat rum—as good a reason as any to volunteer. But many men were just drafted, as Mick would shortly find out, for it would be his turn next. His first ship had been a mighty battleship, and he may never have visualised going to the opposite end of the scale—a midget submarine. Stranger things have happened in the king's navy.

In April 1942, Mick was drafted to the torpedo school HMS *Defiance* in Devonport. Bill remembers one night during the time his brother was at the torpedo school:

> The *Manxman* arrived at Guzz [naval slang for Devonport] and my brother and I had a run ashore down 'Union Street', the Navy area of Plymouth. I remember the large sign on the pub wall 'All drinks are free during air raids'. I was a Chatham rating and didn't know my way about. My brother did. Needless to say the bombers never came that night, so we all had to pay for our drink.

Many sailors were never given the choice to volunteer for submarine service. PO William Byres from Portaferry, County Down, Northern Ireland, recalls:

> Mick Magennis, myself and Leading Torpedo Operator Ervine Fleming from Belfast were all at HMS *Defiance* at the start of the war. Once or twice a week we were all lined up and two or three men were

picked at random to be drafted to submarines. I remember one day a lad from Conlig, County Down called Crawford Henderson being picked. He cried and pleaded with the Petty Officer not to send him into submarines but he was drafted just the same. I only found out after the war was over that he was on board the submarine *Parthian* when she was sunk by a mine while on passage from Malta to Beirut on 10 August 1943; all were lost. There were other oppos of mine including Mick Magennis who were drafted at a later date. I was drafted to the battleship HMS *Nelson,* and later served on destroyers and the cruiser *Capetown*. After the war I was demobbed but joined up again and signed on for a pension. I left in 1958. I am over eighty now and live alone with my dog. But I always feel sad when I think of Crawford Henderson.

Bernard Warwick had joined the navy in 1942. After training in HMS *Raleigh* he was sent to the cruiser HMS *Berwick* and then to HMS *Defiance,* where he met Mick Magennis. He remembers a day well in December 1942 when by a twist of fate himself and Mick were drafted into submarines:

> Mick and myself had our kit bags and hammocks already up on the deck of the *Andromeda* (one of the three ships which, when combined, were called HMS *Defiance*). We had been chosen as two of the new ship's company of the cruiser HMS *Belfast. Belfast* had just finished a very long refit in Devonport dockyard after being mined in the Firth of Forth at the start of the war. We were to join her before she sailed on 10 December 1942 to join the fleet at Scapa Flow. It was not to be. A Petty Officer shouted: 'Hey Magennis and Warwick, your draft has been scrubbed, report to the sick bay for a medical. You are both for the submarine service.'

Bernard Warwick remembers Mick strutting up and down the deck being very angry at having their draft stopped to HMS *Belfast*. They had been told the cruiser was to go to visit Belfast and Mick was looking forward to that. 'Needless to say, after a medical, which was just a farce, off we both were, on the train to the submarine training centre, HMS *Dolphin* at Gosport'. So now in 1942 it was Mick Magennis and Bernard Warwick's turn to be picked out of the line and drafted for submarine training, like Crawford Henderson before them.

FORT BLOCKHOUSE

The two new recruits joined the many servicemen lugging their hammocks and kitbags on and off trains in England in 1942. Both sailors, wondering what their future might be, travelled to Portsmouth via London and then crossed over by ferry boat from Portsmouth to Gosport. HMS *Dolphin*, the main submarine base at Fort Blockhouse, was beside the naval hospital Haslar on the outskirts of Gosport. Mick and Bernard reported to the training section on 3 December 1942.

Mick glanced down along the jetty where he noticed several long grey/black unusual looking conning towers attached to submarines of different sizes and shapes more underwater than above. They looked more like 'water rats' than war ships, Mick thought. It would not be long before he would be at sea in one of them. But first the new recruits had to go through another training course and learn the different escape methods and their duties. Their course would be 3-4 weeks with periods at sea in older H-class submarines. Gus Britton MBE (*Ganges* 1938) remembers when on board the battleship HMS *Nelson*:

> When we were in Pompey dockyard after being mined in Loch Ewe, a group of us boys were wandering round the dockyard and came across this beautiful looking submarine. It was the *Taku*, and we went on board and I can still remember the thrill of going down the fore hatch and smelling that submarine smell and seeing the brass work and bright lights and how friendly and humorous the crew were. I just could not wait until I could join submarines.

The first three weeks Mick and Bernard spent in class learning about the layout of a submarine and its history, which goes back to 1620 when Cornelius van Drebel built an underwater boat which was rowed by twelve oarsmen. It reached a depth of 50 feet when first tried out on the Thames. The first recorded instance of a warship being sunk by a submarine took place in 1864 during the American Civil War when the *Housatonic* was sunk at Charleston. Up to the beginning of the twentieth century naval experts were very chary of using wholly submersible hulls. While they realised their great advantages in warfare, they also knew they were death traps for the men who would serve on board them. Winston Churchill said in a speech in the House of Commons in 1941, 'There is no branch of his Majesty's Forces which in this war has suffered the same proportion of fatal loss as our submarine service. It is the most dangerous of all services.' At the beginning of this century, the idea of a submarine as an instrument of war persisted and many experiments were encouraged. The French government took the lead and produced the Omega class of submarines. These were equipped with eight cylinder petrol engines for surface propulsion, while electric motors propelled the craft when submerged. They were 147 feet long and had a displacement of 400 tons. This in turn started the interest of other naval powers to include submarines as part of their naval forces.

SUBMARINES IN WORLD WAR II

The submarine was an essential part of the World War II navy and the men who served on these craft therefore had to really know their job. Back in 1942, Mick and the rest of the class were told that this was the reason they would be receiving extra pay (given in the form of allowances) which would vary from nine pence, to three shillings and nine pence a day, according to the rank and work they would have to carry out.

In September 1939, the British navy had fifty-eight submarines (one more than the German navy). During the war, the Germans had increased this number to 1,170 U-boats by 1945. Britain however kept adding to the number of submarines they had irrespective of losses, although certainly not on the scale as the German navy, whose U-boat building was a priority over surface warships. British submarines did not receive any names until 1926. At the start of World War II, there were nine H-class and three L-class which were of World War I design. The H-class were 440-500 tons, had four torpedo tubes and a crew of twenty-two. These submarines were only used as training boats. Two of the three Thames class, *Severn* and *Clyde*, survived the war with *Thames* being lost early in the war. *Thames* was the first diesel-driven submarine to exceed twenty-one knots. The Odin and Parthian class, first and second group were 1,870 tons, built 1926-28, and had a complement of fifty-three. *Odin, Olympus, Orpheus* and *Otus* served in the Mediterranean. In 1940 the sole survivor *Otus* returned to home waters. In 1942 *Osiris* and *Oswald* served in the Mediterranean. Five were lost and *Osiris* was later sent east as a training boat. P and R, or Porpoise and Rainbow class, were built in 1929-31 for mine-laying. Their displacement was 2,000 tons, six twenty-one-inch torpedo tubes bow, two machine guns and a complement of fifty-five. All ten of these submarines were brought home from China in 1940 to serve in the Mediterranean.

Signalman Gus Britton piping an oppo ashore
from SM *Scythian*, the mother submarine
to *XE3* in 'Operation Struggle'

In 1938 Leading Telegraphist Harold Diggins DSM C/JX137576 served on a Rainbow class boat in the Far East:

I was the 'sparker' on board HM/SM *Regent* stationed in Hong Kong before the war. The fifteen submarines and the depot ship *Medway* were part of the fourth submarine flotilla. After sailing home at the start of the war, we had eight successful war patrols in the Mediterranean between October 1940 and August 1941. On 22 April 1941 we attempted the embarkation of the British Minister to Yugoslavia at Kotor. I left *Regent* in Alexandria and joined the Turkish submarine *Ulicilireis*. I was to later serve on the *Taku* and the *Ultor*. In 1946 I was demobbed having served twelve years, plus boys service, from when I joined the Navy at HMS *Ganges* in 1932.

There were only two survivors of this class of submarines and they were used for training from 1943; *Proteus* in home waters and *Rover* in the Far East. Eight P and R class were lost. *Regent* was sunk after Harold Diggins left her. She sailed on her last patrol and struck a mine off Monopoli in the South Adriatic on 18 April 1943. All the crew were lost. The three new classes of submarines used continuously throughout the World War II were Triton class or T-class, 1,350 ton, crew fifty-nine, Undine or U-class, 700 ton, crew twenty-seven and Shark, Swordfish and the S-class, 850 ton with a crew of forty-eight.

These three classes of boats were being built before and throughout the war. T-class were built as ocean going patrol submarines. 'Snort gear' based on the German 'schnorkel' used by U-boats was only fitted to British submarines at the end of the war. The first boat fitted with this Dutch invention was *Traunt* in 1945. It enabled the diesel engines to aim at low power and charge the batteries while at periscope depth. Eighteen of the pre-war and later war emergency T-class were either lost in action or wrecked and scuttled. The U-class pre-war and later long hull 1941-42 built boats, along with the S-class were smaller submarines and they main-ly operated in the Mediterranean. Twenty U-class and eighteen of the S-class (war emergency 1941) and later boats were lost. Out of the Porpoise class mine-laying submarines only one, the *Rorqual*, survived. Towards the end of the war the new A-class submarine 1,350 ton with a crew of sixty-one was launched; *Amphion* being launched on 31 August 1944 by Vickers Armstrong of Barrow. The limit that these submarines could go beneath the sea is recalled by Gus Britton MBE (*Ganges* 1938):

The older H and L-class were limited to 100 feet but T-class, although tested to 350 feet dived to 500 feet. U-class could also submerge to 450–500 feet. The S-class were reported to have been deeper and one boat I have heard, the S/M *Sceptre*, was known to have been to 700 feet.

Marine engineers have spent a great deal of time and money in efforts to make underwater craft safe but because submarines have remained the most dangerous type of vessel to serve on, learning the method of escape from underneath the water is of supreme importance. In Mick's day, it began by teaching the men an escape method. This was the use of the Davis apparatus. It was invented by the firm of Siebe, Gorman and Co. (submarine engineers) and was the device most favoured by the British Navy. It was really an artificial lung put around one's neck and tied like a life jacket. Lt. Fraser VC explains:

The apparatus had a yellow bag (rubber) inside which was a canister filled with soda lime. Underneath the bag was an oxygen cylinder. The system works by breathing in pure oxygen and discharging carbon dioxide which in turn is absorbed by the soda lime. The submarine floods and the pressure outside and inside equalises. Then using a canvas trunk which was pulled down from the escape hatch, the first man ducked under, opened the hatch and escaped. The rest followed suit, one at a time. Rising to the surface was controlled by the use of an apron (this was the most dangerous part of the escape, rising too fast could explode one's lungs). The class practised using this device in a 25 foot deep tank of water at the training school.

In 1931 the Davis apparatus proved very successful when the submarine *Poseidon* was rammed by a Chinese steamer off Wei-Hai-Wei in China. Twenty-nine lives were saved by the Davis apparatus although twenty lives were lost. In 1932 the M2 submarine sank off Portland Bill and the entire crew of sixty was lost. There have been other serious disasters in peace time since the Great War. In 1921 K5 was sunk off Vigo in Spain, with fifty-seven lives lost. The following year H42 was rammed by a destroyer in the Straits of Gibraltar, twenty-six lives lost. In 1924 L24 was rammed by a warship off Portland, forty-three lives lost. In 1925 M1 was sunk off Start Point, sixty-eight lives lost. A year later H29 was sunk in dock at Devonport, six lives lost. In 1929 H47 was lost after a collision off the Pembrokeshire coast, twenty-four lives lost. Ten years later the submarine *Thesis* sank while doing sea trials in Liverpool bay, off Great

Orme's Head. Among the ninety-nine lives lost, were civilian dockyard workers. The *Thesis* was later re-floated and renamed the *Thunderbolt*. She later went to her watery grave for the second time in the Mediterranean in 1943.

After World War II a new escape method was used which was called free ascent. The Davis apparatus became obsolete and was considered to be dangerous. In the new method the escapee used his own lungs rather than a false one. This was also used in the conning tower escape where two men could escape at any one time.

DEPOT SHIP *CYCLOPS* H-BOATS

The class passed out, Mick happened to notice nobody failed and the new recruits were well rehearsed in escape procedures. Mick was drafted to the depot ship *Cyclops* in Rothesay, Scotland on 12 January 1943. Although *Cyclops* was mother to the seventh flotilla, her brood of submarines had a dual role for training new recruits and exercising, with anti-submarine ships. Not all submarines were based at Rothesay, but were at ports such as Belfast, Larne, and Londonderry in Northern Ireland and Oban, Tobermore and Scapa Flow in Scotland. Holyhead was where the commander-in-chief had his headquarters. On 7 February Mick joined H50. He quickly found out submariners never called their craft a submarine, the word 'boat' must always be used. H50 sailed and within hours Mick was to have his first experience of being underneath the Irish Sea. Unlike the noise and orders blaring down a tannoy system on surface warships, the calmness with which the officers and ratings went about their duties, gave a feeling of stability and trust. These men knew their jobs. The captain was only a young RN lieutenant and the number one, an RNR sub lieutenant. Two other officers were RNVR. H50 was built in America during World War I. She displaced 400 tons and had a complement of twenty-two. The little boat headed out to deeper water and the crew prepared for diving. The commanding officer left the conning tower last, he pulled the top hatch behind him and pressed the button of the diving klaxon just inside the hatch. The raucous explosion of the klaxon hooter brought the crew instantly to diving stations. The commanding officer shouted, 'One clip on.' Then, 'Both clips on', as he secured the top hatch closed and dropped into the control room and ordered the signalman to 'shut the bottom hatch'. Then to the first lieutenant, 'thirty feet number one.'

HM/SM *Ultor* returning to Malta after patrol, 1943

'Thirty feet, sir.'

'Eight hunded and fifty revolutions, course 350 degrees, let me know when you are happy about the trim number one.'

'Trimmed for diving, sir.'

'Very good. 250 revolutions.'

'Periscope depth.'

'Take a fix.'

'Ship's head 351.'

'Give me a course to reach position well after at exactly 1209. That's five minutes from time of fix.'

'New course will be 315, sir.'

'There is a warship dead ahead, sir. Distance: two and a half cables. She's coming straight at us.'

'Very good, Number One. That's Dickey Dawson who was in my class at Dartmouth in his brand new destroyer the Admiralty gave him for Christmas. He will be playing games with this very old tub all afternoon. If the Admiralty would build more submarines, we might get somewhere in this bloody war. Take her down to eighty feet. We'll stay on this course for two hours then bring her up again to periscope depth and call me before we surface, I'm off for my lunch.'

Having exercised most of that day with the destroyer testing her asdics, H50 surfaced to head back to Rothesay to tie up for the night. The next day and for the rest of that week the submarine would continue exercising with other destroyers in their anti-submarine work up before returning to Rothesay and *Cyclops* and maybe, if Mick was lucky, a run ashore and a few pints of beer at the weekend.

Signalman Tancy Lee recalls H-boats:

> My first training boat was H50. We were attached to the depot ship *Cyclops* in Rothesay Scotland. Lt. Hunt our CO was also my CO on S/M *Ultor* when I joined her. I then served on board the *Unrivalled* and the *Sybil*. Altogether I served six years in boats.

ERA Charlie Reed CGM, who later served on X-boats with Mick, remembers service in H-boats:

> My one experience on board H32 was in Londonderry at the 'Atlantic Sheds,' our base at that time. Going back to Rothesay in Scotland on what we called the egg-run, topping up the torpedo tubes with crates of eggs and butter which seemed easy to get from over the border in Ireland at the time.

After Mick's first week on H50, he gradually got used to the smell of sweat, rum and diesel oil, and spent his time off-duty sleeping in a torpedo rack. During the week at sea he experienced many dives and when the boat returned to the depot ship he joined the spare crew before another week at sea training on H32. Cdr. Edward Young DSO, DSC (RNVR) describes *Cyclops:* (in *One of our Submarines*)

> The depot ship *Cyclops*, nick-named 'cycle-box' by the matelots, was part warship, part liner, part maintenance and engineering shop and general stores. Its function was to repair, fuel and victual submarines. Depot ships kept house for the submarines while they were out on patrol. It fathered the submarines and in naval fashion mothered their crews. *Cyclops* was equipped with all the essentials for repair work, torpedoes, ammunition, spare parts for broken periscopes, engines, air compressors, etc., etc., plus water, oil and food. Her ship's company consisted of electricians, engineers, artificers, shipwrights. Also aboard were workshops, foundries, and surgeries where doctors and even a dentist was available for the submariners returning from exercises or patrol. Without this tremendous support from the depot ship the flotilla of submarines would cease to function.

The officers and ratings on board the training and operational submarines were divided into three watches, red, white and blue. By such an
arrangement, one-third was always on duty at sea or in harbour. The two-
thirds off duty in harbour lived in the depot ship, or shore-side accommodation such as the Atlantic sheds in Londonderry, for maximum relax-
ation and comfort. Many of the submarines just anchored in between
exercises due to lack of shore-side accommodation in many of the other
ports. Most of these ships in service were of pre-World War II design and
some of them were coal burners. *Cyclops* had been built in 1905 and had
served in the Mediterranean until 1939 when she was brought home first
to Harwich for the second flotilla of seven S-class submarines under Capt.
P. Ruck-Kene. Later, she moved to Rothesay for the seventh training
flotilla, where Mick had just joined it.

Mick Magennis was beginning to feel at home in his new underwater
domain. His earlier angry feelings of being drafted against his wish, had
long since left him. He found out he was not alone as most of his new shipmates were all pressed men. A number of stokers, torpedomen, seamen
gunners and even the chief torpedo gunner's mate never volunteered. It
was hard to get these men away from their beloved destroyers, so the
Admiralty press gang had to step in. Only the bunting tosser (signalman),
underwater dishwasher (the cook), the first and second coxswains, chief
ERA, electrical artificer and most other senior rates had been 'in boats'
before the war. Submariner was written all over their faces. The officers
were a mixture of RN, RNR, and RNVR. Their country was fighting for
its very survival, so they might as well make the best of being in this all
together, which is what they did. The comradeship was much closer and
as long as you were known to do your job well enough the pettiness of
being in the right rig of the day – as was the strict routine on some surface
ships – was forgotten. Magennis realised by now he was by temperament
a small ship or submarine man, independent and impatient of spit and
polish and wondered why he had not volunteered for submarines before.

FIRST SUBMARINE VC AWARD

The first submarine VC in World War II was won by Lt. Wanklyn or
'Wanks' as he became known. He was the commanding officer of the
boat, *Upholder*, which sank 140,000 tons of enemy shipping. *Upholder's*
sixth patrol was to win Wanklyn his Victoria Cross, south of Sicily in
May 1941 when he sank the 17,879 ton troopship *Conte Rosse* with
2,800 soldiers on board. Thirteen hundred of them drowned.

Afterwards *Upholder* endured a counter-attack. Thirty-seven depth charges were dropped before he escaped. Wanklyn went on to sink a destroyer and two Italian submarines, *Ammiraglio St Bon* and *Tricheo*, and over a dozen assorted troopships, tankers, supply and store ships. He sank two 20,000 ton troopships, *Oceania* and *Neptunia* in one evening on 16 September 1941 hitting them both with one salvo. His twenty-fifth and final patrol was on 22 August 1942. *Upholder's* four officers and twenty-eight men never returned. On 18 April 1943 the Italians finally claimed one of their torpedo boats had sunk *Upholder*. Wanklyn was the navy's ninth VC winner in World War II.

Unlike surface ships, submarines would slip out of harbour without being noticed, most of them being under water, and would go on patrol for several weeks. According to Gus Britton they were 'like large steel black cats with their engine exhausts bubbling and spluttering,' as the carbon monoxide gases passed through the silencer systems, and alongside the outer casing and ballast tanks. The boats beginning a new patrol saluted the captain of the flotilla with a blast of the whistle and set off to ambush the king's enemies. The captain called 'Good-bye. Good luck. Good hunting'. If they failed to return the convention of the depot ship and the spare crew required that the missing submarine not be mentioned again. However that did not stop loved ones grieving over their missing husbands and sons as this letter in *Picture Post* magazine of 29 March 1941 from Katherine Evans of Moneagh Duvrus, Bantry, County Cork, Ireland, testifies:

My fourth son Alan Evans was serving on the ill-fated submarine *Spearfish*, reported at the beginning of August 1940 to be overdue, presumed lost. Although officially informed of his presumed death, I still hope on. I have heard through the Commander's wife that the Germans announced having survivors. If this letter should come to the notice of any reader of *Picture Post* having a relative serving on the same submarine who may be a survivor, I shall be grateful for any information they can give me concerning my dear son.

Spearfish was sunk off Norway by U-34 on 1 August 1940. Earlier in the year, on 11 April, she torpedoed and damaged the German pocket battleship *Lützow*, north of the Skaw. There was only one survivor, Able Seaman Pester. He became a POW. After the war he died in a motorbike accident.

THREE MORE SUBMARINE VCs IN 1942

In February/March 1942 three more submariners were awarded the Victoria Cross. The T-boat *Thrasher* was on patrol north of Crete and had been successful in sinking a 3,000 ton enemy supply ship. She encountered thirty-three depth-charge attacks and survived. Later the submarine surfaced to charge her batteries. There was a heavy sea and a loud banging noise came from within the casing. Just forward of the casing there lay a 100 pound bomb, 3-4 feet long, stuck inside it. Sub Lt. Roberts and Petty Officer Gould successfully removed it and dropped it into the sea from the bows. On their return a second bomb was found in another hole in the casing. Gould lay on his back holding the bomb in his arms like a baby while Roberts dragged him by the shoulders. The whole operation took forty minutes with the bomb making unusual sounds. Wrapped in a potato sack it was dragged to the bows where it was dropped into the sea like the one before it. Sub Lt. Roberts and PO Gould were both awarded the Victoria Cross for their outstanding bravery. PO Gould was the second and only serving senior rate to win a Victoria Cross in World War II.

Also in March 1942, Lt. Cdr. Miers was commanding officer on patrol on the submarine *Torbay*. He had already been awarded two DSOs for his outstanding success in sinking 70,000 tons of shipping. On previous patrols he sank the Italian submarine *Jantina* and two tankers on 12 March and 5 July 1941. Later, in November 1941, he landed a party of commandos near Apollonio to raid General Rommel's headquarters. Miers sighted three enemy destroyers entering Corfu harbour on 3 March 1942. He followed the convoy at slow speed until dark. He surfaced and entered the harbour then lay on the bottom all night. Coming to periscope depth he noticed that all but one of the escorting destroyers had sailed. Two 5,000 ton transports and one destroyer were ideal targets. As the boat swung round he fired one torpedo at each ship. He hit both transports but missed the destroyer. After enduring forty or more depth charges he made his escape in Nelsonian manner to the open sea after having been in an enclosed harbour for seventeen hours. Miers received the VC on 7 May 1942. All his officers received awards. Lt. Chapman DSO, Lt. Kidd DSC, twenty-four ratings received DSMs or bars to their DSMs. When promoted to commander, Miers went on a fifty-six day war patrol in an American submarine. He was later to be very successful in his naval career reaching the rank of Admiral in 1958. He became a KBE and on retirement became National President of the Submarine Old Comrades

Association. Lt. Cdr. Miers became the twelfth World War II naval Victoria Cross award winner.

ABOVE US THE WAVES

The chances of going to meet your maker while serving in the submarine service during the early years of World War II was a one to one chance. During first sixteen months of the war, up to December 1940, the Royal Navy lost twenty-six submarines or half the original fifty-plus boats they had in commission. The crew situation became desperate. Which was one of the reasons why men like Magennis,Warwick and others were pressed into joining rather than waiting for volunteers. Thirteen hundred officers and ratings, over half the best trained crews, were dead. The year 1941 was to prove a merciful relief, with only ten British submarines sunk, but the greatest destruction was yet to come, for in the seventeen months from January 1942 to May 1943 twenty-eight more British submarines were lost.

Mick's time in the torpedo school HMS *Defiance* before he joined the destroyer *Kandahar* qualified him as a torpedo man. The loading of the 'tin fish' into the tube was only slightly different, although there was far less space to work in than on a destroyer. The submariners slept in empty torpedo racks, hammocks, on top of lockers, tables, or the deck itself in the torpedo storage compartment which also served as a junior rates mess. In this torpedo stowage compartment the junior ratings, torpedomen, radar operators, signalman, telegraphists, seamen gunners and gunlayers, asdic operators, cook and wardroom steward lived, ate and slept. As Signalman Gus Britton MBE, who served on board the submarine *Uproar* in 1944, explains, his mess mates lived

> like unwashed troglodytes for weeks on end. Hammocks covered all the overhead space, their shape distended by the weight of the occupants. Four shiny blue nosed torpedoes contributed to the claustrophobic condition. Dominating everything was the peculiar submarine smell of shale oil, lubricating oil, Brasso, stale food, cigarette smoke, rum, dampness, and the smell of humanity. Unlike the German U-boats, the British boats generally had no distillers to produce fresh water, which had to be rationed on patrol.

Before the torpedo storage compartment lay the tube space. Senior rates and artificers lived in the accommodation space, and nearest to the control room was the wardroom where the commanding officer, his second in command, 'Jimmy the one', torpedo officer and navigating officer lived. In some boats the engineer may have been a warrant officer. Some submarines carried a junior officer usually under training. Just forward of the officers' quarters was the tiny galley. Here the cook prepared and dished out the one hot meal of the day, which was cooked and eaten when the submarine surfaced to ventilate and recharge the batteries, usually after dark. Cooking and smoking was forbidden while the boat was submerged, as it was dangerous and used up precious oxygen. The control room, with its mass confusion and complexity of pipes, valves, switches, pressure gauges, junction boxes and electric wiring, gave the feeling of being inside a spaceship rather than a submarine. This together with the centralised periscope and its well, was the cortex and hub of life within the boat. Down in a tiny compartment under the control room was the pump space where a stoker who, by operating the ballast-pump motor and opening and closing various valves, could flood or pump on any of the trimming tanks throughout the submarine in answer to orders from the control room. Above the control room was the conning tower and a vertical brass ladder which led up to a hatch through to another ladder which in turn led to the upper hatch and on to the bridge. This top hatch was opened at sea while the boat was on the surface. It could be closed quickly when the submarine wished to dive, after the lookout and duty officer descended rapidly to the control room.

The motor room and engine alley were combined and here electricians would group up or group down in operating the boat under water. On Mick's first sight of the engine room, his eyes boggled at the concentration of levers, wheels, depth gauges and other mysterious gadgets that were totally foreign to him and made him thank God he never joined up as a stoker (the word stoker carried over from older days when engineering mechanics had to stoke the boilers of the larger steam ships in the previous war). In the after ends of the boat was a tiny compartment crammed with auxiliary machinery where the stokers lived. The engine alley had two straight eight type, medium speed diesel engines. The unity class had Paxman Recardo; S-class and T-class were Vickers Armstrong and Admiralty English Electric. In the fore and after ends there were the heads (toilets) and two 3,000 pound air compressors which were needed to fill the air bottles. This precious air, was used to bring the submarine up to the surface, where at high pressure, it was used to force the water in the ballast tanks back into the sea again. The crew numbers varied, from twenty-two in an H-boat to nearly sixty in a T-boat, but in war time all submarines carried extra crew. Eating and sleeping times were all on a shift basis and the term 'hot bunking' comes from getting out of your bunk to go on watch and someone else jumping straight in. Extra men would have brought hammocks on board. When the submarine was submerged during daylight hours, it was peaceful with the engines shut down and the engine and motor room served as their bedroom.

The large batteries which were stowed underneath the motor room, wireless office and accommodation deck space, had to be recharged every one and a half to two days and then the submarine had to surface, preferably at night to do a 'charge run'. Usually this took eight hours and was the most dangerous time. Lookouts had to be on constant watch for enemy aircraft. The ideal weather for most boats when on a charge run on the surface is a nice choppy sea, force 2.3. Calm weather was the most dangerous, and heavy seas the most arduous for the crew.

During the greater part of the patrol, the sea would be deserted and the sky empty. The daily routine of surfacing to ventilate and re-charge batteries, the constant watchfulness, and the complicated business of navigating a World War II boat made time pass quickly. But then there comes a day when the hydrophone operator detects sounds from the surface or an enemy ship is reflected in the periscope. The quiet underwater routine steps up to a fierce cold excitement. The torpedo tubes are manned, the commander sights his target through the periscope. Signalman Gus Britton MBE, HM S/M *Uproar* in 1944, explains:

A succession of orders would be given to prepare the boat to fire her torpedoes. The captain would go to the 'fruit machine', the early form of computer, and crank in all the information he had been able to glean from his one look through the periscope and from what the hydrophone listener was telling him. Range, bearing, speed, angle of bow, height of target, course which would give the angle of deflection on firing and ensure target and torpedoes arriving at the same time.

The torpedoes slip away with a tell tale wake behind them. The commander waits just long enough to see if he has scored a hit. Then he dives. Now the boat's presence is no longer a secret. The escorting enemy warships are trying to gauge where she is lying, then the depth charges come thundering down. In seconds the boat would start the underwater dance of death. At best they rack the boat from stem to stern tossing the hull and straining the welds or rivets. Gus Britton survived depth-charging (a 'bollocking', he called it) in *Trident* off the island of Capri in November 1942

'I heard for the first time,' he recalled, 'the cheeping spine-chilling pings of an Asdic transmission in contact, followed by the rumbling of an express train going overhead and finally shattering explosions of a pattern of depth charges going off just above our heads'. At worst the end was mercifully quick as it was with *Spearfish* and many other boats, friend or foe, since the start of the war.

Trident, unlike *Spearfish*, survived the war. During 1941 and 1942, under Lt. Cdr. Sladen DSO & Bar, it sank UJ 1201, UJ 1213 and damaged the German cruiser, *Prinz Eugen*, off Norway. From 1940 to 1944 her crew were awarded no fewer than five DSC's, nineteen DSM's and twenty were mentioned in dispatches. One of those mentioned in dispatches was Belfastman, PO Frances Gerald Rossi. Franks' half-brother, Mr Ralph Rossi from Belfast, remembers his family's Italian background:

> Like many Italians in Ireland my parents settled in Belfast in 1920 and went into the ice cream business. Frank ran off to sea as a boy back in 1930. He later joined the submarine service at the start of the war...He told the family later when the *Trident* next went on patrol against the Italian Navy in the Mediterranean, he was relieved from duty because of his Italian name. *Trident* was the submarine he loved serving on most. I still have Frank's accordion which he used to play to *Trident's* crew in off duty hours. I believe she went to the breaker's yard in 1946, the same year Frank was demobbed.

HERMES AND *ELECTRA* SUNK

Mick's two training courses and an earlier spell at Devonport Barracks had taken up most of 1942. The war was still going on and many more ships had been sunk with lives lost. He heard that one of his earlier ships, HMS *Hermes*, had gone down. The aircraft carrier had sailed out after he left her to join the East India station in late 1941 and was attacked by Japanese aircraft off Ceylon on the 9 April 1942. At 10.30 am she was subjected to very strong air attack whilst sixty-five miles south of Trincomalee and about 10 miles off coast. A shore based fighter squadron could not reach the scene in time to add protection and defence. Forty bombs hit *Hermes* in ten minutes and she eventually sank. HMS *Vampire* and HMS *Hollyhock* and two tankers were also sunk. Over 600 survivors were picked up by a nearby hospital ship and others succeeded in reaching the shore. Two days later one of *Kandahar's* sister ships, *Kingston*, was hit on a bombing raid on Valetta harbour in Malta and destroyed. One month later on 11 May 1942, *Kipling* sank after aircraft attacked in the eastern

Signalman Gus Britton completed seventeen operational war patrols
in *Trident* and *Uproar*, as well as *Tapir*, *Acheron*, *Seascout*, *Truculent* and *Tribune*.

Mediterranean. *Kelvin* and *Kimberley* were the only two of the original eight destroyers to survive the war. HMS *Electra*, Bill's second destroyer was sunk in the Battle of the Java Sea, in action with the Japanese on 27 February 1942. Two months previously she had helped pick up survivors from the doomed *Repulse* and *Prince of Wales.*

FIVE MORE VICTORIA CROSS AWARDS

By the end of 1942, five more Victoria Crosses had been awarded to four officers and one junior rate in the surface navy. The first three were in March 1942 and went to Cdr. Ryder, Lt. Cdr. Beattie and Able Seaman Savage who served on board HMS *Cambeldown*, an old American destroyer loaded with explosives which rammed into the graving dock in St Nazaire as part of a very daring commando raid.

The *Bismarck* was sunk. Her sister ship *Tirpitz* may well have broken out into the Atlantic since there was a dock big enough to take her in France. That was the Normandy graving dock in St Nazaire. On 26 March 1942 'Operation Chariot' consisting of 630 men in sixteen motor launches and *Cambeldown* loaded with explosives and escorted by the destroyers *Atherstone* and *Tynedale* left Falmouth. The operation was highly successful but at a heavy loss of life: 169 men were killed. Besides the three naval VCs, two more VCs were awarded, to Marine Commandos Newman and Durrant who both died. Other awards were four DSOs, seventeen DSCs, eleven MCs, four CGMs, five DCMs, twenty-four DSMs and fifty-one military medals. Fifty-one were mentioned in dispatches, twenty-two posthumously.

Two more naval officers were to win Victoria Crosses separately in acts of bravery in November and December of that year. Lt. Peters was fifty-three years old when he took part in 'Operation Torch' in Oran harbour on 8 November 1942. 'Tramp' as he was called had a career filled with adventure long before he won a VC. He joined the navy in 1904, reached the rank of lieutenant and resigned in 1913. He rejoined in 1914 at the outbreak of World War I. He won the DSO and DSC on board the destroyer *Meteor* at the Battle of Dogger Bank. He resigned again in 1920 to go to the Gold Coast to grow cocoa. Every two years he travelled to London to gamble and enjoy his profit, only to return to grow more cocoa when he was broke. He joined the navy a third time at the start of World War II and was awarded another DSC on board the HMS *Thurlmere* as early as July 1940. He later became Commander of a school for special agents and was a great friend of Guy Burgess and Kim Philby who on learning about the

VC said: 'He was the type of sentimentalist who would have wept at such an honour. Our trainees came to adore him.'(John Winton, *The VC at Sea*)

Back at sea on the 1,000 ton ex-USN coast guard cutter *Walney* he, with Lt. Cdr. Billot, commanding officer of the other cutter, *Hartland*, attacked Oran harbour with parties of US Rangers. *Walney's* boilers blew up. Peters was the only survivor and swam ashore. He was imprisoned by the Vichy French garrison but released a few days later when the Allies took over. On 13 November, flying home, his aircraft crashed at Gibraltar and he was killed. His posthumous VC was gazetted on 18 May 1943. Operation Torch had been Zeebrugge in miniature.

The last honour to be won in 1942 and the seventeenth naval Victoria Cross was awarded to Captain Sherbrooke, the commanding officer of the destroyer *Onslow* on 30 December 1942. Sherbrooke was captain of the 17th destroyer flotilla of five destroyers, *Obedient, Orwell, Obdurate* and the older ship *Achates* were the other four. Also at sea to protect convoys to Russia was the covering force R, consisting of the cruisers *Sheffield, Jamaica* and the battleship *Anson*, commanded by Admiral Fraser home fleet. The cruiser *Cumberland* and other destroyers were on the outer flank of his force.

The convoy JW 51B consisting of fourteen merchant ships heading to Russia was blown off course and reported by U-354. The German fleet under Admiral Kummetz with the battleship *Lützow*, heavy cruiser *Hipper* and six destroyers sailed from the Norwegian Altenfjord for interception on 30 December. During the fourth attack, *Onslow* received a hit behind the bridge with an eight inch shell, which split the funnel and spraying the radar office and bridge with splinters. Sherbrooke's face was split open with his eyeball dangling down his cheek. Onslow was hit again putting B gun out of action and holing the hull under A gun mounting. Sherbrooke ordered his ship to hold his position between the enemy and the merchant men. Hipper turned away for fear of torpedoes. *Sheffield* and *Jamaica* arrived on the scene and were able to hit *Hipper*. One German destroyer was sunk and the German fleet retreated to Altenfiord. Captain Sherbrooke came home on *Obedient* to receive a series of operations on his face and his VC was gazetted on 12 January 1942. *Onslow* carried on to Russia to be repaired.

MAGENNIS'S OPPO JOINS NEW T-BOAT

After training was over in the two H-boats Mick Magennis and his oppo (friend) Bernard Warwick were to part company. Bernard was drafted back to HMS *Dolphin* for further training and then to a brand new T-boat. He explains:

> I joined the T-boat *Telemacus* in Barrow-in-Furness in August 1943. She was a new boat, built at Vickers yard. After sea trials and a work up we sailed for the Far East. On 17 July 1944 we sank the Japanese submarine 1-166 in the Mallaca Straits. Our CO Cdr. William King was awarded the DSO and Eng. Lt. Cdr. Henry Thompson the DSC. The rest of the crew shared five DSMs and nine MIDs in a draw. Later in the Flora Sea Eng. Lt. Cdr. Thompson lost his hand in an accident in the engine room. Two Australian aircraft arrived and while one circled overhead the other flying boat landed to take the wounded engineer ashore. Old Henry only died in 1996 so he lasted well. T-boats *Telemacus* and *Tally-Ho* returned to UK and base, and in 1946 I was demobbed.

Lt. Cdr. Bennington, DSO and Bar, DSC and two Bars, and his crew aboard *Tally-Ho* sank the Japanese cruiser, *Kuma*, the German U-Boat, UIT23, and a number of Japanese transport ships in the Mallaca Straits and off Penang, April–June 1944. His crew were awarded no fewer than eight DSCs, eighteen DSMs and sixteen were mentioned in dispatches. Before the *Telemacus* and *Tally-Ho* went to the breaker's yard, the author remembers them being used for training at Fort Blockhouse when he did his submarine training in 1959. *Telemacus* was scrapped in 1961 and *Tally-Ho* in 1967.

MAGENNIS VOLUNTEERS FOR X-CLASS SUBMARINES: SPECIAL SERVICE

The first X-class submarine was built in 1923 at Chatham. Instead of being a midget submarine, X1 was an experimental submarine of 3,600 tons. It had a crew of 110. The design was influenced by the German submarine cruisers of World War II and took nearly four years to build. The X-craft Mick was to join were nothing like this.

Mick had heard the buzz going around that new smaller submarines were being built and they were looking for volunteers for special service. The little boats were to be called X-craft and carried four crew members and one of these was to be a diver. Mick was spare crew on the depot ship *Cyclops*, he volunteered and next thing he knew he was off to HMS *Dolphin* to register for special service on 15 March 1943. He recalled in

1960: 'Back I went to HMS *Dolphin* at Gosport for a day of medical tests and odd questions from a psychiatrist like "What are your hobbies? What time do you get up at home on Sunday? Do you like cats?" '

Mick Magennis was given his orders to report to HMS *Varbell*, a shore base in Scotland specially being prepared for the X-boat crews to start their training together. This was the Hydropathic Hotel at Port Bannatyne (renamed *Varbell*) not far from where the S/M depot ship *Cyclops* lay off Rothesay, together with a shooting lodge near Loch Striven Head. All midget submariners had to pass a diving course and learn a little about each crew member's vocation. This section of Loch Striven and HMS *Varbell* was an old hydro station taken over as the secret base for midget submarines. A huge area was sealed off and ringed by security patrols. Here were based eight midget boats. Two were prototypes, six were operational craft. They were to be used in Britain's first midget submarine attack on Germany's largest warship in World War II.

When Mick Magennis arrived on 19 March 1943 he first met Lt. Place, Lt. Cameron and Stoker Luck. ERAs Whitley and Reed and RNVR officers whose names he would get to know quickly. The diving course was severe and there were many failures. However he passed out successfully. His instructor back home in the Falls Road swimming baths would have been proud of him now. All his training was not in vain.

The first X-boat of World War II had been launched on the Hamble River near Southampton in 1942. She was fifty feet in length, thirty-five tons in weight and with accommodation for four men. Her diameter was five and a half feet. With a deck board cutting of six feet, it left five feet head room. Mick was five foot four inches and most of the men were of small stature. Having to live in such cramped conditions for days, if not weeks, the smaller you were the better. The engine was a Gardiner 4L/C. The X-craft could dive to 300 feet and had a steaming capacity of 1,200 miles. After learning off the blackboard about these little craft they were all excited to try them out.

Stoker David Snowball (Snowy) recalls his early days in X-craft:

After finishing my submarine training I was drafted to *Cyclops* at Rothesey and then to the submarine *Una*. Later back at spare crew I was drafted to HMS *Varbell* as maintenance staff. We trained using frogman suits at Loch Striven Head. All X-craft had stand-by crews. I trained on board XT5 and later was detailed to X25 but never served in her. The European war was coming to an end and I was drafted to the depot ship *Adamant* out east.

A Clan Line merchantman had been converted to act as Depot Ship to the X-craft. Her name was HMS *Bonaventure* or *Bono* for short. In Loch Cairnbawn they were to practice using these midget submarines. Another depot ship arrived, the *Titania*, to be mother ship to the larger S-class submarines which later would be their tow boats. The first day out on the Loch, Mick was on board X7. His first experience with the 'wet and dry' compartment was very important. He would use this little compartment to enter the sea when the boat was submerged and return again without any inside help. It was different to the conning tower escape on bigger submarines and slightly more complicated. Using it properly was the difference between life and death, as he would find out later on. For months the X-craft and their crews practised diving and doing dummy attacks on friendly warships when they anchored on the Loch. Mick gained more and more experience using the wet and dry compartment, experimenting cutting submarine nets.

ERA Charlie Reed CGM recalls:

In my training period in X-craft, I remember we had just completed our net cutting run and skipper Lt. Ernie Page suggested laying on the bottom in Loch Strivan and having a quiet cup of tea before surfacing. We did this but on trying to surface the rudder guard hooked into an old net. Next thing we knew the boat literally stood on end. Everything loose fell aft. We tried all sorts to break free to no avail and settled on the bottom again thinking of abandoning ship when suddenly for no apparent reason the boat freed herself. Quite a heart-stopping time was had by us all.

There were the towing, navigation and speed trials (surface and submerged). There was the gyro-compass test and tests with side cargoes. Mick felt very proud being among this special group of men, especially when he realised there were not many junior ratings among them. A bond of deep friendship had grown up between the officers and the ratings, which of course was the proper thing. After all, if an officer and a rating were to go out and risk their necks together, it was essential that they should be on the best of terms if the job was to be done properly. Consequently any formality was rather out of place in the great majority of cases, whether he held the king's commission or not, each member of the party was called by his Christian name by everyone else. The only time this did not happen was when there were any officers around who were not special service. Then a respectful 'sir'

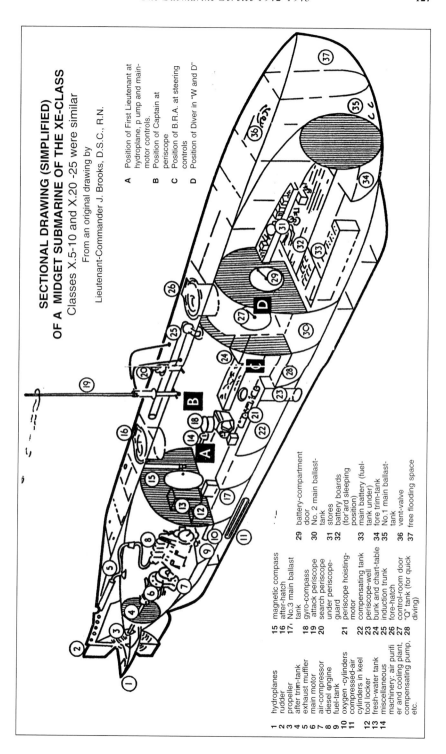

SECTIONAL DRAWING (SIMPLIFIED)
OF A MIDGET SUBMARINE OF THE XE-CLASS
Classes X.5-10 and X.20 -25 were similar

From an original drawing by
Lieutenant-Commander J. Brooks, D.S.C., R.N.

A   Position of First Lieutenant at hydroplane, p ump and main-motor controls.
B   Position of Captain at periscope
C   Position of B.R.A. at steering controls
D   Position of Diver in "W and D"

1   hydroplanes
2   rudder
3   propeller
4   after trim-tank
5   exhaust muffler
6   main motor
7   air-compressor
8   diesel engine
9   fuel-tank
10 oxygen -cylinders
11 compressed-air cylinders in keel
12 tool locker
13 fresh-water tank
14 miscellaneous machinery: air purifier and cooling plant, compensating pump, etc.
15 magnetic compass
16 after-hatch
17 No.3 main ballast tank
18 gyro-compass
19 attack periscope
20 search periscope under periscope-guard
21 periscope hoisting-motor
22 compensating tank
23 periscope-well
24 bunk and chart-table
25 induction trunk
26 fore-hatch
27 control-room door
28 "Q" tank (for quick diving)
29 battery-compartment door
30 No. 2 main ballast-tank
31 stores
32 battery boards (for'ard sleeping position)
33 main battery (fuel-tank under)
34 fore trim-tank
35 No.1 main ballast-tank
36 vent-valve
37 free flooding space

would creep into Mick's conversation with his own officers, and a surname would be used here and there by the commissioned ranks.

18th NAVAL VC

In the early months of 1943 while Mick Magennis was still training, the eighteenth naval VC was won by another submarine commander. Tubby Linton spent the last eight years of his life as a submarine captain. At the start of the war he was out in China on board *Pandora*. All these O and P boats, ten in all, were recalled to the Mediterranean in 1940. After five patrols from Alexandria he was to join the eighth flotilla at Gibraltar. By May 1941, Linton had done eleven patrols spending 196 days at sea out of 251. In 1942 he spent 254 days at sea. He won a DSC for sinking two Italian supply ships. He was promoted to commander and given a new T-class submarine, *Turbulent*. His success at sinking enemy ships increased. On one patrol four ships, two destroyers and two merchant men, in all 100,000 tons of shipping, were sunk. *Turbulent* also destroyed three trains by gunfire. Her eighth patrol lasted thirty-five days and he was awarded a DSO. *Turbulent* sailed on her tenth and Linton's twenty-first patrol in the Tyrrhenian Sea in February 1943. She ran into a minefield. He had been hunted 13 times and 250 depth charges were dropped on him. On 24 February 1943, after six days silence, *Turbulent* was reported lost. Cdr. Linton's posthumous VC was gazetted on 25 May 1943.

Cdr. Linton's son William joined the submarine service after the war and was doing his submarine training on the submarine *Affray* when she failed to surface in the English Channel on 17 April 1951 during routine exercises.(John Winton, *The VC at Sea*)

TIRPITZ MISSION: OPERATION SOURCE

Germany had invaded Norway in early April 1940 and within months their occupation was complete. From then on they kept naval forces, including capital ships, in Norwegian ports and fiords, ready to break out and attack the Arctic convoys which were going to Russia at the time. The *Tirpitz* and several other warships were stationed in the Altenfiord, North Norway. The success of St Nazaire meant Norway was *Tirpitz*'s only outlet now. In October 1942 an operation of two-man torpedoes (chariots) belonging to the same special group as X-craft, carried out an unsuccessful mission against *Tirpitz* in Trondheimsfiord, supported by the fishing vessel *Arthur*. In 1922 the Washington Treaty was passed by the League of

'Operation Source' - Against German battleship *Tirpitz*
in Altenfjord, Norway, November 1943

The Operational and Passage Crews of *X.7*
(Back row, from the left) Sub-Lt. R. Aitken, Lt. B.C.G. Place,
Sub-Lt. L.B. Whitham, Lt. P.H. Philip.
(Seated, From the left) Leading Seaman J.J. Magennis,
Stoker Luck, E.R.A. W.M. Whitley

Nations to limit all countries' new capital ships to under 35,000 tons. Germany did not keep to this treaty and therefore *Bismarck* and *Tirpitz* were two of the most powerful warships afloat, 44,000 tons each at the beginning of World War II.

Rear Admiral U.U.P. Patterson received the Order of the Bath for his part in the sinking of *Bismarck* in 1941. Now the time was right to have a go at Germany's other big warship, the *Tirpitz*. In August/September 1943 RAF reconnaissance aircraft based in Russia kept constant photographic survey on the movements of *Tirpitz* and other ships. In September word came through that *Tirpitz*, *Lützow* and *Scharnhorst* had just returned to Altenfjord from a gunnery exercise in Spitzbergen. The time was right to attack. Mick had been nine months with the X-craft. Some of the others had been preparing eighteen months for this moment. One day in September 1943, six little X-craft left Loch Cairnbawn towed by their mother submarine and headed out into the unfriendly North Sea. They had 1,000 miles ahead of them before they could reach their target. Mick was on board the X7. With him was Lt. Phillips and Stoker Luck. The weather was good and the six craft made good speed. Three or four times in twenty-four hours the little boats had to come up to ventilate. They stayed forty feet deeper than the mother submarine whilst on passage.

At night time the larger submarines stayed on the surface charging batteries. There were four S-class and two T-class parent boats. On the fourth day X8 broke her tow with *Sea Nymph*. It took fourteen hours of searching before the tow was fixed again. The following morning 16 September, X9 broke her tow with *Syrtis* and she was never seen again. She had been carried below the danger limit and her casing probably imploded: the inrush of water would have done the rest. X8 began to have buoyancy problems and they decided to scuttle her. The three crew came on board *Sea Nymph*. The attack on the pocket battleship *Lutzow* would not now go ahead.

Mick Magennis recalled the 1,000 mile underwater trip, to David Francis in 1960:

> From the start we ran into trouble. We were zooming up and down first breaking the surface, then plunging dangerously close to the 150 feet limit where the water pressure would damage the explosive charges and blow us up. Mac Phillips, our South African Captain, flooded in more ballast. The weight gave us greater stability. We were kept up by the pull of the tow, a six inch nylon cable. But when the tow broke we had a terrific scare. I was operating the planes, stoker John Luck was

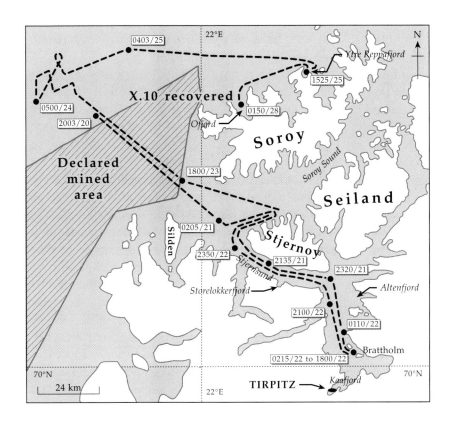

ATTACK ON *TIRPITZ*
Operation Source
showing movement of X10
September 20-28 1943
All times are GMT

sat at the steering and periscope controls, Lt. Phillips was dozing on our one bunk above the batteries. We took it in turns to change round. Lt. Phillips ordered to blow all tanks. The depth gauge still rose 110 feet, 120 feet, 130 feet. I was in a cold sweat as it approached 150 feet and slowly we started to surface. The third time we broke the line we dived well below the limit of 160 feet. It was a hair-raising, horrifying experience. At an angle of sixty degrees with the tail down, there is nothing worse than a sub that goes into a back slide. I was standing alongside the periscope to work the blows. John Luck dropped back into the engine room. He had to fall into it because of the crazy angle we had taken up. The engine clutch was jamming. We could get no drive from the propellers. John was working on the clutch itself. The props started to turn and slowly we surfaced. Lt. Phillips had to get on deck to fix the new tow. Rough seas made it dangerous to open the hatch. On the tiny lurching deck he had only the upright induction tube to cling to. He was out there for a whole perishing hour. Another damper was a collision with the tow submarine. It was yawing frighteningly. One crash and it would have sent the midget to the bottom. So it went on for eight weary days. Only when we heard a hand grenade exploding in the water did we know where to surface off Alten Fjord Norway. That was the signal to surface. Beneath a starry sky at 10 o'clock on 21 September the operational crew paddled themselves across in a rubber dingy to take over from us.

Lt. Phillips, Mick Magennis and Stoker Luck were taken on board *Thrasher* after eight days on board the little midget. They had travelled 1,000 miles. Lt. Place, Sub Lt. Aiken, Sub Lt. Whitham and ERA Whitley were now on board X7. They were to be the operational and attack crew. The following day *Thrasher* with X5, *Truculent* with X6 and *Sceptre* with X10 all changed crew. They were all at the entrance to the fiord. The mother submarines just had to keep at their patrol station and wait for them to come out after their mission was over. Admiral Barry was to later state:

The passage crews of the X-craft deserve great credit for the way they stuck the long and weary passage and for the efficient state of the craft when they were turned over to the operational crews. The passage crews played a big part in the subsequent success of the operation. I consider this passage a fine example of seamanship and determination by all concerned.

TWO MORE NAVAL VCS

The target now for X10 was the *Scharnhorst*. *Tirpitz* was to be attacked by X5, X6 and X7. X6 and X7 succeeded in entering and navigating the fiord and with great difficulty placing their charges under the 44,000 ton warship. Lt. Place on X7 succeeded in reaching his objective after being entangled in nets. Place broke surface briefly to find himself inside the protected berth with *Tirpitz* thirty yards away. X7 crashed into the warship's side below B turret where Place released one charge, before going astern to release the other under C turret. Lt. Cameron on X6 also succeeded in placing both charges under the battleship, despite being hindered by a defective periscope. The Germans spotted X6 but the hail of small arms was ineffective. However, Cameron and crew abandoned X6 and escaped. Lt. Cameron won the Victoria Cross, Sub Lt. Kendall the DSO, Sub Lt. Lorimer the DSO and Lt. Wilson the MBE. X7 sank and Lt. Place escaped. Aitken escaped two and a half hours later from the bottom of the fiord using the Davis escape apparatus. This was a miraculous escape from 120 feet. Aitken had given both the other crew members instructions through the correct escape drill: 'I gave Chadwick (training instructor) and his training full marks. He had made us realise that the pressure at 120 feet was a mere nothing.'

Sadly Sub Lt. Whitham and ERA Whitley both drowned. Aitken's experience as a diver undoubtedly saved his life. Lt. Place was awarded the Victoria Cross, Aitken the DSO and the two drowned officers Whitham and ERA Whitley were both mentioned in dispatches.

Six officers and men were captured and brought back on board the battleship for interrogation. Lt. Place looked a fine example of an officer representing His Majesty's Senior Service. Standing with no trousers on, a pair of navy long-johns and pair of soggy fur-lined boots he borrowed from another submarine officer called Uncle Peter who paid five guineas at Gieves in London for them (He had no chance of getting them back until after the war was over!), the German naval officers treated them with the greatest respect and honour. Hot coffee and schnapps was provided. While all this was happening the German battleship's captain had ordered his officers to move the *Tirpitz* from her moorings. Being such a large ship the time element needed to shift her berth was insufficient. The large explosions, caused by four two-ton Amotol explosive charges dropped underneath the 44,000 ton warship by the two X-craft, damaged the underside of the hull. This damage was to put the large battleship out of action until April 1944 when she was only able to limp from her anchorage to be further damaged by carrier-borne aircraft of the fleet air arm. This kept her out of action until she crawled away to Tromso in October 1944, and was finally destroyed on 12 November by the Royal Air Force, using Barnes Wallis armour-piercing bombs.

The six survivors of the raid spent the rest of the war as POWs in Dulag Nord in Germany. Lt. Place was repatriated after the war and later described the attack on *Tirpitz*: (in Capt. Fell's *The Sea is our Shield*)

> In this particular operation the chance of return was better than many others, because the training had been long and thorough, and the design of the boats was such that we could come back under our own steam. But in this rather novel type of warfare it is impossible to plan for everything. One of the difficulties we encountered was minor mechanical failures, which had not been bowled out during the 'working up'. In passage to the operation we were submerged for twenty-three hours out of twenty-four for ten days on end.
>
> The actual attack took place in daylight, in the most heavily defended anchorage of the German north Norwegian fjords. In the essentials, the attack was simple. A question of getting under the *Tirpitz* and laying heavy mines which exploded after a time lag. I myself encountered some difficulties in the form of net defences, which were rather more complex than we had thought, and my eventual form of attack was to pass underneath them which took longer than I had anticipated. It was, in fact, these close net defences which made it impossible for me to get out after the completion of the attack.

Lt. Cameron's story of his part in the attack is equally understated:

> My difficulties were mechanical. My periscope was flooded and one of my explosive charges had flooded, which added to trimming difficulties and gave me a fifteen degree list. We managed to navigate the outer defences, more by luck than good judgment or skill, and found ourselves outside the steel nets which surrounded the ship herself as her last line of defence. Fortunately there was a gap in the close defences used for the passage of small craft. We learned subsequently that this gap had been opened about half an hour previously to admit normal boat traffic to and from the *Tirpitz* and the surrounding ships. We passed through and in turning to attack, betrayed our presence by grounding on an uncharted sandbank. The alarm was raised on *Tirpitz*

by an observant lookout who reported 'a large fish' to the officer of the watch. As large fish were apparently extremely uncommon in that particular area, he was told not to be a blooming fool. However the buzz had got around of something unusual. Due to our navigating apparatus being out of action when we grounded, we were totally blind and floundered around inside the nets.

We were forced to carry out our attack against *Tirpitz* on the surface. We closed in on *Tirpitz* from fifty yards range under constant barrage. Laying ourselves alongside, we dropped our charges with a time setting of one hour. Having laid the charges and considering the chance of escape with the craft to be negligible, I decided to scuttle the craft on top of the charges to prevent her falling into enemy hands. We did this, and were picked up by motor launch and taken on board *Tirpitz* for interrogation. I was in *Tirpitz* being interrogated when the charges exploded.' (*The Sea is our Shield*)

X5 unfortunately disappeared and was never seen again. She was probably destroyed by depth charges or enemy fire. X10 had trouble with her tail clutch and flooding in her periscope compartment. She had to call off the attack and return to sea where she met the mother submarine *Thrasher* for a tow home. Mick recalls X10's rescue:

Back on board the *Thrasher*, X7's passage crew had all lost weight, and we saw the sense of having a passage crew. We were 'flakers' (exhausted). *Thrasher* circled the entrance to Altenfjord for two days. Boldly she sneaked on the surface as far as she could up the fjord. A flashing light led her to the rescue of X10. Lieutenant Phillips, Stoker Luck and myself were put on board to try to bring her home. First we were showered by spray from a sudden leak. There was a horrible hissing of water under pressure. We surfaced and repaired the leak. Then the tow rope broke and in our efforts to fix a new one, *Thrasher* crashed down on us. I thought we had had it. The planes were jammed. Fortunately for us we managed to abandon ship before X10, the sixth and last midget sub, plunged to the sea bed.

Mick met his brother Bill shortly afterwards:

Ten days later I was on leave having a pint with my brother Bill in a pub near Chatham Barracks. He was the only one in my family to know I was in special service. We were talking about home in Belfast when the radio came on. 'Here is the news and this is Alvar Lidell reading it. For the first time the Admiralty have revealed the existence of midget submarines. They announce they have carried out an attack on the main units of the German navy in their well protected anchorage at Keefjord in Altefjord. They have travelled 1,000 miles from their base, penetrated minefields, dodged nets, gun defences, and listening posts, and negotiated intricate fjords. Within a range of 200 yards, and inside the final screen of protecting nets, they delivered their attack and damaged the *Tirpitz*, which reared out of the water unable to escape. The submarine commanders scuttled their craft and were taken prisoner.'

In total six X-craft were lost and ten men died. Only one German sailor died on board *Tirpitz*. A number of other awards were given. It was later discovered that the *Scharnhorst* had moved her berth and X10 would not have achieved success anyway. The Admiralty was pleased with the outcome and some military historians were to say that these little craft should have been used earlier in the war because of their destructive force with such a minor use of materials, money and manpower. Mick Magennis told the *Daily Mail* in 1960:

Ever since the operation I had been wondering if it had been successful. The news in the pub left no doubt that it had. People in the bar thought I was mad. I let out a rip-roaring 'hooray'. The *Tirpitz* was out of the war for good. Our awards for being the tow crew on X7 and X10 were an MBE for Lt. Phillips with John Luck and myself being 'mentioned in dispatches'.

An extract from a signal from the commander of Western approaches stated:

Will you please convey to the twelfth submarine flotilla my warmest congratulations and profound admiration for their unique and successful attack on the *Tirpitz*. The long approach voyage in unparalleled conditions culminating in the successful attack on the target, called for and produced the highest degree of endurance and seamanship skill. While deploring with you the loss of officers and men whose gallantry is unsurpassed in the history of the submarine service, I rejoice at the success which crowned this magnificent feat of arms– Sir Max Horton. (C.E.T. Warren & James Benton, *Above us the Waves*)

NAVAL WAR LOSSES

By the end of 1943, 465 British warships had been sunk including ten capital ships: *Hood, Repulse, Prince of Wales, Royal Oak* and *Barham* and aircraft carriers *Ark Royal, Courageous, Eagle, Glorious* and *Hermes*. Twenty-five cruisers, 107 destroyers, fifty-eight submarines, two escort carriers, one monitor, 157 trawlers, twenty-five minesweepers, three minelayers, thirteen coastal craft, two depot ships, twenty-five corvettes, fourteen drifters, twelve sloops, nine gunboats, three cutters and three fleet tugs. Numerous warships had been damaged and millions of tons of merchant shipping and their crews lost during the U-boat campaign. By this time however, the naval losses of four years had been replaced. Nine hundred new warships of all kinds had been completed since 1939. The shipyards all over the country were working day and night, including Harland and Wolff in Belfast. The beginning of 1944 saw the reopening of the Mediterranean and the surrender of the Italian naval fleet, gains which had far reaching consequences all over the sea front.

Mick was able to go on leave for Christmas 1943. He travelled to Bradford to be with Maisy and Rosemary. Mick's brother Bill also remembers this time:

> My brother came down to visit me in Chatham barracks once in early 1944. He had been to a wedding of one of his shipmates. After the wedding he paid me a visit. Later I was drafted into submarines and joined the submarine depot ship *Cyclops* at Rothesay in Scotland.

Back at Devonport there were homecoming scenes when *Glasgow* and Mick's old ship *Enterprise* returned in triumph from the Bay of Biscay Battle after defeating a force of German destroyers. On 28 December 1943 they sank three German destroyers and damaged others.

After leave Mick was to become diver on the XT1, a training midget boat, to practice, as new operational XE craft were being built for future missions. Bill had been drafted to HMS *Elfin*, a submarine tender at Blyth and in May 1944 joined the submarine *Tribune*. During this period both Mick and Bill were allowed weekend leave and they travelled to Bradford to visit their mum and sister. Maisy and Rosemary had come over from Belfast to England to find work and they travelled over with Molly McIntyre to Bradford where Molly's sister Ena Baxter lived, in Whetley Hill, Manningham. It was not long before they found work in the wing section of the GEC aeroplane factory. The factory had moved up from Coventry which had been almost destroyed in the Blitz by the German Luftwaffe. Jimmy McIntyre recalls:

> My dad and I were left at home. We had moved from Mulhouse Street to live at 74 Glenmachan Street off the Donegall Road. My brothers Eddie and Joci along with Jim's brother Tony had joined the navy at the beginning of the war. Our two families were very close and all the navy boys including Jim and Bill used to spend their leaves at my Aunt Ena's house at Whetley Hill, Manningham, Yorkshire. I was just too young or I would have been with them all in the navy as I sat many a night listening to all their experiences when they came on leave.

Jimmy's sister Maureen remembers the large terrace house at 112 Whetley Hill:

> My brothers Eddie and Joci and I lived with Aunt Ena and her husband Tommy Baxter at Whetley Hill. Eddie served on the Russian convoys and Joci was in minesweepers. I was married to Harry Rigby and we moved to 59 Thornton Road in 1940. After 1942 the McGinnes brothers and my brothers used Whetley Hill as a home base. None of them went home to Belfast, all their leave was spent in Bradford.

Ena Baxter was a kind woman and her home had an ever open door for all the navy boys and their friends during the war years. Now both families were helping in the war effort.

X-CRAFT AND CHARIOTS

The next missions in 1944 proved without a doubt the success of X-craft. Although Mick was not on these missions his old friend Ginger Coles was the engineer on X24. Sub Lt. Brooks, Lt. Shean and Sub Lt. Ogden were the other three crew members.

One day while the craft was out practising, they thought they would play a trick on the large flag ship, the battleship *Duke of York*, which was anchored in the loch during a break in her North Atlantic patrols. It is the custom for one ship to acknowledge the other while passing. Lt. Mac Shean, while close to the battleship on the surface, stood up by his periscope and saluted the mighty man of war. The next thing all the crew had been ordered on deck to acknowledge the salute including the

Commander-in-Chief Home Fleet Admiral, Sir Bruce Frazer whom Shean did not even know. He picked up his Addis lamp and signalled to the warship, 'What a big bastard you are'. He received the formal receipt-of-signal code group and no acknowledgement. Next morning *Bono* received a signal from the Commander-in-Chief, 'RPC request the pleasure of the company of the commanding officer of that little twit of a submarine X24 for dinner tonight'.

OPERATION GUIDANCE

X24's mission was Bergen, a Norwegian harbour. In the harbour was the Laksevaas floating dock which was needed to repair the German U-boats after their patrols in the North Atlantic. The mother submarine was *Sceptre*. Two and a half days out from Shetland where they rested for a while, they changed crews and the X24 proceeded for thirty-five miles to the target, the floating dock which was anchored in a fjord a few miles from the port of Bergen. The attack went exactly to plan. They found the target, dropped their four ton charges and slipped out of the fjord again to be met by *Sceptre* and thence towed back to base. ERA Ginger Coles DSM remembers the operation well, with humour and with relief:

> Just before the attack Lt. Shean raised his periscope to take a last reading and we were only a few feet from a German patrol boat. The sight that met him was a German sailor relieving himself over the side. It was lucky for X24, because had the sentry been facing seaward, we might have been spotted!

It was later to come to light that instead of the intended drydock, Lt. Mac Shean destroyed *Barenfels*, a 7,500 ton ammunition ship, carrying a cargo of high explosive and much needed torpedoes for the German U-boats who were patrolling in the Atlantic. Lt. Shean received the DSO, Sub Lt. Brooke the DSC and ERA Coles the DSM. The fourth crew member Sub Lt. Ogden was to receive the MBE at a later date (Operation Struggle). Tragically, the Germans thought it had been the work of the Norwegian resistance and rounded up fifty Norwegian men and shot them.

'Operation Bigot' was carried out by X20. Lt. Hudspeth carried out beach reconnaissance on the D-Day landing beach. Later, 'Operation Gambit' was carried out by X20 and X23. Lt. Hudspeth and Lt. Lyne carried out beach marking on D-Day and prior to the D-Day landings.

After the success of 'Operation Bigot' by X20 and 'Operation Gambit' by X20 and X23, the planned invasions eventually took place on 6 June 1944, D-Day, when a total of 176,000 British, Canadian and American troops were carried by waves of aircraft and a vast armada of ships across the English Channel to Normandy. Casualties were relatively light except on one of the five landing beaches, Omaha, and bridgeheads were successfully established to be consolidated and extended over the coming weeks. At the end of July, Allied troops finally broke out through the encircling Germans, whose position in France deteriorated further when another invasion landed in the South of France on 15 August 1944. On 25 August, Paris was liberated and on 3 September, Brussels.

CHARIOTS: TWO-MAN TORPEDOES

The other branch of the Special Service was also to have success. Sub Lt. Greenland DSO, RNVR and Leading Signalman Fevrier CGM sank the Italian cruiser *Ulpio Traiano* in Palermo harbour on 2 January 1943. In the same action Sub Lt. Dove DSO, RNVR and Able Seaman Freel CGM sank the Italian SS *Viminali*. On 28 November 1944 Sub Lt. Causer DSO RNVR and Able Seaman Smith CGM sank the Italian cruiser *Bolzano* in La Spezia. Other chariot operations were carried out at Askvoll, north of Bergen in Norway based on MTB 675 in October 1943. Lt. Bramwell DSC and Able Seaman Harrison, Petty Officer (Mech) Knowelden, Ordinary Seaman McNeill were awarded DSMs. Leading Seaman Freel and Able Seaman Worthy were captured after the raid in Palermo Italy. They both escaped and joined the Italian partisans. Both were later mentioned in dispatches. In October 1944 four chariot men sank two Japanese supply ships in Phuket harbour: Sub Lt. Eldridge DSC, Stewart A. Brown DSM, Petty Officer W. S. Smith DSM and Petty Officer Woollcott DSM.

OPERATION HECKLE

In September 1944, Lt. Westmacott, the new commander of X24, went back to Bergen and the floating dock was blown up along with another stores ship. He also escaped, met the now nicknamed 'Bring them back alive', S/M *Sceptre* and returned to base and the depot ship *Bono*. Westmacott received the DSO; Sub Lt. Dening RNVR DSC, ERA Davison DSM. Sub Lt. Purdy RNZVR the diver was lost overboard on passage. He was replaced by Sub Lt. Robinson RNVR DSC.

THREE COASTAL COMMAND VCs

The year 1944 had ended with four more great successes of the X-craft. On 22 February 1944, Lt. Place and Lt. Cameron, X7 and X6 were gazetted for the Victoria Cross. They were repatriated after the war and presented with their medals on 2 June 1945 at Buckingham Palace. Place and Cameron had become the nineteenth and twentieth naval VCs.

Other VCs connected with submarines were won too. The German submarine service had lost a lot of U-boats to aircraft depth-charging. Therefore they were ordered to stay on the surface and fight it out with attacking planes. This is what happened when Flying Officer Trigg VC attacked and sank U-68 in 1943. In June 1944, north of the Shetlands, Flight Lt. Hornell of coastal command attacked U-1225. It stayed on the surface and fought back. Both aircraft and submarine destroyed each other. All U-1225's crew were lost. Six crew survived from the aircraft. Unfortunately Hornell died from his wounds. His posthumous Victoria Cross was gazetted on 28 July 1944.

In July 1944, Cruickshank, another pilot, attacked U-347 in the Arctic Ocean, west of Narvik. His navigator and bombardier were killed on his first attack. He circled the submarine and on the second run dropped depth-charges on it. The U-boat was lost with all hands and Cruickshank flew his Catalina back to the Shetland Islands although wounded himself. He survived to accept his Victoria Cross from the king at Holyrood Palace on 21 September 1945. These three VCs, although working for coastal command, were all RAF officers.

After the success of the D-Day landings and the later advance into Germany by the Western Allies, the Italian campaign, although much slower, was over. Germany surrendered on 7 May 1945. The Battle of the Atlantic was over and the final cost at sea of the five and a half year war was to be counted. The German navy's strength had been its submarine branch with only fifty-seven submarines, one less than Britain, in 1939. By May 1945, Germany had built some 1,170 U-boats, 863 of which had been commissioned as operational boats. They sank 2,840 Allied ships totalling 14,315,964 GRT. Among these were two battleships, three aircraft carriers, five escort carriers, six cruisers and forty-one destroyers.

JOHNNY WALKER

Capt. John Walker CBE, DSO and three bars of the second escort flotilla consisting of *Starling, Magpie, Wildgoose* and *Wren* between them sank some twenty or more U-boats. Capt. Walker on board *Starling* (flotilla leader) hunted, depth-charged and sank six U-Boats during February 1944. U-264 surfaced briefly before her final end. Starling rescued many of the doomed boat's crew. Capt. Walker died five months later in Liverpool and was given a hero's funeral. He was later buried at sea from the destroyer *Hesperus*. The Atlantic war was brought to an end by the heroic efforts of officers and men on board these small cramped overworked frigates and corvettes. Their home bases were Liverpool, Londonderry and Belfast. From these ports they sailed to seek out and destroy the strongest arm of the German navy, their U-Boat flotillas.

No roses on an ocean wave
No poppies on a sailors grave
Loved ones wail, cry and weep
Bones lie forever in the ocean deep

(German U-Boat song)

In all, 630 U-boats were lost in action, 123 were put out of action in harbour. Two hunded and fifteen were scuttled by their captains at the end of the war under the code word 'Regenbogen' to prevent them falling into enemy hands. One hundred and fifty-three U-boats were captured and 115 were scuttled after surrender in Loch Foyle in Northern Ireland and Loch Ryan in western Scotland. Of 40,000 U-boat servicemen, 28,000 lost their lives, 5,000 became POWs and the remainder surrendered in May 1945.

The European war was over but the war in the East against Japan continued and Mick Magennis was now to travel out to the Pacific on board the mother ship *Bonaventure* on another secret mission.

SIX

'The little guys with a lot of guts.'
(Admiral J. Fife, USN)

FOURTEENTH SUBMARINE FLOTILLA

In late 1943 and early 1944, six new X-craft were built and began to arrive by train to Loch Cairnbawn to join the mother depot ship *Bonaventure*. These new craft were to be used in tropical waters and were called XE instead of just X. They were slightly longer and had a type of air conditioning in them to cope with condensation in the tropics. The new XE craft were to be sent on a top secret mission against Japan. Mick had been chosen for this new mission and was promoted to leading seaman. He was an unusual choice as his duties before in X-craft and in 'Operation Source' were that of tow crew. When Mick applied, back in March 1943, for special service, only officers were allowed to be divers and the only NCO's on any operational crew were engine room artificers. He explains himself:

My job, when not on two-crew operations, was part of the training team to help new officers for midget submarines. In 1944 one of those officers was Lt. Ian Fraser from New Brighton, Cheshire. He had new ideas. 'Magennis', he said one afternoon, 'you are a leading torpedo operator and know all about the electrics. It would be a good thing if I had a man aboard who could do another job beside diving.' 'That's what I want, sir, I replied. Next day I was on my way to Hornsey Island, Portsmouth, for a special diving course. I did a physical reaction test. When the body pressure was equal to that at sixty feet under water gave me the first symptoms of oxygen poisoning. My lips twitched, I had pins and needles, I could scarcely hold my mouthpiece. Soon, I knew, my arms and legs would be twitching involuntarily, my head would feel like a sledgehammer, I would go into convulsions and then black out. I was about to give in when they hauled me out to hear those terrific words, 'You've, passed.' Back at HMS *Varbell* on the Isle of Bute we all trained during the summer of 1944 (while the D-Day landings were going on) at cutting through the submarine nets.

There was friendly rivalry among the divers to break the record of seven and a half minutes needed to cut a hole for an X-craft to pass through and one day Mick was hauled in front of Captain S [Capt. Fell] for trying to work too fast. He recalls:

> I quickly finished the first cuts. My wrists ached and I was breathing deeply, smothering. I shot to the surface. The rescue boat came alongside. 'I'm going back', I insisted. As I was struggling into my wet and dry compartment my breathing bag strap caught on the hinge of the hatch. I broke the straps and slowly, breathlessly slipped into the compartment. I flooded down and crawled into the midget boat. Captain S said, 'Let this be a warning. Don't be too clever. If this had happened on an operation it would have given the whole job away.' My mistake served as a lesson to all divers. Everyone was ordered not to race, not to over-exert themselves.

After six months of hard training the crews of the six small submarines had Christmas leave in 1944, and by early 1945 all X- craft and crews were on board the depot ship *Bonaventure*, ready for their next mission. On 21 February 1945 the *Bono* sailed from Port Bannatyne, Scotland.

Able Seaman John Clarke (now eighty-four) joined the Royal Navy in 1940 as an HO (hostilities only). He served on HMS *Welshman* running stores to Malta during 1941/42 and was then drafted to HMS *Bonaventure* as ship's company. He recalls sailing from Scotland in February 1945:

> I remember Mick Magennis and other X-craft men. We thought very highly of them. They were brave men to go to sea in such small submarines. When we left the UK for the Pacific on board *Bonaventure* the living space was cramped. The stokers' and seamen's mess and ERA's mess were right aft of the poop deck, it was makeshift for this one mission and we were living on top of one another.

The *Bono* looked an inelegant ship (she was after all just a tramp steamer). She had the four little submarines secured on the deck, with two more in the hold, and had strong cranes to lift them in and out of the water. All the X-craft were covered up and marked aircraft to add

Mick Magennis

to the secrecy. Mick describes the journey when he writes to his brother Bill in Sydney, Australia, in September 1945:

Bill, I will now give you a brief idea of what happened to *Bono* since we left UK. First stop from Scotland was Azores, next Trinidad. We spent two weeks here to see how boats would stand up to tropics. This was the first diving the divers had done in shark infested waters and were we shaky! It was also the first time we had tried out our new idea of sticking small mines on enemy craft. So we had tons of work to do. The only thrill I had was when I saw some small sharks and later a barracuda while under, they both sniffed around me then lost interest, but I was honestly scared to death. Next we went through the Panama Canal, a wonderful sight, it puts the Suez into the shade.

Stopped at San Diego two days, by the way had no leave in any of these places, left for Honolulu, Pearl Harbour had shore leave there, disappointed, no dusky maidens under palms, just palms and yanks, more commercial and warlike than romantic, no beer just hooch. Next stop Ellice Isle just above the line, Japs had been on here, next intended stop Brisbane, Aussie land. Arrived there 27 April, 0300 hours, distance steamed 14,888 miles.

Horrible buzz going around that we are too late, craft not required, no targets, etc.. Even the officers admit it, I was fed up to the teeth. Pubs open two hours here, no beer, horrible nightmare situation. Plenty of food in Australia though, and fruit, like England in peacetime.

It was here they found out their new boss was Admiral Fife, US Navy. However, much to their dismay, he had decided against using them. Mick explains what happens next when they left Brisbane.

Left here 14 May and proceeded to Townsville, small port north-east coast of Australia, left next day for the island of Cid on the Barrier Reef. Arrived following day. Commenced working up again, but nobody interested. Have got the impression that we have been dumped here till they consider what they will do with us. The skipper is flying all over the various areas pleading for targets, sort of hawking his wares.

Lady Luck was with them, however, for the Americans needed someone to cut the under sea telecommunication cables running from

The King inspects charioteers on board HMS *Bonaventure* in Loch Cairnbawn

Saigon and Hong Kong. Captain Fell and his little group of men and XE boats (now designated the fourteenth submarine flotilla) had a job to do. Mick and the other divers had practised cutting their way through anti-submarine nets before, but telecommunication cables they would have to practice on. Mick's 'own personal thought was, a tough job this, only to be clearly backed up later'.

The *Bono* sailed out near the Barrier Reef where an old cable was lying on the sea bed to start practising cutting it. Sadly, whilst working on the cable two of their divers, Lt. Enger and Lt. Carey, were lost, believed drowned. Mick explains what happened:

> Seventeenth of June arrived Moreton Bay, commenced cable job. Had a go at it myself, done it OK but realise how slow one must go. Working too hard on oxygen at over thirty feet is dangerous, liable to black out. Had another couple of goes at this found it OK. Lt. Carey RN, our first lieutenant and second diver very keen to have a go. These second divers are not properly coursed divers, are merely blokes who are very keen. Lt. Carey had done quite a lot of diving with me and was good. Twenty-third, Carey went out, was away at cable twenty minutes, when skipper saw him through periscope coming back, he swam into wet-and-dry compartment, gave thumbs down then seemed to tumble out again. Surfaced the craft and went down with other divers but found no trace of him. Presumed oxygen exhaustion. Next day Lt. Enger, another second diver done exactly same thing only he surfaced then sank, never found him. One more experienced diver baled out and just made the surface, another blacked out in W & D.

It was later presumed oxygen poisoning led to their unusual behaviour before they both drowned.

Morale was low after this unfortunate accident. However the *Bono* sailed to Subic Bay in the Philippine Islands and then on to Labuan Island in North Borneo and waited. The orders came through in late July that the cables were to be cut off Saigon and Hong Kong. As well as this, they received orders for an even more hazardous mission: an attack on heavy Japanese cruisers in the Johore Straits of Singapore. Mick later explained:

> Captain S [Captain Fell] gave us a pep talk, told us we were on big things now. Things were humming up, had got to be ready to slip on

the first operation on the 26th. Our own craft skipper Lt Fraser got all the XE3 crew up in his cabin and told us we were after a 10,000 ton cruiser *Takao* of the Japanese Imperial Navy tied up in Singapore.

The *Takao* and *Myoko* were 9,850 ton heavy cruisers of the Atago class. Four were built in the early 1930s. They had been constructed in the naval yard at Yokosuko, Japan. With a complement of 630 officers and men, *Takao* had eight inch guns in both her forward and aft turrets. She was also well armed against air attack and had four aircraft. She had a triple hull and extra armoured plating. When built she cost the Japanese tax payer £2.2 million. She was anchored close into the Singapore side of the straight.

The warships were in shallow water and partly aground at low tide, so the timing of the tides was important. Neither ship had been to sea for some time and it was thought the Japanese had placed them beside Johore Causeway expecting an attack by British troops under Lord Louis Mountbatten as the supreme commander. (He had not been given another ship but was appointed to this job by the British Prime Minister, Winston Churchill.) The Japanese themselves had conquered Singapore Island by advancing soldiers on bicycles across the Johore Causeway. XE1's mission was to destroy the *Myoko* and XE3's was the *Takao*. The submarines *Start* and *Stygian* were to be the parent boats and were to tow the XE-craft to their attacking positions. XE5, which was to proceed to Hong Kong and cut cables there, was left at Subic Bay in the Philippine Islands. The *Bono* was also now flying the flag of Admiral Fife USN who gave them all a speech on the morning that they departed on their dangerous mission. His final statement was 'You're the little guys with a lot of guts. Good luck'.

Now the little craft were lowered over the side and attached to their mother submarines. The distance from Borneo to the Singapore Straits was some 650 miles. The towing boats with the XE-craft sailed at noon on 26 July 1945 and it was four days later that the towing crew and the operational crew changed places about forty miles off Singapore. The passage crew on XE3 was Sub Lt. Ogden RNVR, ERA Nairn, Able Seaman Dee and Stoker Hughes. On the *Tirpitz* mission Mick had been passage crew but now he was the diver and one of the operational crew. He was now twenty-five years old and the most experienced diver on the team. Lt. Fraser was two years younger and the commanding officer. He had already been awarded the DSC for his services on the submarine *Sahib* as a Sub Lt. The S-boat *Sahib* had itself been successful in sinking several enemy

Lt. Ian Fraser on the casing of XE3 before Operation Struggle 1945.

supply ships and on 21 January 1942 sank U–301 west of Corsica in the Mediterranean.

Sahib was scuttled after a depth charge attack by Italian corvettes to the north of Sicily on 24 April 1943. Lt. Fraser was not on board that day, he had been left ashore with a broken foot. Like Mick he had served on destroyers and other H-class submarines before volunteering for X-craft special services. The third crew member was to have been Lt. Carey, who would have been the second diver and navigating officer. He had died earlier off the Barrier Reef. His place was taken by Sub Lt. Kiwi Smith, a New Zealander. ERA Charlie Reed was to be the engineer and crew member number four. All four men were veterans of other X-craft missions and very experienced.

OPERATION STRUGGLE BEGINS

After the 650 mile tow from Borneo and four days at sea, the X-craft crews changed and the more dangerous part of the mission began once the two X-boats slipped their tows. They were now alone. Fraser stayed on the surface trimmed well down using his diesel engines and making five knots. ERA Charlie Reed recounted:

Kiwi Smith was seated aft. His job would have been to operate the motor/engine controls, the hydroplanes, and the pumping systems, forward. I would have been on the starboard side of the control room just forward of the periscope well and would be concentrated on the wheel and on the gyro-compass repeater. Mick Magennis the diver's job on passage was to plot the course and bearings on the chart. Fraser being the CO would have directed orders to all the other three.

The sea was so peaceful and the warm air aroused a mixture of sweet smells of mangoes and spices and aromas known only to the East. Trimmed as well down as could be XE3 presented as low a silhouette as possible as she headed towards her target through the calm and tropical sea. In the early hours of 30 July the tiny submarine hugged the coast until she reached the narrows of Kuala Johore. The boat's position now was a few miles to the south-west of a lighthouse called Pualmangi. And so XE3 spent her first night of the operation creeping up to the entrance of the straits. Singapore Island is twenty miles by ten miles; the city is to the south and to the north beside the causeway was the captured British naval dockyard where Mick had spent some time on board HMS *Enterprise* before the war. Its high cranes and barrack-like buildings sat out like a landmark. Johore lay across the strait and the only connection with the mainland was three miles from the dockyard. Here was a concrete and rubber pontoon-like causeway.

Takao lay anchored to the east of the dockyard. XE3 would have to travel from the boom gate up the channel about eleven miles. Fraser hoped to pass through at first light if possible. By 7.00 am on 31 July, without sleep all night, Fraser took the XE-craft to the bottom for three quarters of an hour and all the crew took benzedrine tablets. This meant they felt refreshed when they came up to periscope depth. Mick had a good sleep curled up like a cat in the engine room. Everyone slept except Charlie Reed and the benzedrine tablets had taken full effect and their morale was reawakened. The air in the submarine had become thick and heavy so a tin of protosob was installed in the fan intake to get rid of excess gases and replenish the oxygen content. Now they had to make good time and race against the tide to reach *Takao* before she lay on the bottom of the harbour.

'Stand by to get under way and I hope the luck of the Irish is with us. Up periscope,' said Fraser.

Mick pressed the switch to operate the long brass periscope, until the eye piece was above the deck. After taking a fix, the tiny submarine dived again to forty feet to press on towards the boom. Once or twice when Mick brought the periscope up to catch a quick look, Fraser 'notices the grey ugly and inhospitable buildings of Changi prison on their port side. He could see the grey tower in the prison yard with its flagstaff.' There flew the Japanese Imperial flag with its rising red sun. Changi prison had its own horrific story to tell later where mostly British and Australian women and children were held in horrendous conditions. The men had been sent to work and die on the ill-fated Burma railway.

At 0930 Fraser finally sighted the boom from which the wire mesh hung and which Mick would have had to leave XE3 to cut through had it been closed.

'The gates are open, we're in luck', Fraser said with a sigh of relief. That was one job less that Mick had to do. Fraser's remark a moment later told a different story, 'Hell, there are a couple of Japs leaning over the side of the boom vessel. Down periscope. Let me know when we have been eight minutes on the course, Magennis.'

Mick started the stopwatch. The time was 1030 and at a slow and silent speed, the midget submarine slipped underneath the boom vessel and passed through the boom gate. They crept slowly round the curved channel north of Singapore Island and heard the thrashing of propellers overhead as the noise died away. Fraser gave Mick the order to put on his frogman suit. They had been below now some seven hours and the air was hot and clammy. Fraser clearly remembered the events of that day:

> I felt sorry for poor Magennis, as he struggled as best he could into the thick rubber suit - a job difficult enough in the open air with plenty of space and an assistant, but here, in the confines of an X-craft control room, twenty times harder. When I next looked at Magennis the suit was half on, his face was red and streaming with sweat, and his long hair dangling like a pair of horns over his eyes. His chest fairly heaved as he panted for breath in the oxygen-scarce atmosphere of the boat and the muscles of his arms gleaming and rippled as he pulled the tight rubber neck piece up under his arms.

Fraser gave the order to submerge to forty feet and helped Mick to dress. Then he gave the command to bring her up again. Mick, now dressed, less hood, stood by the periscope. Up she rose out of the water with Fraser's keen eye over the eyepiece and there suddenly was *Takao*. She was in the exact position as on his chart. He was relieved that every-thing up to now had gone to plan. Now they had the real job to do. *Takao*

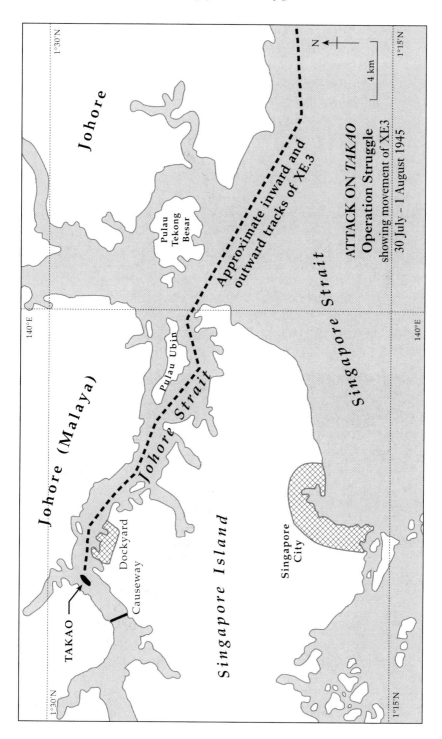

N

4 km

ATTACK ON *TAKAO*
Operation Struggle
showing movement of XE3
30 July – 1 August 1945

Johore

Pulau
Tekong
Besar

Singapore Strait

140°E

1°30′N

1°15′N

Approximate inward and
outward tracks of XE.3

Johore (Malaya)

Pulau Ubin

Johore Strait

Dockyard

Causeway

TAKAO

Singapore Island

Singapore
City

1°30′N

1°15′N

140°E

had been damaged earlier in the war by an American submarine and as a warship she was not much of a threat but where the Japanese had anchored her, just a few miles from the causeway, she was a tremendous threat to any advancing army trying to capture Singapore Island from the Malaysian jungle as the Japanese themselves had captured the islands nearly four years before.

In the eighteenth and nineteenth-centuries naval operations Blue Jackets were sent ashore to spike the enemy guns. The four man miniature submarine was about to do just that in a more modern way. The Allied troops were in Rangoon and, as an invasion was shortly to take place on the Malaysian coast, it would only be weeks before Mountbatten could take Singapore. These two 10,000 ton cruisers, with their eight inch guns could have caused immense destruction to an advancing army. So putting them out of action was of tremendous importance.

When *Takao* was about abeam, Fraser started to prepare for the attack. Mick finished dressing then moved back to operate the periscope, the slide rule and stop watch to Fraser's orders. Fraser could see a number of other smaller warships through the periscope and then as *Takao* came nearer and nearer he noticed her pagoda like structure, her huge bridge work and thick funnel to the rear. Stuck upwards vertically were two tripod trellis-work masts. 'She looks as big as a bloody battleship', he thought.

'Start attack', Fraser ordered. Mick Magennis started the stop watch.

'Up periscope, down periscope.' Mick changed the degrees into yards using the slide rule. 'Length 1600 yards, sir', said Mick.

Fraser swung the periscope.

'Bloody hell, there is a boat full of Jap sailors going ashore. She is only about forty or fifty feet away in the starboard bow. One of the sailors is trailing his hand in the water. I don't know how they don't see us', he said.

XE3 touched the bottom and the *Takao*'s keel both fore and aft was touching the sea bed with an opening in the middle. On Fraser's first try he was brought up short. He could have dropped the charges as with previous missions but instead he tried again and was successful in putting the X-craft right in the middle under the large ship. They were sitting on the bottom with *Takao*'s keel a foot above their heads.

Mick was ready. He fitted his hood on and entered the wet and dry compartment. The door was closed and she started to flood as the pumps transferred water from the ballast tank into the wet and dry compartment. Captain Fell on board *Bonaventure* records on his report sheet exactly what happened:

Magennis flooded his compartment and tried to raise the hatch above

XE3 crew. *(left to right)* Mick Magennis (diver), Lt. Kiwi Smith RNZN (navigator), Lt. Titch Fraser (commanding officer), Charlie Reed (engineer).

Japanese heavy cruiser *Takao* which was attacked by XE3 on 31 July 1945 in Singapore Harbour

his head in order to get out, but he found that after going up a short distance it hit against the cruiser's bottom and did not leave room for him to get through. Taking a deep breath of oxygen he took off his breathing set and found he could just squeeze through the gap with it removed. Outside he replaced his breathing lung (a thing that had never been done by a diver before). *Takao's* bottom was one mass of barnacles, weed and razor sharp shells on which he tore his hands to pieces and cut his suit starting more leaks. He found that the magnets that had been designed to hold the mines in position would not hold on to the filthy bottom, and kept sliding away in the slight tidal stream. Working and thinking like lightning in the mud and pitch darkness he returned to the wet and dry compartment, (repeating the same operation with his breathing apparatus) he then got some rope and, repeating the performance of breath holding, he squeezed out again with great difficulty, noting that the gap was narrower than before owing to the falling tide. He now lashed two mines together and put one on one side of *Takao's* keel and the other on the opposite side where they held well. He repeated this four more times and then returned to XE3 having great difficulty in getting in.

Mick later said this of that part of the operation:

My first impression was how murky the water was. The bottom of the target resembled something like an underwater jungle and I had to clear a patch of undergrowth and barnacles off six places in order to make sure the magnetic limpets would stick on. Getting them on was quite like my old training days when I had stuck many dummies under our own ship. It took me about three quarters of an hour altogether before I got back to XE3.

When finished he closed the hatch and started to drain down. Lt. Fraser later realised that when he chose Magennis as his diver he had picked exactly the right man for the job. He recalls:

Looking back on the limpet-placing part of the operation, I see how wonderfully well Magennis did his work. He was the first frogman to work against an enemy from a midget submarine in the manner designed; he was the first and only frogman during the whole X-craft operation ever to leave a boat under an enemy ship and to attach limpet mines. In fact, he was the only frogman to operate from an X-craft in harbour against enemy shipping.

Frogman suit Mick Magennis used during Operation Source.
Now in the Imperial War Museum

Lt. Fraser had great difficulty in freeing the midget submarine from under the cruiser's keel, and only managed by blowing his ballast tanks, thereby coming to the surface momentarily. They then settled back on the sea bed a short distance from the *Takao*. Fraser now gave the order to release both side carriers, the two tons of Amatol explosive and the empty limpet mine carrier. The Amatol fell away correctly but the empty carrier refused to drop clear. They could not make their escape with the empty carrier still attached to the submarine. The carrier had apparently become flooded during the delay and, unless released, the craft was in dire peril with no possibility of escape. The limpet mine carrier had to be released now from the outside. Lt. Fraser decided he would go out and release it. He describes what happened:

> Magennis was still sweating away in his suit, and I felt he had done enough to make the operation a success. As Reed had little or no experience of underwater swimming in the frogman gear, and Smith wasn't particularly good at this either, I considered that it was justifiable for me to take the risk of leaving the boat for a few moments, even if I was the commanding officer. Should anything happen, I had the confidence in Smith to know that he could get her out to rejoin the *Stygian*.
>
> Come out of the way, Magennis, I'll go out and release it myself. Get me the spare set from the battery compartment. 'I'll be all right in a minute Sir', said Magennis, 'Just let me get my wind.' What a wonderful lad he was! He said this with a most hurt expression on his face, quite obviously meaning that since he was the diver it was up to him to do the diving. And so we sat quietly for five minutes, and when he was ready I replaced his hood and perspex face. 'Thanks', he said and into the wet and dry compartment he went for the second time.

Mick had this to say about his own effort in this hazardous situation:

> When we found that the limpet mine carrier had jammed, Lt. Fraser immediately volunteered to go out and clear same–but knowing it was my job I went out and did it.

Refusing ERA Reed's offer also to leave the X-craft, Mick left the submarine for the third time and with a large spanner managed to release the limpet mine holder. He gave the thumbs up for the last time and climbed back into the wet and dry compartment and closed the lid.

Mick Magennis explains twenty years later to a *Daily Mail* journalist:

The water was muddy but when I looked closely I saw the lifting clips had not fallen away. I unclipped one, then the other. The midget submarine started to float away. I was still astride the side cargo. I had to swim for my life. Luck was with me. I made it. When I drained down in the wet and dry compartment and climbed back into the main section of the submarine, I was barely conscious. I remember Lt. Fraser saying 'You're a gem, Mick'. A few hundred yards from the cruiser we hit the surface. We had been going steadily. Suddenly we were all over the place. 'We'll soon know if we have been spotted', said Kiwi Smith, working the hydroplanes but unable to keep her steady. We were in a fresh water pot in the river without any buoyancy. Ten minutes later we had to crash dive. A fast Japanese launch approached. We thought we had been spotted but it passed without incident.

'Starboard twenty, steer 090 degrees, half ahead group up', Fraser ordered with excited relief in his voice.

'Aye, aye sir, twelve hundred revolutions.'

'Let's get the f*** out of here', Mick said under his breath.

XE3 slid out across the bank and, in another race against the tide, headed back to sea. Lt. Fraser successfully navigated the strait and at 2100 hours passed the boom which was still open, then went a mile or so further, then surfaced and opened the hatch. Whoosh it went as they had been building up pressure inside. It opened with an explosion. Mick remembers:

Happily we steamed on. Lt. Fraser lashed himself to the induction trunk on the casing. At 23.50 we picked up our parent submarine HM/SM *Stygian*. She was using an infra-red lamp as a signal. It could only be seen by us wearing special goggles. Hours later we transferred to *Stygian* and the tow crew took over. We had been fifty-two hours without sleep except for the doze I had before the attack.

XE3 and her crew of four extremely brave men had achieved 100 per cent success. They felt the tension release and started chatting to one another.

'What will you do when you get back No 1?'

'Sleep for three days', replied Kiwi Smith.

Before leaving for Operation Struggle Lt. Fraser had drawn the crew's rum ration and back on board *Bono* lay a one gallon stone jar of rum under his bunk.'I think I'll get a jar of rum from under my bunk and swig the lot', said Fraser.'And I'll help you', said Mick. Back on board the mother submarine, Mick remembered later:

> The boys on board *Stygian* told us they had heard an explosion at 2130 hours and had seen a big glow over the headland. We felt happy. There were tots of rum all round, big eats and lots of sleep. Later we learned we had blown a sixty feet by thirty feet hole in the *Takao* and put her guns out of action. One man inspired us all on that mission: Lt. Fraser. He was cool, real cool.

Later in the letter to his brother Bill he casually explains everything in a few lines:

> 31st July 2300 proceeded up Johore Straits all very happy, at last we are here. Under target 1400 1st August. Clear of boom and out 2130. 2200 till 2300 loud explosions and clouds of shit. Joy in our hearts.

XE1 was unable to attack *Myoko*. Instead they dropped their Amatol charges under *Takao* and had great difficulty in contacting submarine *Start* for a tow back to base. XE5 could not cut the cables off Hong Kong but XE4 had been successful in cutting the cables off Saigon. When all the boats returned without loss of life, celebration was the order of the day, but not for long. Captain Fell informed the crews of XE4 and XE3, the two successful boats, that they were going back in again to finish off the *Myoko*.

In the Far East the war was in its final stages. In India after desperate sieges at Kohima and Imphal, the British fourteenth army drove the Japanese back into Burma where they surrendered in Rangoon in May. After the Battle of Leyte Gulf, the Americans continued to drive the Japanese from the islands they had occupied. The eventual capture of the Mariana Islands brought Japan itself within range of American bombers. Between November 1944 and August 1945 they destroyed 275 square kilometres of Japan's cities with incendiary bombs, killing hundreds of thousands. Despite these appalling losses, the Japanese prepared to fight on. There were still four million men in the armed forces and there was a home army for the defence of the Japanese Islands. In view of the very large number of casualties which invasions of Japan would cause, the Americans decided to use a new kind of weapon to force the Japanese to surrender. The newly developed atomic bomb was dropped on the city of Hiroshima on 6 August 1945 and another one on Nagasaki three days later. Appalled by the terrifying power of the bombs and unaware that the Americans had no more bombs ready for use, Japan's supreme war council reluctantly decided to surrender to the Allies. Emperor Hirohito announced his country's surrender on 15 August. Back on board *Bonaventure* preparations were being made for XE3 and XE4 to return to Singapore to sink the *Myoko* when the news came through that Japan had surrendered. The war was over. In Mick's letter to his brother Bill from Sydney he explains:

> Arrived back at Brunei and were informed that the other craft had not reached its target, so XE3 our boat and another boat XE4 would have to go back in seven days for the other cruiser, also cut Singapore cable. On the seventh day the boats were stored and ready, and we were just about to be hoisted out when Cdr. 'X' came running along and washed everything out. Some days later peace was declared. Later we scrapped five of the X-boats, the remaining one is show boat in Sydney. So that Bill is our brief history out here. I'm afraid it is not as good as we expected, we thought we were going to sink half of the Jap merchant fleet.

Of the eight and a half million tons of Japanese shipping sunk in World War II American submarines accounted for nearly 5,000,000 tons. Out of 288 submarines of the United States Navy, fifty-two were lost. I would like to mention here that the largest ship ever sunk by a submarine was the 68, 000 ton Japanese aircraft carrier *Shinano*. A feat unrivalled to this day by Commander Joe Enright and the crew of US/SM *Archerfish* when they fired a salvo of six torpedoes thus sinking the ship during the Pacific campaign.

As Mick Magennis stated they did not do as well as expected, but then in the European War the British Navy's submarine service had sunk 1,300,000 tons of German and Italian shipping at the loss of forty-one British submarines. Had the fourth submarine flotilla stayed in China at the beginning of the war Singapore may not have fallen so easily to the Japanese. However two men, of the Royal Navy, one an officer of high rank and one a seaman of low rank both from Northern Ireland played their part in destroying two of the last heavy cruisers of the Imperial Japanese Navy in 1945.

Six weeks before Mick Magennis and the crew of XE3 attacked the 10,000 ton cruiser *Takao* at Singapore, Cdr. 'Baldy' Hezlet (later Vice Admiral and today president of the twelfth area Irish division RNA) was on patrol in the new T-class submarine *Trenchant* not far away in the Banka Strait near the island of Sumatra.

Cdr. Alister Mars DSO, DSC and Bar remembers Hezlet's exploits on board *Trenchant* in his book, *Submarine at War*:

> The 13,000 ton *Ashigara* was one of Japan's heavy cruisers with an exemplary war record, she was transporting some 5,000 Japanese troops back from Indonesia to defend Singapore and Commander Baldy Hezlet on board *Trenchant* was lying in wait. *Ashigara* was only going at half speed because of the shallow strait and did exactly as Hezlet had hoped for, even making a navigational change of course around a shoal at the proper time. At approximately 3,000 yards Commander Hezlet fired a salvo of eight torpedoes, and five found their target. Then reversing *Trenchant* in order to bring his stern tubes on target, Commander Hezlet fired two more torpedoes, but missed as the warship had changed course to try and run onto the beach. But alas she sunk in half an hour with great loss of life. A Kamikaze class destroyer hunted *Trenchant* with depth charges unsuccessfully and as the victorious British submarine made its escape, a guard vessel picked up some of the few remaining survivors.

Cdr. Hezlet was decorated with a bar to an already awarded DSO for sinking U–859 off Penang on 23 September 1944. Other officers and ratings of his gallant crew also received decorations for both these brave deeds plus a number of other successful war patrols. Both Cdr. Hezlet of *Trenchant* and Lt. Fraser of XE3 were awarded the USA Legion of Honour, the highest award from the USA to a non-American officer. Admiral Fife USN was in command of the British fourth and fourteenth submarine flotillas during the war. There were no awards given to Royal Navy ratings by the USA who served under the United States flag during World War II.

OPERATION RIMAU

Unknown to the officers and men on board *Bonaventure* during the final days of Operation Struggle nine captured frogmen from a previous mission in September/October 1944, Operation Rimau, were being ceremoniously beheaded. These nine men were the survivors of a twenty-three-man team led by Colonel Ivan Lyon who had set out for Singapore harbour to sink Japanese shipping. The operation went drastically wrong and fourteen frogmen died. Because of the brutal and inhuman way the Japanese treated the POWs, a court martial was held after the war. Possibly beheading would have been the fate of the crew members of Operation Struggle had they been caught.

Back on board the *Bonaventure* Mick remembered that day in 1945 well, as he explained to David Francis of the *Daily Mail* in 1960:

'The war is over', someone shouted, as we all were playing tombola (bingo) in the recreation space. The Japs had surrendered. Captain S.W.R Archie Fell ordered a bottle of beer for every man.

The *Bonaventure* returned to Sydney after calling at Subic Bay to collect XE5 and her crew. After the five XE-craft were scrapped, the scrap metal was later used as reinforcements to build a sea wall in Garden Island, Sydney. One X-craft was for a short time put on display and later scrapped. HMS *Bonaventure* was returned to the clan line to become a cargo ship as originally intended.

Three submarines were based in Sydney, the *Virtue*, the *Vox* and the *Voracious*. They were tied up alongside the old cruiser HMS *Adelaide* at the Sydney Yacht Club. Most of the X-craft crews were drafted to spare crew or to one of these boats. Mick was drafted to HM submarine *Voracious* and on 19 September 1945 he wrote a letter to his brother Bill:

HMS/M *Voracious*   19th September 1945

Dear Bill, Received your very welcome letter, pleased to know that your wife and yourself are on par, and my congratulations to the new arrival when one comes, you are certainly working fast. I suppose by the time you get this, your 'demob' should be ready. I shall be looking forward with great interest to meeting the young McGinnes some day. I only hope you get a decent house soon, as I know how hellish it can be living in apartments, shades of 'Gamble St'.

Well Bill, as you can see from above I am now on a big boat, doing my best to pick it up. When the peace was made absolute the *Bonaventure* was in Brunei, Borneo, from where but a week before we had just completed our first job. We then steamed up to Subic Bay, north end of the Philippines, then to Sydney. Two days after arrival some officers spilled the beans to newspapers, this was slightly premature to the plans of the 'Higher Ups' and a big stink was kicked up about it. However the job was a general press release after that.

Two days later I was Sydney spare crew with two boats being in the harbour Vox and ourselves, done three days spare crew and then found myself on here. We have one petty officer torpedo operator here and several acting leading seamen, this PO will be leaving shortly and I will be taking over.

As I write this the *Voracious* is on her way to Hobart in Tasmania. We are on a sort of goodwill cruise, spent seven days in Melbourne, great place, after the cruise we go back to Sydney and get docking leave. Though I'd much rather go home.

I am sending you some cuttings from Aussie newspapers, after you have read them will you send them on to mother. Well, Bill I hope you find a new home all right and settle down to living life happily. I will probably see you in about eighteen months time.

Cheerio,
All the best
Jim [Mick Magennis]

When Mick wrote this letter he had not the slightest idea that he and Lt. Fraser had won the Victoria Cross. No junior rating in the submarine service had ever had been awarded a Victoria Cross. There had been a number of CGMs and most of these awards had gone to men in chariots. Mick first heard about his award one November morning in 1945:

I was having breakfast when above all the chattering sailors I heard my name being mentioned on the radio. I thought I had misheard. Later as I was repairing an electric oven a sailor came to tell me Lt. Fraser wanted to see me up top by the gangway. I was in overalls. Lt. Fraser held out his hand and congratulated me. 'You have won the Victoria Cross.'

I was too staggered to speak at first, and as Lt. Fraser walked away I asked, 'What about you, sir?'

The engine room of a midget submarine.

An XE-craft at speed on the surface during exercises.

'Oh,' he replied casually, 'I have been awarded the Victoria Cross as well. Sub Lt. Kiwi Smith has won the DSO and ERA, Charlie Reed the CGM.'

I never did get back to repair the electric oven. After that it was just one round of receptions. All the submarines cleared lower deck. I had to stand beside the captain as he gave out the news and read all our citations. They had come through from Buckingham Palace on 13 November 1945. Mine read:

Citation

The King has been graciously pleased to approve the award of the Victoria Cross for valour to:

Temporary Acting Leading Seaman James Joseph Magennis, D/KX 144907.

Leading Seaman Magennis served as diver in His Majesty's Midget Submarine XE3 for her attack on 31 July 1945 on a Japanese cruiser of the Atago class. Owing to the fact that XE3 was tightly jammed under the target the diver's hatch could not be fully opened, and Magennis had to squeeze himself through the narrow space available.

He experienced great difficulty in placing the limpets on the bottom of the cruiser owing both to the foul state of the bottom and to the prominent slope upon which the limpets would not hold. Before a limpet could be placed therefore Magennis had thoroughly to scrape the area clean of barnacles, and in order to secure the limpets he had to tie them in pairs by a line passing under the cruiser keel. This was very tiring work for a diver, and he was moreover handicapped by a steady leakage of oxygen which was ascending in bubbles to the surface. A lesser man would have been content to placed a few limpets and then to return to the craft. Magennis, however, persisted until he had placed his full outfit before returning to the craft in an exhausted condition. Shortly after withdrawing Lt. Fraser endeavoured to jettison his limpet carriers, but one of these would not release itself and fall clear of the craft. Despite his exhaustion, his oxygen leak and the fact that there was every probability of his being sighted, Magennis at once volunteered to leave the craft and free the carrier rather than allow a less experienced diver to undertake the job. After seven minutes of nerve-racking work he succeeded in releasing the mine carrier. Magennis displayed very

Lieutenant Ian Edward Fraser DSC, RNR
and Leading Seaman James Magennis
photographed at the Admiralty.

great courage and devotion to duty and complete disregard for his own safety.

After listening to the citation being read Mick remembered:

I was proud but embarrassed. It was an ordeal for a matelot to be thrust into the limelight. Admiral Bruce Fraser C-in-C Sydney asked me to see him. Gins flowed in the wardroom; strange surroundings for a matelot used to rum and beer. There was just one whirl of parties, sherry, champagne, cocktail parties the lot. No-one expected me to work. I was excused everything. I did not seem to belong to my ship. Later I took off to visit friends at Newcastle a few hundred miles from Sydney. When I returned two days later a policeman hurried up to me on the street. 'The whole city has been searching for you. A plane is standing by to fly you home,' he said.

LAST NAVAL VC

The last Victoria Cross to be won in 1945 was by Lt. Robert Grey RCNVR, a Canadian with the fleet air arm, at Onavara Wan Hon Shu in Japan in August 1945. He was killed in action when his plane was shot after sinking a Japanese destroyer. His Victoria Cross was presented to his parents by the Earl of Athlone, the Governor General of Canada in Ottawa in February 1946.

Lt. Fraser RNR and Mick were to fly home to be presented with their Victoria Crosses by the king. Eighteen officers (fourteen RN, three RNR and one RNCR), two petty officers, two leading seamen and one able seaman were awarded this high award for valour in World War II in the Royal Navy and Mick Magennis was proud to be one of them.

SEVEN

Homecoming

NEWS REACHES HOME

James Kelly was a journalist for the *Irish News* in 1945. In his book *Bonfires on the Hillside* he remembers receiving news of the VC award:

> A Stormont civil servant who had served as a captain in the navy in World War I phoned me one night in Belfast to tell me the embarrassment of his political bosses at the news that an announcement was about to be made that a Catholic Navy man had been awarded the Victoria Cross.

Maisy and Rosemary had moved back home to Belfast after working in England during the war. They had found a house at 8 Ebor Street off the Donegall Road. The telegram arrived inviting them to Buckingham Palace and within hours all the street knew. Journalists from the main Belfast newspapers were up interviewing Maisy and Rosemary. When asked by one of the journalists what she thought about going to Buckingham Palace, Maisy replied:

> I felt terribly proud of Jimmy when I got the news but I was also a wee bit sad for I knew he must have been through a lot to get a Victoria Cross. As for going to Buckingham Palace, myself and Rosemary will have to be looking our best, but dear knows where we will get the coupons for new clothes.

Mrs Magennis applied to the Board of Trade for extra coupons so Rosemary and she could buy some new clothes to go to meet the king.

Unfortunately they got no reply and some friends in the street eventually helped them out before they were to travel to London.

On 13 November 1945, the day Mick's VC citation was published in the *London Gazette*, the *Belfast Telegraph* interviewed Mick's mum and gave a write-up in the newspaper. 'The proudest woman in Ulster today is Mrs Magennis since last Friday when she received a letter from the Admiralty telling her of her son's award.' The article gave a full report of all the family and mentioned the school Mick went to in West Belfast and the Falls Road swimming baths where his mother said he spent all his time during his school days. It went on to praise him and his fellow crew members on board the midget submarine and Operation Struggle. 'The deed for which they have been honoured will go down as one of the most amazing in naval history.'

The paper reported the noble contribution of the Magennis family during the war; of Bill and Tony's fourteen years service between them and how both Maisy and Rosemary had worked in England in a munitions factory.

BELFAST CITY COUNCIL MEETING

In the Belfast City Hall on the evening of the 14 November 1945, a special meeting of the General Purpose Committee took place. Those present were Alderman R. Byrne MP, Alderman L. McCurdy and Sir Crawford McCullagh, the Lord Mayor. These great Unionist figures prided themselves that they had done their bit for making Belfast a healthy law-abiding city. One item on the agenda that evening was brought up by Alderman Henderson, another member of the council. He produced the *Belfast News Letter* and read the story relating to James Magennis going to the investiture ceremony at a later date to be awarded the Victoria Cross and to meet the king. As the minutes of General Purpose Committee recorded:

> Alderman Henderson referred to a report in this morning's press that Leading Seaman Magennis of 8 Ebor Street, Donegall Road, Belfast had been awarded the Victoria Cross for bravery in the war recently ended and on the motion of Alderman Henderson, seconded by the Deputy Lord Mayor Alderman Hinds, the town clerk was instructed to convey, on behalf of the council and the citizens to Leading Seaman Magennis their hearty congratulations.

Recognition also came from Northern Ireland's Prime Minister who sent a telegram:

Heartiest congratulations on your award of the Victoria Cross. It is the highest honour paid to heroism, courage and devotion to duty. We are proud of you.

Basil Brooke

HOME MINISTER QUESTIONED

Mick was still in Australia and already his VC was beginning to stir up trouble. He had not even received his award at Buckingham Palace when a row broke out in the Northern Ireland Parliament (Stormont) on Friday 23 November 1945. The *Belfast Telegraph* reported:

The Minister of Home Affairs (Mr Warnock KC) was asked at Stormont by the Nationalist MP, Mr T. J. Campbell, whether Leading Seaman Magennis VC of Belfast on returning home from service throughout the war will be free to reside in Northern Ireland, if he so wishes, without the necessity of obtaining a permit from the Ministry. Mr Warnock in reply, said he was proud to say that the honour of the first VC to come to Belfast had been won by one of his constituents. It was absurd to suggest that there could ever be any question of the right of Leading Seaman Magennis to return to Northern Ireland. The permit system did not apply to him at all. Special provision was made to safeguard the position to any person ordinarily resident in Northern Ireland immediately prior to joining HM Forces. Mr Campbell asked if the Minister was pleased that this particular Irishman was not bound by this irritating and insolent restriction.

Mr Warnock, 'I am pleased indeed that he is a citizen of Northern Ireland and hope he will come back to stay here for many happy years.'

Mr Campbell, 'Do you claim him as one of your supporters?'

Mr Warnock, 'I have no doubt at this time Leading Seaman Magennis through the ballot in secret voted for another ex-service man.'

On 26 November in reply to this Stormont outburst, Mrs Magennis's next door neighbour in Ebor Street, Mr G. Gallagher, wrote to the *Belfast Telegraph*:

Mrs Magennis and Propaganda –
Strong Protest Issued in Her Name

Sir, speaking with the full knowledge and consent of Mrs Magennis
mother of Ulster VC hero we wish to disassociate ourselves from the
remark passed by Mr T. J. Campbell KC MP (Nationalist Central
Member of Parliament) and to protest in the strongest possible terms
against what may be regarded as the exploitation of her son's name for
propaganda purposes from which no good can come. Outbursts like
these tend to keep our people apart. I am a close friend of Mrs
Magennis and have been answering letters of congratulations etc. from
many sources including one from J. K. Warnock KC MP in the last
week and I can say without fear of contradiction that not one came
from any nationalist representative or body for that matter. In conclu-
sion a word of advice to my own representatives in the 'Maiden City'
why not try asking for the freedom of the city for Magennis. I am a
Derryman myself and employed in Queen's Island.

STOP OFF AT SINGAPORE

The Sunderland flying boat landed at Singapore after the one stop
flight at Darwin from Sydney. They both had a few hours of a break
before their next flight was to leave for England. Lieut. Fraser states: 'I
was requested by the admiralty to go and see the results of our mission.'

The navy had already moved into the dockyard and a lot of clearing up
was going on. The *Takao* was lying like a beached whale with her pagoda
like superstructure looking top heavy. It was an eerie yet exhilarating feeling to be there. The officer in charge had arranged transport and he congratulated them on the excellent job they had done. The Japanese inter-
preter informed them that there had only been a skeleton crew on board
the *Takao* and there was very little loss of life. The navy officer was sad-
dened when he heard of all the brutality that the Japanese had used on
British POW's and local Chinese and Malayan people. The *Myoko* and the
hulk *Takao* were being used to hold Japanese prisoners. When the
Japanese POW's were repatriated both these ships were towed out to sea
and sunk.

NIGHT OUT WITH BBC STAFF: MEETS QUEEN MARY

Back in England the flight from Singapore arrived at Poole in Dorset.
Mick recalls:

After all our arrival at Poole, Dorset was an anticlimax. No one met us. No one knew we were arriving. We had no money; not even a rail ticket. Lt. Fraser phoned a nearby naval station. They loaned us money and the RPOs of all people (regulating petty officers were notorious disciplinarians) gave us a real welcome. 'Have a tot.' he said passing the bottle round, while we waited to catch a train to London.

The evening before the investiture ceremony Mick and Lt. Fraser were invited onto the BBC 'Tin Town Tonight' programme. The BBC staff then took them out on the town. First was the Bolivian Cocktail Bar; then off they went to the Phoenix Theatre where Mick was welcomed by the manager. In between acts Mick was introduced to Cecily Courtneidge the actress. While they were chatting word came round from the Royal Box that Queen Mary would like to meet him. He was taken round and introduced. Queen Mary greeted Mick cordially.

'You are Magennis, how do you do, young man? I feel deeply honoured to shake your hand.'

After a lengthy discussion he told Queen Mary he was looking forward to his brother Bill coming down from Bradford and his mum and sister coming over from Belfast the next day for the investiture ceremony. But most exciting of all he told her he was his going to meet the king. Queen Mary replied,

'Young man, I think my son will only be too delighted to meet you. Goodbye and God bless you'.

Mick was touched by her warmth and friendliness, so unlike what he would have expected from royalty. Just down to earth like most of us he thought.

On 15 December the *Illustrated London News* published 'One of the War's most daring exploits; the British midget submarine attack which gained two VCs'. Two full pages of drawings by artist G. H. Davis covered the event.

The plane on which Maisy and Rosemary were travelling was held up at Sealand Airport, Chester, because of fog and Mr Henderson of the Northern Ireland Office waited three hours at Croydon. They came on to London by train but they were not going to be able to get to the ceremony on time. Maisy and Rosemary had been having some lessons in curtsying just in case the king would speak to them. Now it was all in vain but many a joke and laughter would be talked about in days to come. They were met at the station and arrangements had been made for someone to take them to meet both Mick and Bill at the gates of Buckingham Palace.

INVESTITURE CEREMONY

That morning three Victoria Crosses and two George Crosses were presented by the king. They headed a long line of 350 men and women who passed before His Majesty at the investiture which lasted one and a half hours.

Lt. Fraser was the first to pass before the king and next it was Mick's turn. The king asked Lt. Fraser, 'How long did the whole business take?'

'Sixteen and a half hoursl,' Lt. Fraser told him. Watching Fraser receive his award were his father, his mother and his wife.

Micks remembered the event later:

The most nerve-racking part of the investiture was when the citation was being read out. It seemed interminable. I was six feet from King George. He smiled understandingly when I stepped forward to receive my award. 'Congratulations, Magennis,' he said. Chatting with Mick, after pinning on his Victoria Cross, the King asked him how long he had been at this work.

I replied I had been in the submarine service since late 1942. He wanted to know what I was going to do and I told him I was a regular sailor who had trained as a boy at HMS *Ganges* and I still had four years to serve,' HMS *Ganges* has produced many fine men for the Senior Service. Well done my lad,' said the king.

The third Victoria Cross was won by Colonel Newman who had been at St Nazaire and had been a POW until April of that year. The George Crosses were awarded to Flight-Lieutenant Wilson, bomb disposal expert and Mr Joseph Mott, formerly a private in the Essex Regiment.

Maisy was disappointed that Tony was not able to be there. His ship was still at sea. Bill had just been demobbed and came down by train from Bradford. He did not need coupons for new clothes as the navy had kindly provided him with a demob suit. It did not fit well and the hat they gave him made him feel like an American FBI agent. With Bill being in the submarine service, Mick and his brother had a lot in common; so he was looking forward to a few drinks and a bit of crack about old times. The family had made arrangements to stay with friends in Wandsworth that night. With tears of joy in their eyes, Maisy and Rosemary could not help but think of the day they stood waving good-

The original crew of the XE3.
*(from the left)*Leading seaman Magennis, Lt. Fraser,
Lt. Carey, Engine Room Artificer Maughan.

Outside Buckingham Palace December 1945
Bill (brother), Mick Magennis, Mary (mother), Rosemary (sister).

bye to their son and brother, as he climbed up the gangway of the Belfast Liverpool ferry ten years before when he first joined the Navy at only fifteen. There were many hugs, kisses and greetings when the family of four met at the gates of Buckingham Palace.

After the ceremony the press was waiting to take photographs. Maisy and Rosemary looked really elegant.

Maisy wore a black stole and Rosemary had a wide rimmed hat like you would see at Ascot, or on Belfast's Malone Road. The rest of the day was spent catching up with the family news. Mick and Bill were having a good laugh at Bill's demob suit. 'They give you a Victoria Cross and look at what I got. It doesn't even fit.' laughed Bill. The crack was going to be good for the next few days. Soon they would all be heading home to Belfast.

BACK TO BELFAST: A THREE DAY HERO

Reporters and a small crowd gathered at Larne harbour as the news was that that was the way they were coming, but instead they came on the night boat from Heysham. The boat was packed with servicemen and women coming home, some on leave, others being demobbed. The larger demobilisation had happened earlier in the year after VE day and Mick got the feeling nobody was talking about the war with Japan being over. Anyway the bar stayed open most of the night and very little sleep was had by anyone.

When Mick arrived at his mother's house in Ebor Street he saw all the bunting but the street was empty. However once the word got out he was home, the street just filled up with people from everywhere. Here was beginning a day he would never forget. The people of Ebor Street treated their hero Mick Magennis to a reception as only the working class people of Belfast know how. A man from Stranmillis Road brought over the White Ensign. He put it up beside the red merchant navy flag (The Red Duster). They flew side by side to represent the Battle of the Atlantic where both Merchant and Royal Navy men had lost their lives. All the women had baked and cooked the night before in preparation for the great day ahead. The neighbours had put up bunting and hung out Union Jacks and navy flags. The air raid shelter was decorated and painted with 'Welcome home our Belfast hero'. Like the Grosvenor Road area of Belfast, many men from the Donegall Road had served in the navy. Some of them would not be coming home. The majority of people who lived in Ebor Street were Protestants and usually this sort of celebration only hap-

The Lord Mayor of Belfast, Sir Crawford McCullagh reads the letter
from Sir Basil Brooke, the Prime Minister of Northern Ireland,
to Mick Magennis at the reception in 1945.

pened, in their Donegall Road area of the city, on the Twelfth of July. But the people did not care; they were going to treat Mick Magennis as just as much a hero as they would King Billy. Someone even suggested changing the name of Ebor Street to Magennis Street.

Mick felt touched but very embarrassed when he saw the sign, 'Welcome home our Belfast hero'. All his friends and friends of the family came over from Majorca Street and the Grosvenor Road to join the party. The day was non-ending. Jimmy McIntyre recalls:

> I wore my brother's sailor's cap and now I was of age the war was over. I was so proud of Jim and so were all my family. Someone from the little street I lived in had won such an honourable award. The party went on to the early hours of the next morning. Jim and his mum and sister had to have some sleep because the next day they had to see the Lord Mayor of Belfast.

At Belfast City Hall the next morning, Mick arrived with Maisy and Rosemary to be given a mighty cheer from the crowds gathered outside.

> Magennis was all but mobbed when he reached the City Hall. Scores of women were waiting his arrival at the entrance and when he was seen approaching in the Lord Mayor's car scores of others rushed from the streets to catch a glimpse of him. (*Belfast News Letter*, 15 December 1945)

The Lord Mayor, Sir Crawford McCullagh, greeted him as he stepped out of the car. The high sheriff, councillor R. B. Alexander MP, and members of the Corporation wearing their robes walked in procession from the hall to a specially erected dais near the main entrance. The presentation committee and the Minister of Home Affairs, Mr E. Warnock, were also present. Flanking both sides of the dais were hundreds of people eager to see the gallant sailor and they gave him rousing cheers. The Lord Mayor read a letter from the Prime Minister, Sir Basil Brooke, expressing regret at being unable to attend owing to a previous engagement. The Mayor congratulated Mick as did some of the Corporation. He told him, the public and the press about the shilling fund that was being set up and that at a later date he would present a monetary gift from the people of Northern Ireland. 'You did your duty without counting the cost, and you have added lustre to the annals of the British Empire. You took great risks without for a moment thinking of your own safety,' said the Lord Mayor.

Procession to Belfast City Hall. Mick, his sister Rosemary, the Lord Mayor and local councillors, with crowds looking on.

Night out with the Lord Mayor of Belfast at the Group Theatre.

Then Mick spoke to the public:

> I am very proud indeed that it was I who brought a Victoria Cross to
> this city and I am proud to be a Belfast man, [and continued amid
> loud applause] I hope when my service is finished in the Navy I will
> come back and settle down in the city I was born in. I will be in the
> navy for three more years and may sign on for another ten years to
> qualify for my pension. (*Belfast News Letter,* 15 December 1945)

After the press session and photography were over, Mick and his
family, with the Lord Mayor and councillors, went back into the City
Hall where a reception was laid on. Jimmy Webb, a former classmate of
Mick at St Finian's school, felt proud of his achievement and describes
the occasion:

> I went to the City Hall that day for the civic reception and I could
> see that Jim hadn't changed that much as he accepted the hand-
> shakes and the pats on the back with the same modesty I had seen in
> him at school. (the *Andersonstown News,* 8 June 1996)

In the afternoon all the family visited friends in Mulhouse Street, and
Majorca Street. They were welcomed with open arms and there were so
many people to see but Mick even had time to call into Kelly's and see
Sally Hannigan and some of the locals. That evening, the people from
Donegall Road held a reception at Windsor Cinema. This started at the
midnight matinee. Mick was presented with gifts from the Ebor Street
and District Home Welcome Fund and the proceeds of the matinee went
to swell the fund, which it was 'confidently anticipated, will be popularly
supported by the workers in city firms large and small'. The programme
was given free by Messrs J.D. Finney, Major Finney and Mr Hegarty.
Others sent donations, including Linfield and Belfast Celtic Football
Club, Greyhound Racing Co., Lisburn Picture House, Mr McAlinden's
Furnishing Co., L. Roddy and staff, A. Dalzell and P. Hogan. There were
many local artists who gave their services for the occasion: Sam and Jean
Murphy, Arthur Martin, Gordon and Morris, Roberto and Reno, Ethel
Bullick, Melda Davey, Joan Willis, Jim McKenna, J. Forte and lastly
William the Wizard. The Right Hon. Edmond Warnock KC Minister of
Home Affairs and member for the division on behalf of the people of the
district presented Mick with a wallet of notes, and a gold watch. Mick
thanked Miss Noble and members of the committee, Mr Hegarty and the
director of the theatre. He told them that he would remember the past

Mick meets his old HMS *Ganges* instructor CPO Watkins at the Belfast Recruiting Office at Clifton Street in 1945

three days for the rest of his life. He was leaving the day after to spend the final week of his leave with his brother Bill in Bradford before returning to his new draft in HMS *Dolphin*, Gosport, Hampshire.

On the third day Mick and his mum went to visit his old school on the Falls Road, St Finian's. He met most of his old school teachers but did not feel at home and it was not an entirely happy occasion. Gerry Oates, a schoolboy, who was there recalls:

It was a cold morning, damp with fog. At eleven o'clock there was a knock on the classroom door and a party of four were ushered into the room by the head master: an elderly lady, an official of the Belfast Education Authority, a naval officer in full regalia with shining buttons and coloured service ribbons immediately catching the eye, and a shy, handsome young man in ordinary seaman's uniform with bell-bottoms and open-neck front; it was him, Leading Seaman Magennis.

Nobody rose; we sat and we watched in awe as the naval officer told us in a swanky English accent what we already knew. Young

Magennis smiled inoffensively and said he was glad to be back in his old school and the party left to visit another class.

I remember feeling proud that I was Irish and that I hadn't honoured king and country by standing up, but there lingered an uneasy feeling inside me that I had hurt the poor, young lad Magennis in some way, and for years afterwards I could still see his kind, smiling face and his elderly mother by his side as we sat stubbornly in our seats.

After lunch Mick was invited by the *Belfast Telegraph* to meet Lady Montgomery. Field Marshall Montgomery's mother had travelled down from Moville in County Donegal to meet him. They met on the steps of the *Belfast Telegraph* offices.

'I am very glad to have the opportunity of meeting you and please accept my congratulations,' said Lady Montgomery. Mick expressed his thanks and Lady Montgomery asked him had he met the Field Marshall during his travels. Mick told her that although he may have been near him he never met him.

'Well when I'm writing again I'll have the greatest pleasure in telling him that I met young Magennis, VC. God bless you, my boy,' said Lady Montgomery as they departed, leaving a knot of spectators.

Mick walked round to Clifton Street to the recruiting office to meet his old *Ganges* instructor CPO Watkins. Watkins was overjoyed that one of his former *Ganges* lads had won such a high honour: what a way to finish his career. This was his final year after twenty-two years service. He showed Mick the book where he had signed on the dotted line and asked him did he remember that day. Mick said he certainly did. 'Ten years ago, I was given 3s.9d. I felt a rich boy.' They had their photograph taken and then went round the corner for a couple of drinks to finish off the remarkable coincidental meeting.

The next day Mick and the family travelled over to Bradford to spend Christmas 1945 with Bill. Before his leave was over he travelled back to Belfast to be guest of honour for the Irish ex-servicemen's comrades association club in Divis Street, Belfast, where he was presented with an illuminated address and made a life member of the association. Tributes on behalf of the British Legion were paid by Captain J. L. Bennet OBE, Major H. R. Haslett, chairman Belfast branch. This association closed down at the start of the recent troubles, and the illuminated address was presented to the RNA, Great Victoria Street, Belfast, by Paul Magennis after his father James Magennis died in 1986.

EIGHT

After the War

While on leave in Bradford during the war, Mick had met Edna and they had been very close but had decided to wait until after the war before they married. They were married in 1946 and Edna came down to live in Portsmouth while Mick was based at Fort Blockhouse. Soon Edna and Mick were to have their first son, James, and Maisy became a grandmother. Mick was to serve on two more T-class submarines in 1946/47. He served on board the *Trenchant* and the *Tantulus*.

REUNION WITH OLD SHIPMATES

Mick's old friend Ginger Coles DSM who was on XE4 came back from Australia. They had some good nights together ashore in Gosport. One night Ginger asked Mick if he could bring a few friends on board to see his Victoria Cross:

> After leaving *Virtue* in Australia I became the ERA on the new T-Boat *Tireless*. The day we tied up at the jetty at Fort Blockhouse in December 1946 Mick was there to meet me. He came aboard to drink my tot, and we then all headed ashore to the pub The Yorkshire Grey. Myself and some other shipmates wanted to see his Victoria Cross (we had never seen one before) so after the pub closed we all came back on board Mick's boat *Tantulus*. But Mick could not find the little bronze Victoria Cross. Eventually it turned up in a kiddy's toy box Mick had bought for his son James. Just like the old Mick I knew. Easy come, easy go, except when it came to diving, Mick knew his job.

Tancy Lee, the first boy Mick met on the train when joining *Ganges* and with whom he served on HMS *Kandahar*, met him again after the war at Fort Blockhouse. He too had joined submarines and had served on *Ultor*, *Unrivalled* and *Sybil*. The gunlayer on board the *Unswerving*, Leading Seaman Sid James DSM remembers 'many's a night ashore with Mick in the Old India Arms in Gosport. Myself, Ginger Coles and other oppos of Mick's from spare crew and men from other boats which had much to talk about, most of us were only still in our early and mid twenties. We had lost many friends.'

Seventy-four British submarines lay on the sea-bed marking memorials to the three thousand officers and ratings who would not be coming home. Mick would have remembered especially the thirty-nine officers and ratings lost in special service (X-craft and chariots). The surviving submariners would have had much to share with each other. Their reminiscences would have been of funny sea stories of past happenings, sadness and sorrow and maybe even the odd tear (who said submariners are all tough guys with no emotions?). Past grievances with fellow shipmates would be gone because it is bad luck to speak ill of the dead. Some of the men would have been serving extra time as they had joined before the war in the seven and five scheme and were in their five years of reserve time when the war ended and were saying their goodbyes to return to civvy street. Some would be signing on as they had no home to go to. Many of their loved ones died in the blitz. Some were orphans and had joined the navy from Dr Barnardo's and other children's homes before the war as boys in HMS *Ganges*. To them the navy was their life, peace time or war time, but at least they had a choice. Their oppos (shipmates) on the ocean

James Magennis celebrates Christmas with two of his sons.

floor did not. Mick Magennis O/N DJX 144907, John (Tancy) Lee O/N DJX 144904 and Don Wynne O/N DJX 144906, the three boys who had travelled down to HMS *Ganges* on 5 June 1935 had all survived the war.

After leaving *Ganges* John (Tancy) Lee had lost touch with his class-mate Don Wynne until 1945. He recalls:

> I was on board the S-boat *Sybil* in Trincomalee and I bumped into Don on the dockside. He was a PO sparker (telegraphist) on board the minesweeper, *Friendship*. They were on their way to Singapore. Don had been a survivor when the destroyer, *Defender*, sank after aircraft attack off Tobruk on 12 July 1941. We had a great evening together talking about old times at *Ganges*. Don had free beer tickets for the PO's mess Naafi canteen, so for one night I became a petty officer, I borrowed one of Don's jackets with his badges on. No one noticed.

In the Royal Navy more Victoria Crosses were awarded to officers than to men on the lower deck. Of the fourteen won in the submarine service in both world wars only one went to a junior rating. Some of these officers went on to reach high rank. Lt. Place VC on X7 and Cdr. Mires VC on S/M *Torbay* were to become Rear Admiral and Admiral. On the lower

Giving a speech at the launching of a new submarine at Barrow-in-Furness 1946.
Lt. Fraser and Lt. Place in the background.

Barrow-in-Furness 1946. Three VCs in a row.
Leading Seaman Magennis, Lt. Fraser, Lt. Place.

A-class submarine *Anchorite* being launched at Vickers Armstrong Shipyard 1946.
Magennis attended this launching ceremony.

Out for a stroll in London. *(left to right)* Buster Crabb OBE, GM, Lt. Place VC,
Leading Seaman Magennis VC, Tom Waldron, Lt. Fraser VC. James Gleeson, Lt. Cameron VC.

Four VC's share a drink together

Four X-craft VCs have a cup of tea together.
(left to right) Lt. Place, Lt. Fraser, Lt. Cameron, Mick Magennis

Three Naval VC winners at Vickers Armstrong 1946.
Lt. Place, Lt. Fraser, Mick Magennis.

Three VCs view model of A-Class submarine at Vickers Armstrong 1946.
(from left) Lt. Fraser, Mick Magennis, Lt. Place

deck on the other hand, to hold such a prestigious award can create envy and resentment coupled with flattery from other ratings. Mick Magennis held the rank of leading seaman. He also had one good conduct badge which was awarded for four years good service. The most one can have is three for twelve years service. As Lt. Place and Cdr. Mires climbed the ladder of success Mick had to go the other way and suffer the humiliation of being reduced to the ranks. (Being busted in the navy is quite common and the door is left open for promotion again, more so at the lower end. Good conduct badges are only given so that they can be taken off you again.)

POMPEY DETENTION QUARTERS

In late 1947 Mick was in the rattle again for drunkedness. He was immediately put on a charge and later at the captain's table the cards were stacked against him. The usual preliminaries and naval routine with regards to being in the rattle were gone through: first, officer of the day's report, second, first lieutenant's report and finally captain's report. The further up the ladder you go the less chance you have of escaping with a telling off for being a bad boy. With cap in hand as numerous sailors before and after him have experienced, one humiliated five feet four inch VC winner stood on one side and a battalion of 'scrambled egg' on the other. They busted him. Loss of his killick's rate, loss of his good conduct badge and to crown it all twenty-one days in Pompey detention quarters with its Victorian conditions and run by anachronistic barrack stanchions (sailors who never go to sea) in HMS *Victory*, the Portsmouth naval barracks. This was the second time Mick had been seriously in the rattle. In November 1944 while at HMS *Varbell* he lost a good conduct badge and received fourteen days cells for another misdemeanour.

Ginger Coles DSM now belongs to the leading branch of SOCA. One of his old shipmates recently died and his last words to another shipmate Nobby Langfern were, 'Keep in step Nobby or I'll put you in the effing rattle'.

Stoker David Snowball recalls:

I ended up myself in the rattle while serving at *Varbell*. Three of us went out one night to Dunoon in a borrowed truck from the officers' quarters without their permission. We all were put on a charge and landed in cells. It was while I was locked up my old mate Stoker Higgens, along with Able Seaman Carroll and Lt. Staples lost their lives on board XE11 on 6 March 1945 in a sad accident. The X–craft came up under a boom defence vessel and smashed her casing, then sank to one hundred and twenty feet in Loch Striven. Sub Lt. Morrison and ERA Swatton escaped.

It is here the author identifies with detention. While serving with the fourth submarine flotilla in Sydney, Australia, the submarine I was a crew member on, HM S/M *Tabard* was in drydock in a place called Cockatoo Island (an old prison island). Being left on my own all week-end I was lonely so I got 'Brahms and Liszt'. The commanding officer was not sympathetic and I was put on a charge for being drunk in charge of a submarine which happened to be in dry dock. I ask you: can you imagine knocking someone down in that? Sentence was loss of my only good conduct badge and twenty-eight days detention in a place called Holdsworthy. It had been an internment camp for the Japanese. Three rolls of barbed wire and four machine gun posts. After the war the Australian services used it as a detention camp. After my release I went absent without leave for three weeks to see my newly found 'Sheila'. (What Jack will do for love!) On my voluntary return I received another forty-two days starting with the usual first three days of bread and water, punishment diet number one. Number two was slightly better, porridge, porridge and more porridge.

The naval code of good conduct does not in anyway represent the criminal code of civilian law. Most commanding officers however can only judge each case before him by what has been told by other officers and NCOs and the level of their truthfulness or exaggeration thereof can usually defend or sink the offender. Unfortunately for Mick, being a VC did not stop him from being put in the rattle. Also, what might be seen as humorous and petty by some officers, e.g. the officer of the day on board HMS *Glasgow* and the Marquis of Milford Haven on Mick's earlier ship HMS *Kandahar*, may in another situation by other officers be seen to be a much more serious offence. However, humour lies in the eye of the beholder, I think, and I am sure readers would agree. A VC holder of low rank calling out the duty watch over the command of his superiors is very funny (a Victoria Cross winner has the right to call the guard or duty watch out irrespective of his rank or seniority) and I might add extremely brave (having a punch up with the duty petty officer). As Vice Admiral Fife USN quoted earlier said, 'Those little guys with a lot of guts', even if it was to cost Magennis his hook, badge and twenty-one days detention.

It is also worth mentioning that although officers may never be sent to detention quarters, their punishment can be just as severe with loss of rank, privileges and a set back for future promotion. The officer or rating who climbs the ranks in HM Navy without being in the rattle has not been born yet. However, Garry Owen (*Ganges* 1933) nearly made it: 'In my sixteen years in the Andrew (navy) as a boy telegraphist up to PO (tel.) acting chief, I can boast that I was only once in the rattle, the case being dismissed. That was in HMS *Commonwealth*, Kure, Japan.'

Even members of the gentry have been known to get the boot but I have never known any of them to ever go to Pompey detention quarters. But then neither have I heard of any civilian authority that presents Victoria Crosses. Wartime over, the petty trivialities of a peace time navy returned. The naval routine of spit and polish merchants were back in power again and worse still, they were even creeping into the submarine service. They train men to blow up warships, to risk their lives for their country. When it is all over they want them to behave like Sunday School boys, without understanding the mental pain and anguish some of them have been through.

In the Royal Navy drunkenness was a way of life both in Victorian times and in Mick's time. The issue of rum was a part of one's pay packet. The moral attitude to the use of alcohol in the Royal Navy was very hypocritical. Drunkenness among both officers and men was accepted, except when on duty when under naval law it was a crime punishable by removing rank, or if that was not possible then a period of time in Pompey detention quarters. Therefore excessive drinking was in itself not wrong, only the time when the person chooses to do it. The navy decided to stop the rum ration in 1970 due to a combination of moral pressure and the requirement of total sobriety for more technical jobs. Regarding this, Lt. Fraser VC of XE3 makes this statement:

> It is an odd thing but during the whole long five years of the war, servicemen and civilians alike had to put up with a thousand and one hardships, but I never once heard of a sailor missing his tot of rum. Even in besieged Malta with everyone starving and the only food for 100,000 people being brought in by an occasional ship or submarine, Jack still drew his full tot.

When submarines came in from patrol, it was a well known fact that officers turned a blind eye when their crew went on a bender. Living in such unnatural conditions, not knowing if you were even going to come back alive every time your boat went on patrol, certainly the booze up was more than just a social event. It must have released a certain amount of built-up tension every time a patrol was finished and you knew you were safe, at least until the next patrol. Many men cracked up and extremely unnatural behaviour was common amongst men serving on submarines in World War II. John Lee recalls two such incidents:

> One crew member on board a boat kept urinating in the captain's cabin when he got drunk. On another submarine the coxswain was drunk out of his mind one day we went to sea. He nearly sank the submarine himself as he was on duty operating the hydroplanes. Needless to say both men were put in the rattle.

The Royal Navy was the only one of the three services to issue rum free to its men on the lower deck before 1970, an anachronism carried over from Victorian days when most bluejackets could neither read nor write and food was deplorable. The modern navy of the twentieth century during the war and up to 1970 must have lost a certain percentage of its efficiency due to this outdated tradition.

Three Victoria Cross winners are recorded to have died of suicide. One man named Boyes killed himself shortly after being court-martialled and dismissed from the service for what would have been perceived as petty nonsense, a boyish escapade of climbing over the dockyard gate at night. Only one man in the history of naval Victoria Crosses had to forfeit his award. He was Midshipman Daniel who had his VC removed on 4 September 1861. His life ended in disgrace and death from alcoholism in New Zealand. King George V expressed his absolute distaste at taking a medal back from a hero. I wonder would some of the spit and polish merchants, post-war officers, and non-commissioned officers have removed Mick Magennis's Victoria Cross if they could?

RETURN TO GENERAL SERVICE

After Mick was demoted and finished his detention, he was transferred back to general service in September 1947 on HMS *Drake* in Devonport. He was then drafted on board HMS *Orion*, a Leander-class cruiser, which had just returned home from the Mediterranean to go into the reserve fleet. The cruisers *Newfoundland* and *Cumberland*, the battleship *Howe*, and many other warships, were laid up and most of the older ones were later to be scrapped. On board HMS *Orion*, Mick was attending the sick bay for ear treatment. Petty Officer J. A. Smith, the sick bay attendant on board *Orion*, remembers:

> I knew Mick Magennis as he had to attend the sick bay for treatment to his ears. I was the sick berth Petty Officer and remember treating him. He was, as far as I recall, medically downgraded from the submarine service because of damage to his ear drums.

When Mick was busted and given twenty-one days detention HM submarine service was finished with him. He was no longer considered to be of any use to them. On 1 September 1947, the day he was transported over to Pompey detention quarters in Victoria Barracks, to begin his twenty-one days detention, the deed of betrayal was written in black ink right across his service papers: 'Discharged back into general service'.

Mick Magennis became the only Victoria Cross winner to have spent time in Pompey Detention Quarters. John Daly, a P.O. stoker on board the cruiser *Cumberland*, remembers Mick:

> Like many other Irishmen he got into trouble with his superior officers and the powers-that-be. Unwanted in submarines he was discharged back into general service. He was detached to my department, i.e. the engine room to do small electrical repairs. He was very much a loner and like many at that time wanted to get out of the service. The slogan at that time was 'Roll on my twelve'.

After spending eighteen months on board *Orion* and *Cumberland*, Mick spent the final months in the navy serving on board ships of the reserve fleet. His wife Edna and son David were able to move into No 1 Bute Road, Mutley, Plymouth, and Mick returned to Drake Barracks on 15 September to prepare for demob on 24 November 1949. During his final years in the navy Edna had two more baby boys. David was born in 1947 and Paul in 1948.

DEMOB

Mick left the navy, I think, a sad man, in 1949 after spending his final two years in general service. I believe he was more than glad when his demob came through but at least he was alive. Some of his classmates at HMS *Ganges* and shipmates in the navy were never coming home. They had crossed the bar long before their lives had really begun and only their families would ever remember them. In 1945 his ambition was to finish his twenty-two year career in the navy but by 1949 circumstances had changed his mind. Not being allowed back into the submarine service which he loved so much resulted in his leaving the navy, a decision made by many, as Gus Britton MBE explains:

> The peace time navy with all its pomposity and ceremony, the unfortunate social gap between the lower deck and wardrooms, all too prevalent in surface ships and occasionally submarines, was too much to endure for the reward of a none-too-generous pension.

When Mick returned to Belfast in 1949, he found employment in the RN air station at Sydenham and he lived with his mum and sister at No. 8 Ebor Street and later until 23 June 1951 along with his wife Edna and sons David, James, and Paul he moved to a new Corporation house, No. 32 Carncaver Road in the Castlereagh/Cregagh area of East Belfast. Settling into civilian life after fifteen years in the service is far from an easy task as most men who have been through the experience will agree. The first three to four years are really a period of uncertainty and many men even think of rejoining the navy. His brother Bill did just that and served on the cruiser *Cleopatra* in the early 1950s. Having brought his wife Edna over to Ireland and being with his family (mum and sister and son), Mick probably felt it his duty to stay.

Then tragedy struck: his son David was knocked down and killed by a trolley bus on the Cregagh Road. Mick and his wife were devastated. His brother Bill remembers this sad tragedy:

> I travelled over to the funeral. It was a sad time but one thing stuck out in my mind was the work Jim [Mick] had put into his garden; the lawn and flowers and vegetable garden. I couldn't believe him being a sailor could have such green fingers.

THE VICTORIA CROSS IS SOLD

By 1952 the generous gift he received unconditionally seven years before from the people of Northern Ireland was gone. He had shared it among his family and friends as unconditionally as he had received it. He was broke (a common occurrence among working class people). He lost his job and shortly after that he sold his Victoria Cross for £75 to a dealer in Smithfield Market. Mick saw no shame in selling his medal to make ends meet, just as Mary Cunningham had no shame in pawning her husband's false eye (it too had been a gift from His Majesty's Government). The area where he was brought up had as many pawnshops as other establishments. In the poor areas of Belfast the pawnshop was a way of life. These places and second-hand shops were a way of buying and selling for the 'lower classes'. The middle class on the other hand saw shame. The press got hold of the story and the dealer duly returned the cross to Mick when it became clear that there was not universal approval at his selling it in the first place (a rumour soon circulated that Viscount Furness had paid £100 to have the cross returned). Sotheby's 1986 catalogue of medals repeated the story: 'after hearing about Magennis's story about selling his medal a well-wisher bought it back for him.'

The dealer disputed this rumour and told the *Belfast Telegraph* (18 September 1952):

> I had received offers from Viscount Furness to buy the medal from me so that it might be given back to the man who won it but I turned him down.

Later the *Belfast Telegraph* reported that

> Mr Joseph Kavanagh, Smithfield dealer, is presenting the VC to the Ulster Museum. Now the bronze cross will remain for all time the property of Magennis' native Belfast.' Mr J.A.S. Stendall OBE, curator of the museum agreed it was the right place for the cross and anyone who wants to see it can do so.

This was not to be. So Mick got his cross back, but not without suffering the price of having the whole world know about the unfortunate incident. A Belfast journalist was about to capitalise on the story.

A PUBLIC SHOW

For the benefit of everyone but Mick, the return of his Cross was to be done in front of the dealer, a photographer and journalist. We can only wonder what the effect of all this was on him. The press who when he returned to Belfast in 1945 with his VC had praised him, now used this sad incident to disparage him and made sure the world knew about it. His enemies from both sides of the political and religious divide revelled in his misfortune. Mick explained why he sold his VC, when interviewed by David Franks of the *Daily Mail*, in 1960:

> My health broke down, I was broke and it didn't seem right to go begging from the British Legion after the people of Belfast had collected and presented me with a monetary gift of £3,066 back in 1945. When I returned to Portsmouth in early 1946 I had just married Miss Edna Skidmore from Barnsley. As we moved around, living in digs, this was a steady drain on the money I had received. Those post-war years were for living it up and sharing my gift with my family and friends. Navy pay was very poor and those three years after the war, money was for spending if you had any, which I did. However back in Belfast, some six years later in 1952, I was laid off work due to illness. My wife, myself, and family were broke. You can't eat a Victoria Cross. So I sold it to a dealer in Smithfield Market for £75. The dealer had promised to keep quiet about it, but after a few weeks he announced publicly he would present it to the Belfast Museum. My name was on it and everyone knew it was my VC. What a stink it caused; what a blow-up. The world protested. I received hundreds of letters condemning me. Some were sympathetic, others rude and scurrilous. Then an influential friend [Viscount Furness] told me I must have my VC back. I don't know what went on but the dealer returned my VC to me. It leads my row of medals and there it stays.

VC GOES ON DISPLAY IN ULSTER MUSEUM

However that was not the end of the story, as the *Telegraph* told its readers (18 September 1952):

> Before the dealer informed Magennis that he was going to give him back his medal he talked with Mr T. A. S. Stendall OBE, curator of the Belfast Museum to whom he had promised it. Mr Stendall said that it would be quite all right to return it as far as he was concerned. 'So I got in touch with Mr Magennis immediately and told him that I wanted him to have the medal back.' Then the medal was taken from the safe where it had been ever since the Belfast hero sold it. The dealer handed it over.

Because the dealer had so openly promised the VC to the Belfast Museum, Mick Magennis loaned his VC to the Museum so it could be displayed for

Photograph which appeared on the front page of the *Belfast Telegraph* in 1952
of Magennis being handed back his Victoria Cross.

a short time. Later, he received it back for a reunion in England and the
coming Queen Elizabeth II Coronation in 1953.

This was the beginning of a period of re-evaluation for Mick. The
people of Belfast did not seem to hold him in high regard; some people
even tried to downgrade his act of bravery. He realised that the limelight he had briefly basked in was gone forever. It almost appeared that
many people in Northern Ireland thought a Victoria Cross was an award
for good behaviour or a guarantee for credit rating instead of an award
for valour earned in wartime.

LEAVES BELFAST FOR GOOD

His critics had come out into the open and he now knew where he
stood. It was clear that he was not wanted in Protestant Unionist East
Belfast and neither was he wanted in Catholic Nationalist West Belfast.
That uneasiness about a former pupil winning a high decoration for
bravery in the British armed forces felt even by the teachers and pupils

in his old school St Finian's was hardening into something else, as attitudes in Northern Ireland themselves hardened. He was the little guy in the middle caught in a strange religious and political trap. The only thing was to go to England.

He moved on 7 February 1955 to 17 Beech Road in Rossington, near Doncaster, where he and his wife were made much more welcome than in his home town of Belfast. He found work as an electrician down the coal mines at Rossington Colliery. Here he found the comradeship of the Yorkshire miners very much akin to his early experiences in submarines.

WELLINGTON BARRACKS PARADE, JUNE 1956

In 1956 the Victoria Cross centenary celebrations opened in Hyde Park on 26 June and over 300 of the 400 living holders of the VC were guests of the government. Mick's frogman suit, which he wore during Operation Struggle and which is permanently on display at the Imperial War Museum, was included in an exhibition of over 1,000 items covering the one hundred years history of the VC.

That grand day in London Mick Magennis walked to the assembly point for VCs prior to the Hyde Park review by the queen with his medals in his pocket, because, he said, 'I didn't wear them coming here because it makes people look at you in the street.' (*Belfast Telegraph* 26 June 1956) Shy and quiet (just like the midwife, Miss Glasgow, had predicted all those years ago) he stood among the scores of other VC winners on the parade ground at Wellington Barracks and pinned the VC and other medals on to the jacket of his neat grey suit. When asked by the reporter about his X-craft service, Mick told him: 'Yes, I do look back on those days in midget subs and it is like looking back to another world and another existence.' Of his great feat he said humbly: 'I think I would be too nervy to do it again.'

Looking around at the gathering of the VC winners, Mick picked out other naval holders of the award. He saw Commander D. Cameron, X6, and Commander Place X7, whom Mick was with in the *Tirpitz* exploit, Operation Source. Also in their company was his commanding officer on XE3, Lt. Fraser, in Operation Struggle. Other Army and RAF officers and men were still in their uniforms. The men from the great war wore dark suits and bowler or trilby hats. Some of the much older VC winners moved slowly with the aid of sticks. John Murphy remembers the grand occasion:

Mick with other VC winners with silver tankards presented to them during
the Victory Anniversary Reunion and Victoria Cross Centenary.
(from the left) Lt. Col. H.M. Ervine-Andrews (1940 Dunkirk – East Lancs Rg.), Robert Quigg
(1916, Hamel, France - Royal Irish Rifles), Brigadier J.A. Sinton (1916, Mesopotamia - Indian
Medical Service) and Robert Scott (1900, S. Africa - First Bt, Manchester Rg.)

When Jim (Mick) attended this parade and also others I was always given leave from my Post Office job to attend. Once I remember him standing beside the New Zealander Capt. Upham who won two VCs during World War II.

It is interesting to note the low profile Mick took when he left Northern Ireland to live in England. He could not be found and he was even presumed dead. Rumours and some local newspaper articles assumed there was a lost VC winner living in the Yorkshire area. However his recent sad experience in Northern Ireland did not let him drop his Irish identity as this letter written to a local newspaper confirms:

> June 4th 1956
> James J. Magennis
> 17 Beech Road
> Rossington, Doncaster

Dear Sir,
Many thanks for your letter of the 1st June. I will certainly be present at the Centenary Celebrations and have intimated as such to the War Office quite some time ago. So perhaps when you made your

query they had assumed I was English as I had applied from an English address.

However this will clear things up and I will be definitely attending with my wife and will be there for the best part of a week.

Yours sincerely,
James J. Magennis

Having moved home from Rossington in the late 1950s, Mick, his wife Edna and two sons moved to Exe Street and later Newtown Street in Bradford. In the late 50s another son was born called Michael and Mick found employment as an electrical and television engineer with a firm in Bradford. David Frances of the *Daily Mail* sought Mick out at the time and wrote:

The hero in the cloth cap called quietly over the bar, 'Pint of bitter please'. The landlord at the new inn was pleased to see him. 'Mick, the telly's gone. Can you fix it?' Mick Magennis the telly repair man was well known in the small world round Manchester Road, Bradford. But Mick Magennis VC was almost unknown. 'That's the way I like it', he said, quietly sipping his pint in near obscurity. Sixteen years had passed since that eventful day in July 1945. Only the way he wore his cloth cap, Pussers-style, as ordered in the seaman's Bible, the Admiralty Seamanship Manual, reminded the journalist of the swash-buckling sailor who stirred the hearts in 1945. Even his talk had changed. Then it had been tots of rum, of bars and beer, and girls and runs ashore with his oppos (friends). Now it was of broken tellys and tomato growing, of his wife Edna and boys, their home and the garden, of family life. The reason for the change is typical of many men. Its simple. 'I'm 42. I have settled down.' Family man Magennis had bought his own house, was keen to get on as a TV engineer, was happy to get his feet up these dark winter nights. He only visited the local pub when friends called.

'I get a bottle in now and again from the corner shop. That's enough for me now. Things were much different shortly after the war. I had been kindly presented with many gifts by the people of Belfast. My family and friends lived it up for a few years since that's what a gift is for anyway, not to hoard away in some bank. Life is too short and I was only one of the lucky ones who survived the war. Many of my oppos and boys I served with at HMS *Ganges* never made it home. They are all still in the big drink at the bottom of the sea.'

Mick Magennis at the Royal Navy Submarine
Research Museum, Gosport, Hampshire–
standing in front of the midget submarine X24.

Mick Magennis has a chat with the Queen, Jubilee year, 1977.

The Magennis family visit the Submarine Museum 1982

THE FINAL YEARS

Mick had continued to receive official recognition as a VC winner. In 1962 Queen Elizabeth had also invited holders of the VC to attend a garden party at Buckingham Palace. This was a splendid occasion since it was as long ago as 1920 that the VCs were last invited to the Palace. Mick also attended annual reunions of the Victoria Cross and George Cross holders. Admiral Place VC , X7, who later became President of the HMS *Ganges* Association, and Lt.Fraser VC, XE3 were also present. Unfortunately, Commander Cameron VC, X6, the fourth special service award winner, had died the previous year at Haslar Naval Hospital. He was buried at sea from his submarine.

By 1969 the electrical firm closed down. He was 49 and made redundant. He told the *Daily Telegraph* (21 July, 1969):

It is the first time I have been on the dole, drawing £12 a week. I hit on hard times after the war in Belfast and parted with my VC medal. It was bought back for me by a well-wisher, but no matter how hard times get now I will not part with it again. All I want is a quiet life. And when I go for a job I don't play on the fact I have a VC.

Later, he found work in an electrical firm for a number of years and moved to live in Greenwood Avenue, Bradford. Finally in 1982 he was made redundant. He was a sick man with chest complaints and at sixty-two was not to work again. In 1976 in a new housing estate in Gosport, Hants, fourteen streets were named after the fourteen submarine VCs recipients of both world wars. At the submarine base in Rosyth, Scotland, sheds at the dockyard are all named after the fourteen First and Second World War VC winners. The following year was the queen's silver jubilee and all VCs were presented with a jubilee medal.

CROSSING THE BAR

Magennis's final years saw him involved in another battle requiring a different kind of courage and endurance; the struggle against acute bronchitis. He finally succumbed to the disease on Wednesday 12 February 1986 in Halifax Infirmary at the age of sixty-six. Just before this, his heroism was honoured by the issue of a special first day stamp cover by the Royal Naval philatelic officer at Yeovilton in Somerset. He had been looking forward to the stamps being issued and had signed more than one thousand personally.

Along with family and friends, Lt. Cdr. Ian Fraser VC, Mr Bob Pounder, national chairman of the Submarine Old Comrades Association, and Captain Wood, Naval Regional Officer were at the funeral. The Revd. Alan Kitchen, Vicar of Manningham, conducted the service, paying tribute to Belfast born Magennis, who lived most of his life in Bradford. He showed a great sense of loyalty to the country he loved, said Mr Kitchen.

At his memorial service in Bradford Cathedral in October 1986, the Submarine Old Comrade Association (West Riding Branch) erected a plaque in remembrance of him. The plaque made of Welsh slate was supplied and installed by ex-submariner Tommy Topham MBE. Rear Admiral Place VC, CB, CVO, DSC unveiled it in a brief but moving ceremony in which he paid tribute to Leading Seaman James Magennis VC. Petty Officer Nat Gould VC was also there and one ex-submariner, Mr Gerry Haigh, the only representative from Belfast Royal Naval Association, was able to come over from Belfast to attend the memorial service. John Murphy remembers that sad but proud day:

> Both Eddie McIntyre and myself (his two school friends) were sad but proud to be asked by Bradford City Council to attend the wonderful memorial service at Bradford Cathedral. It was a tribute to a great wee man in every sense. Eddie and myself were called to the side chapel to witness the exposure of his great achievement. Pride and sorrow were the emotions at the time and still remain to this day.

As so often happens, death transformed Magennis: some expressed regret while others adopted a more generous attitude. Gerry Haigh, told the *Belfast Telegraph* (17 October 1986):

> It would be good and proper that James's home city should honour his name. I'd say Belfast should have paid its respects before anyone else thought of it.

Ireland's leading daily, the *Irish Times* (10 December 1986), under the headline 'Belfast War Hero Ignored, Remembered in Bradford,' noted:

> James Magennis who left his home in Belfast thirty years ago to live in Yorkshire was commemorated at a service in the Anglican Cathedral in Bradford on Sunday without any official recognition from his native city.

Rear Admiral Place VC, Nat Gould VC and the Lord Mayor of Bradford at the Memorial Service to Mick Magennis in 1986.

Plaque of rememberance in Bradford Cathedral

A year later, the *Belfast Telegraph* (27 March 1987) said:

The current edition of the *Navy News* describes James Magennis as Bradford's only naval VC. However you can't blame Bradford for claiming him as its own and the *Navy News* for recording how the city feels about a courageous wartime sea-dog, for Belfast appears to have forgotten him. You'd think somebody would have got round to putting up a memorial to the man in his home town before now.

Every year at Remembrance Day, James' three sons Paul, James and Michael, attend Bradford Cathedral. There they hold a service in memory of their Dad, submariner, and former *Ganges* boy.

In 1976, HMS *Ganges* closed its gates for the last time. Since the establishment opened at the beginning of the century 200,000 boys and 'hostilities', had been trained to serve in ships of HM Royal Navy. Many gave their lives for the freedom of others in two world wars and in other conflicts. In World War II, 100,000 Royal Navy and Merchant Navy men lost their lives. In April 1996 over one thousand *Ganges* boys and men attended a twenty year reunion. Bill McGinnes now aged eighty was there to represent his brother James Magennis. (*Ganges* 1935)

HMS *Ganges*, West Yorkshire Group 1994.
(second from left) Sect. Norman R Wilson. *(far right)* Bill McGinnes

EPILOGUE

During World War II only three junior ratings were awarded the Victoria Cross: Able Seaman Savage at St Nazaire and Leading Seaman Mantle on board the auxiliary cruiser *Foylebank*. Both died in action, which left Leading Seaman Magennis the only junior rating to win a VC and survive World War II. This must have been a tremendous burden, and being of a quiet nature, adulation was probably an embarrassment to him. Officers who survived the war and stayed in the service usually climbed the steps of promotion and their rank protected them from jealous and resentful remarks coming from fellow shipmates. This was not the case for Magennis on the lower deck. The Cross did not protect him from spiteful remarks, even if his award aroused fierce national, country, local and family pride. It generated frantic newspaper correspondence. Everybody wanted to pass comment, applaud or attack. In such an atmosphere, hearsay quickly became fact. An unchecked newspaper cutting with wholly imaginary information can become accepted research material. After his last experience in Belfast one can imagine his relief to resettle in Yorkshire and become just a quiet little Irishman from Belfast.

It is over fifty years since that remarkable day in Ebor Street when everyone celebrated his achievement but few people in Belfast remember James Magennis today. Yet he was an ambassador for his native city and he brought both sections from the religious divide together, however briefly. They all had gone through a terrible war and many lost loved ones. James Magennis returned to Belfast in 1949 when the euphoria at the end of the war was evaporating and Northern Ireland was once again setting hard into its old ways. The Belfast that Magennis returned home to was a city where attitudes had been hardened and polarised by the declaration of the Republic of Ireland and the passing of the Government of Ireland Act in 1949. To the Protestant Unionist authorities having a war hero from Catholic Nationalist West Belfast, if not an embarrassment, certainly did not fit in with how they preferred to remember the 'Ulster' war effort.

James Magennis VC became a religious and political pawn and the first chance to disparage him and his award came on the day he sold his VC for £75. The press of the day backed by the powers-that-be made sure the world was going to know about it: front page coverage 'Frogman gets his VC back', *Belfast Telegraph*, Thursday 18 September 1952. When James Magennis left Northern Ireland to settle in the north of England they were delighted to see him go. So too were hard-line Irish nationalists. What his award stood for contradicted their cherished beliefs.

FREEDOM FOR VC RAISED AT CORPORATION

His commanding officer was given the recognition and freedom of his own borough of Wallasey in England. This was not to be the case in Belfast. During another meeting at Belfast City Hall concerning the homecoming of Mick Magennis, a proposal was made to the Corporation by Councillor Clark Scott; the *Belfast Newsletter and Northern Whig* of 4 December 1945 records:

> The city has conferred the freedom of the City on many notable personages and now you have the opportunity of honouring one of the common people. Leading Seaman Magennis has performed a great feat and his heroism should be recognised by the citizens. I move that the General Purposes Committee should consider the question of conferring the Freedom.
> The Lord Mayor, Sir Crawford McCullagh replied to Councillor Scott:
> 'The General Purpose Committee will consider it. They will do it without your asking.'
> Scott replied:
> 'But I am not a member of that committee and I am entitled to move the motion.'
> The Lord Mayor:
> 'That is not how the freedom of the city is conferred.'
> Councillor Clark Scott:
> 'But this is Mr Magennis, not Alexander or Montgomery.'
> The matter was dropped.

The Lord Mayor was also the Grand Master of the County of Belfast Grand Orange Lodge. The reason for his snub against Councillor Scott was because previously in his own room along with other Unionist Councillors he had decided what award to give Leading Seaman Magennis and it was to be his own contrivance, not the freedom of the city nor anything voted by the Corporation. This was the shilling fund,

> supported by workers in the city firms large and small. The subscription limit was to be £1. The reason for this, some of larger contributions might deter others from giving more modest terms. The first person to give to the fund was Miss T. Gatey, Lismain Street, Belfast. She gave a shilling. (*Belfast Telegraph*, 19 November 1945)

The Lord Mayor set himself up as treasurer and eventually a total of £3,066, collected by the ordinary people, was presented to their VC hero. It does not seem likely that the Lord Mayor and his councillors ever thought that such a large sum would be collected, with money so scarce so shortly after the war. What did it say for the Corporation who had refused him freedom of the city and instead left it to the people to collect money for him? Why did the Lord Mayor and the majority of his council rebuff him when he had just been awarded the highest honour by the king? The answer lay in differences of 'class' and 'creed'. Sir Crawford McCullagh and his Unionist councillors did not agree with Queen Victoria's choice of award going to an ordinary Catholic, not withstanding the VC register's own description of the award as one which 'bore no religious significance and contained no rank within itself, to be highly prized and eagerly sought after by officers and men of the crowned armed forces'. At the time and since the Belfast authorities could not bring themselves to consider a fitting tribute to Mick Magennis.

'HE DIDN'T DO IT FOR IRELAND'

The tragedy was that not only was James Magennis from an ordinary background and the wrong religion to receive the Freedom of the City but neither was he respected by the very community in which he was born and raised. Gerry Oates, the boy in the classroom of St Finian's school, today a school teacher himself, recalls:

'I was a nine year old pupil in St Finian's school on the Falls Road the day that James Magennis returned to visit us after receiving his VC and I have been affected by that visit ever since.'

He remembers his master describing Magennis's bravery that cold December morning back in 1945:

The master recounted in detail how brave the young man who had
sat in those very seats had been; 'Bravery beyond the call of duty,
they describe it', said the master. 'He is a brave man, nobody can
deny that, but,' and there was a tremor in his voice, 'he didn't do it
for Ireland'. The class sat in silence. Not a hand was raised to ask the
usual questions. We sat there expectantly, proud and strangely sad at
the same time.

COMMEMORATION AND REMEMBRANCE

He did not do it for Ireland nor for Ulster nor for Belfast; he did it for
twenty-two Allied countries. It should also be remembered that he won
his Victoria Cross while under the command of Admiral Fife USN and
so was in fact fighting for the USA–in other words for the country to
which nationalists today look for support. His commanding officer was
also awarded the American Officer's Legion of Honour Medal.

During World War II, 42,973 from the Irish Republic joined the
British armed forces, as well as 100,000 men and women who worked in
munitions factories to help in the war effort. Although there was no con-
scription in Northern Ireland, 39,000 enlisted. Travelling recently
through the Republic, it was heartening to notice memorials erected in
towns and villages to pay homage to many of those men and women who
died in World War II serving with the Allies. The southerners who
entered military service in World War II won a total of 780 decorations
including five Victoria Crosses.

TRAPPED BY HISTORY

To understand the predicament that Magennis was in and the reactions
to him, we must remember that Northern Ireland is a place of political
turmoil and sharply divided allegiances, fractured along religious and
political lines. A history stretching back four hundred years, to the
Plantation of Ulster, still holds the north of Ireland in its grip, meaning
that no one is judged on his merit as a human being–or as a war
hero–but on what tribe he belongs to. For the Unionist establishment
who dominated Northern Ireland since Partition in 1920, the hallmark
of acceptability and individual worth was the Protestant religion and the
Orange Order.

Both the Unionist Party and the Orange Order had made great play
of the part played by Ulstermen in World War I. The deaths of many

Protestant men of the 36th (Ulster) Division, particularly at the Battle of the Somme, is still important to the unionist community to this day. That these were Ulster Protestants dying for the British Empire is emphasised to the exclusion of Catholics who did the same. A stone memorial tablet was installed in St Anne's Cathedral, Belfast, to all the 36th (Ulster) Division VC winners from the 1914-18 Great War. No cathedral in Great Britain is used as a regimental church as is St Anne's in Belfast, yet it is not attached to any army barracks. In this cathedral lies the grave of Sir Edward Carson one of the founders of the new Protestant state. In Carson's new state all political support came from religious division.

In such a situation, the Unionist establishment had no place for a Catholic hero. This is one reason why Magennis was so unsettled in Belfast after the war. It is also the reason why to this day Unionist politicians–those on Belfast City Council–find it hard to acknowledge the achievements of a hero who was neither Protestant nor Orange.

Yet Magennis found no comfort from among his own people nor in the Republic. The development of Irish nationalism was based on the glorification of those men who rose in rebellion against British rule in Ireland, particularly those who fought in the War of Independence 1916-1922. It was they who were remembered and honoured. Those who had served in the British armed forces were written out of history and ignored, if not condemned outright as 'traitors to Ireland'. If the North had room only for heroes who were Protestant and Orange, the South wanted only those who were nationalist and more often than not Catholic.

One writer, Pól O Muirí, has noted

> that amongst Nationalists there is a great ambiguity towards remembering openly any Catholics who died fighting in the British armed forces...The case of James Magennis who was awarded the Victoria Cross for his actions against the Japanese Navy during World War II is a case in point. Indeed, Magennis's deeds also seem to have given some Unionists cause for concern challenging as they do the common sectarian stereotype of 'disloyal' Catholics. (*Causeway*, Autumn 1997)

So it is that trapped by a heritage of bitterness and hatred, Magennis, and those like him, were banished to a no-man's land, remembered by all but a few with embarrassment or derision. After his three days of glory in Belfast amidst the post-war euphoria, only in England was he seen simply as a war hero and honoured as such.

THE WINDS OF CHANGE

However, the winds of change are blowing through Ireland, clearing away the cobwebs of the mind and the dust on memories. The Irish government holds ceremonies for Irishmen who served in both World wars, showing that the Republic has changed its attitude towards men like Mick Magennis who served with the Allied Forces in the World War II. Those living in the Republic are now able to talk openly of their fathers and grandfathers who fought or died in British uniform in two world wars. Yet on the northern side of the border attitudes frozen in time are thawing much more slowly. An ex-pupil of St Finian's wrote to the *Belfast Telegraph* on 6 July 1984:

> On June 20th featured on the main news on ITV at 1.00 pm and 10.00 pm was a school on the Falls Road, St Finian's Boys, concluding the story it was mentioned that Gerry Adams (leader of Sinn Féin) was a former pupil, however what was not mentioned was another former pupil who merited a few lines, James Magennis of Majorca Street who was awarded the Victoria Cross in the 1939-45 war.

Here was another ex-pupil who felt deeply proud of James Magennis and he had to wait forty years to be able to express his feelings.

Majorca Street in West Belfast, where Magennis was born is now a carpark. The children today know nothing about James Magennis, but they are still playing in Dunville Park as they did in his day. I was there recently and as I left the park, I thought I heard a Belfast children's song from James Magennis' boyhood days:

> She is handsome, she is pretty.
> She is the girl from Belfast city.
> She is courting, one, two, three.
> Please won't you tell who is she?

CAMPAIGN FOR A MEMORIAL

Inspired by Magennis's achievement, the author undertook to try to persuade Belfast City Council to give belated but due recognition to this son of the city. In 1995, a letter writing campaign began directed at the councillors and also to local and national newspapers in order to arouse an interest in Northern Ireland's only VC winner and gather support for a memorial. After two years of campaigning (some newspaper article headings - see Appendix four)–a story that must be told elsewhere–in February 1997, the Belfast City Council voted to erect a suitable memorial to James Magennis VC.

The James Magennis memorial will be the first ever erected by Belfast City Council to a Catholic from a common background. The last memorial erected in the City Hall grounds was on 26 January 1943 when a Portland stone column was dedicated to the arrival of the American Expeditionary Force. It was rededicated by President William Jefferson Clinton on 30 November 1995 when he visited Northern Ireland. It is presumed that the James Magennis memorial will also be of Portland stone and will be erected, as is the American memorial, beside the statue of Queen Victoria at the entrance to the Belfast City Hall. Both memorials together will symbolise Britain and USA's joint fight against fascism during World War II, one that will mark the beginning of a process of reconciliation between the two communities in a divided city.

GLOSSARY OF NAVAL RANKS, TERMS & ABBREVIATIONS

LOWER DECK JUNIOR RATES

1st and 2nd class	Boy seaman
OD	Ordinary seaman
AB	Able seaman
HO	Hostilities only
Killick	Leading rating
Jaunty	Leading regulating rating
GI	Gunnery instructor
Jack dusty	Stores rating
	(Different ranks)
PTI	Physical training instructor
RM	Royal Marine
	(Different ranks)
LTO	Leading torpedo rating
LEM	Leading electrical mechanic

SENIOR RATES

PO	Petty Officer
CPO	Chief Petty Officer
ERA	Engine Room Artificer
	(Different branch names are added to rank)
RPO	Regulating Petty Officer
Master at arms	Chief Regulating Officer

UPPER DECK

OOD	Officer of the day
CO	Commanding officer
DO	Divisional officer
WO	Warrant officer
Midshipman	Junior officer
Sub Lt.	Sub lieutenant
Lt.	Lieutenant
Lt. Cdr.	Lieutenant commander
Cdr.	Commander
Capt.	Captain
VICE/REAR.	Admiral
	Admiral of the fleet

AWARDS WORLD WAR 11

UPPER DECK

CBE	Commander of the British Empire
DSO	Distinguished Service Order
DSC	Distinguished Service Cross
OBE	Order of the British Empire
MBE	Member of the British Empire

LOWER DECK

CGM	Conspicious Gallantry Medal
DSM	Distinguished Service Medal
BEM	British Empire Medal

UPPER AND LOWER DECK

GC	George Cross
VC	Victoria Cross

NAVAL TERMS

Green rub	Hard luck story
Jolly Jack Tar	Sailor dressed up in his best suit
Rattle	In trouble with senior officers
Devil's elbow	dangerous part of mast
Kye	Hot choccolate drink
Pussers hard	Navy soap
Pusser	Anything owned by the Navy
Lash up	Tie up
Stonakie	Rope end
Ho	Halt
Rabbits	Presents to bring home
Dhobey	Wash one's clothes
Brag-tags	Campaign medals
Oppo	Friend
Faith hope and charity	Three rows of steps used for running up and down when under punishment (Shotley routine)
Shotley routine	Class punishment *Ganges* Style
Poteen	Illegal alcoholic drink
RIC	Royal Irish Constabulary
Scrambled egg	Gold leaf on senior officers' caps

216

BIBLIOGRAPHY

After the Battle No 55: U–Boats, Battle of Britain Prints.

Captain W. R. Fell CMG, CBE, DSC, RN, *The Sea our Shield*, Cassell, London.

End of the Second World War, The Commemoration of VE Day and VJ Day, DOE, Northern Ireland.

Maurice Cocker, *Destroyers of the Royal Navy 1893-1981*, Ian Allen Ltd., Shepperton, London.

C.E.T. Warren and James Benson, *Above Us The Waves*, George G. Harrap and Co. Ltd., London.

Ian Fraser VC, *Frogman VC*, Purnell & Sons Ltd., London.

Waldron and Gleeson, *The Frogmen*, Pan Books Ltd., London.

John Winton, *The VC at Sea*, Michael Joseph Ltd.

Paul J. Kemp, *Midget Submarines*, Arms and Armour Press, London.

Edward Young, DSO DSC, *One of our Submarines Penguin Books* The Whitefriars Press Ltd. London.

Alister Mars DSO DSC and BAR, *Submarines at War*, Corgi Books Transworld Publishers Ltd London.

James Kelly, *Bonfire on the Hillside*, Fountain Publishing, Belfast.

Jimmy Webb, 'Raglan Street', *Andersonstown News*.

Seedie's List of Submarine Awards for World War Two

Picture Post 1940 Vol 9 No 1, Vol 9 No 9, Vol 5 No 13, 1939

Illustrated 3 July 1954

Belfast Telegraph

Belfast News Letter

Daily Express and Sunday Express

Irish News

Andersonstown News

Northern Whig

Evening Courier, Halifax, Yorkshire, West Riding.

Navy News July 1991

The HMS Ganges Association Gazettes, 1989-1996

SOCA News, the newsletter of the Submarine Old Comrades.

APPENDIX I

THE VICTORIA CROSS

In Hyde Park in London on 26 June 1857, sixty-two officers and service-men of Britain's army, navy and marines stood in line and each one in turn was presented to the Queen of England who pinned onto the lapel of their jacket uniforms a new award for valour named after herself, the Victoria Cross. The first man to win this award for valour was Midshipman Lucas on board HMS *Hecla* in the Baltic on 21 June 1854 during the Crimean War. Charles David Lucas was born in Drumargole, County Armagh, Ireland on 19 February 1834. He became a Rear Admiral and died at the age of eighty at Great Culverden, Kent on 7 August 1914 and a memorial to this first VC winner can be seen at St Lawrence's Church, Mereworth near Maidstone, Kent. Another one of these sixty-two men was Cdr. Talbot Burgoyne who had just been appointed executive officer in January of that year to the battleship of line HMS *Ganges* which was waiting to sail on its last commission in the Pacific.

HMS *GANGES'* FIVE VCs

Cdr. Burgoyne had won his VC with three others during the Crimean War at the Sea of Azov in June 1855. He was serving on board the eight gun steam sloop *Swallow* as senior lieutenant. The three other VC winners in the said action were Lt. Buckley and Boatswain Cooper on board the four-teen gun steam corvette *Miranda* and Gunner Robarts of HMS *Ardent*. Later during HMS *Ganges'* career four more VC winners served on board the ship and later the training establishment of that name. The second was Surgeon Capt. Maillard VC who served on the ship in 1898. Before and after World War II three more VC recipients were to have their names associated with *Ganges*: Second Class Boy Seaman Magennis who served as a boy under training 1935-36 won his VC in 1945, Lt. Cdr. Cameron VC Divisional Officer 1948-50 and Captain Place VC (later Rear Admiral), Captain of HMS *Ganges* 1962-64. Both these officers won their awards in 1943. Before 1856 awards such as the Order of the Garter, the Order of the Bath, Knighthoods or Companionage were awarded only to the upper ranks of military and naval officers for services rendered to the Crown.

The Victoria Cross was in 1857 a new award for valour where rank was unimportant. Bravery in the field of action over and beyond the call of duty was its only qualification. The award for valour therefore was a cross or medal for every man. All persons were on equal footing. Neither rank nor long service nor wounds nor anything else save conspicuous bravery would qualify a man for the Victoria Cross. When the new medal was being designed Queen Victoria took great interest. She also voiced her opinion in the original warrant on 26 January 1856. 'There was no way of adequately rewarding the individual gallant services either of officers of the lower grades in our naval and military service or of warrant and petty officers, seamen and marines in our navy, and non-commissioned officers and soldiers in our army.'

The Queen's decision to have the motto 'for valour' rather than 'for the brave' was accepted during the design process. A total of 1,354 Victoria Crosses have been awarded to all three services since 1857. During World War II five VCs were won by officers and men from Éire: they were Captain H.M. Ervine-Andrews (Dunkirk), Fly/Officer D.E. Garland (Maastricht), Captain J.B. Jackman (Tobruk), Private R. Kelliher (New Guinea) and Flight Lt. D.S. Lord (Arnhem). One hundred and twenty-four Royal Navy officers and men have received the award. Twenty-three VCs were awarded to naval officers and men in World War II and are mentioned in this book. Nine of them were from the submarine service. Only three junior ratings were awarded the VC during World War II, two of whom died in action, Able Seaman Savage and Leading Seaman Mantle. The third and last was to survive the war. He was ex *Ganges* boy J. J. Magennis VC. Since Midshipman Lucas won his VC on 21 June 1854, Leading Seaman Magennis was the 163rd and last Irishman to date to win a Victoria Cross on 30 July 1945.

James Magennis was the second winner of the VC to come from Belfast. The first, Private Patrick Carlin, has long been forgotten. Carlin was born in Belfast in 1832 and was serving with the Somerset Light Infantry, Prince Albert's own regiment, during the Indian Mutiny. He won his VC on 6 April 1858, when he went out to rescue a Naik (an Indian soldier) of the 4th Madras Rifles. After killing an enemy sepoy, he carried the wounded naik back to safety. He was presented with his cross by General Sir Colin Campbell. Carlin returned to Belfast after his service with the army and spent his later years at 47 Ward Street in the Falls/Grosvenor Road area. He died on 11 May 1895 in the Workhouse Union Infirmary, which today is the City Hospital. He is believed to be buried in Friar's Bush cemetery behind the Ulster

Museum in an unmarked grave in the paupers' plot. His VC was sold in 1903 for £63.

SUBMARINES & FIVE VC AWARDS IN WORLD WAR I

During World War I the submarine service was awarded five Victoria Crosses. Four of these were won during hostilities against Turkey and in that area ten British and Australian submarines sank two battleships, one destroyer, one gunboat, seven transport troopships and 197 other ships. The first ever submarine VC was awarded to Lt. Holbrook on B11 when he sank the Turkish battleship *Messudiyeh* on 13 December 1914 at the Dardenelles. The second was to Lt. Boyle on board E14 in April/May 1915, in the Sea of Marmara. *E14* sank a 5,000 ton troop ship with 6,000 Turkish soldiers on board. The third was to Lt. Cdr. Smith on E11. He sank no fewer than eleven ships and the battleship *Heweddin Barbarosa*. The fourth VC was won by Lt. Cdr. White who was the new commander of E14 in the Dardenelles. In 1918 E14 was scuttled and White lost his life. There were fourteen survivors who became POWs. The last was won at Zeebrugge when Lt. Stanford on board the old submarine C3 rammed the viaduct. He set the fuses and the crew made their escape on board the destroyer HMS *Phoebe*. His second in command, Lt. Howell-Price was awarded a DSO and three crew members were each awarded the CGM. Sadly Stanford, who received his award from the king in July 1918, died of typhoid on 23 November 1918 in Cleveland Hospital, Grangetown, Yorkshire.

At the outbreak of the Great War the submarine was still a weapon of unknown capabilities. However their unrestricted use against commercial shipping was, in the words of Lord Jellicoe, 'the greatest peril which ever threatened the population of this country'. Germany realised this and between September 1916 and January 1917, 170 Norwegian, 29 Swedish and 50 Danish ships were destroyed by U-boats. Eighty-six British ships were sunk in home waters. In September and October 1917 Norway lost 5 per cent of her mercantile fleet. Methods of protection of a convoy and the use of Q-ships were hastily devised. These methods helped but by the end of the 1914–18 war, 5,408 British, Allied and neutral vessels were sunk by submarines.

APPENDIX II

THE SAILING SHIP HMS *GANGES*
AND THE MAIN ESTABLISHMENT

The first boys' training ship had been a ship of the line, laid down in Bombay, India in 1821. She was the first English man o' war to be built of teak. Previously ships of the line had been built of oak, but as the traditional 'hearts of oak' became more difficult to obtain (900 oak trees were required to build a first rate ship of the line), India with its vast teak forests provided a plentiful supply of timber. Ships were built for the Royal Navy in India and sailed back to England where they were fitted out with the necessary ordnance transforming them to men o' war, ready to take up their role in defence of the realm. HMS *Ganges* completed active service as flag ship on the South Atlantic Station. She became the last British sailing ship to carry a flag officer and indeed was the last British man o' war and ship of the line to round Cape Horn under sail.

After four years on the reserve list, HMS *Ganges* became a RN boys training ship based at Falmouth in 1866. Before this time in the eighteenth century boys as young as ten went to sea. Nelson himself went to sea as a boy of twelve.

Brutality was a way of life which touched pressed men, boys and regular volunteers alike. It did not differentiate between them. By the age of thirty lower deck ratings were past their best. Many suffered from wounds received in battle. Disease, such as scurvy, and the harsh living conditions aboard a man o'war took their toll.

RULES FOR THE GUIDANCE OF BOYS

(1) On first entry boys are to make themselves acquainted with the Printed Orders posted up in the Establishment for their information, a careful consideration of which will prevent their getting into trouble.

(2) Boys letters are to be addressed with their Christian and Surnames in full: their number on Ships Books and the number of their Mess being written underneath their names.

(3) Silence is to be kept after lights out. Boys are to turn out smartly when the hands are called in the morning.

(4) Prompt and unquestioning obedience to orders is essential. Talking and skylarking when on duty or when fallen in are forbidden.

(5) Should boys ever require any information or advice upon any subject what-
ever, they should go to their Instructors or the Officers of their Division.

(6) Boys are on no account to enter any of the Ships Company quarters.

(7) Watches, articles of value and any sum in excess of 2/6d are at once to be
taken to the Regulating Office to be turned over to the Accountant Officer
for safe custody.

(8) Any boy receiving a postal order is immediately to take it to the Mail Office
to be stamped and cash it at the Canteen at the first opportunity. He is
never to retain more than 2/6d in his possession.

(9) Boys are prohibited from procuring clothes, knife-lanyards or other articles
of their kit, or cigarettes and matches, either from their friends or by pur-
chase on shore and all such articles found in their possession will be con-
fiscated. Boys are not to carry knives.

(10) During leave on shore boys are forbidden to enter public houses or clothes
dealers shops: they are not to lounge about or assemble in groups in the
streets or pathways. They are not to trespass but keep to the highways and
public paths.

(11) A boy missing any article of his clothing however small should at once
report the fact to the Instructor of his class: and anything found is to be
taken without delay to the Regulating Office. It is regarded as a serious
offence for a boy to be in possession of any gear belonging to another boy.

(12) Boys are on no account to alter their uniform. They should always appear
neatly dressed and keep their clothes well marked, properly made up and
stowed away.

(13) Borrowing or lending money or private property (including article of kit)
or any form of exchanging, selling, or giving away, is forbidden.

(14) Fighting, quarrelling, gambling, tattooing, bad language and the use of
intoxicating liquors are forbidden.

(15) No boy is to leave his class or place of duty without first obtaining permission from the Instructor or whoever is in charge. Any boy wishing to report
sick is to report the fact to his Instructor.

(16) Boys should never break their leave, or abuse privileges and must remember that by being steady they will not only avoid getting themselves into
trouble, but will be doing what they can to ensure future success in life.

APPENDIX III

General service ships Mick Magennis served on
before and during the war 1936 – 1942

HMS *Royal Sovereign* was one of five battleships built 1914 - 1916, 29,150 tons. She served in both world wars and went on loan to the Soviet Navy in 1944. On her return in 1949 she went to the breakers yard at Inverkeithing. Sister ships: *Royal Oak, Revenge, Resolution* and *Ramillies.*

HMS *Dauntless* was one of eight cruisers built 1917 - 1919, 4,850 tons. Served throughout the World War II. She went to the breakers yard at Inverkeithing in 1946. Sister ships: *Dispatch, Delhi, Durban, Diomede, Dunedin* and *Dragon.*

HMS *Enterprise* was one of two cruisers built 1919 - 1920, 7,550 tons. Served throughout World War II. She went to the breakers yard in 1946 at Newport. Sister ship: *Emerald.*

HMS *Hermes*, aircraft carrier built 1919, 12,000 tons. She was sunk on 9 April 1942 off Ceylon by Japanese aircraft.

HMS *Kandahar* was one of eight destroyers built 1937-39. 1,690 tons. She hit a mine off Tripoli 19 December 1941 and was sunk next day by HMS *Jaguar.* Sister ships: *Kelly, Kashmir, Kelvin, Khartoum, Kingston, Kipling* and *Kimberley. Kelvin* and *Kimberley* were scrapped at Troon in 1949.

Ships Bill McGinnes served on

HMS *Hostile*, one of nine destroyers built 1935-37, 1,505 tons. Struck a mine and sank off Malta 23 August 1940. Sister ships: *Hardy, Hasty, Havock, Hereward, Hero, Hotspur, Hunter, Hyperion.* Seven were lost in action.

HMS *Electra*, one of nine destroyers built 1933-34, 1,375 tons. Sank in action (Battle of the Java Sea), 27 February 1942. Sister ships: *Echo, Eclipse, Encounter, Escapade, Escort, Esk, Exmouth, Express.*

HMS *Renown*, one of two battle cruisers built 1916, 32,000 tons. Sister ship: *Repulse* sunk 10 December 1941. *Renown* was scrapped 4 March 1946, Faslane, Scotland.

HMS *Vanquisher* (Admiralty V class), one of twenty-eight destroyers built 1917, 1,090 tons, 34 knots, was scrapped after the war.

HMS *Manxman* (Fast mine-laying cruiser). Sister ships: *Abdiel, Apollo, Ariadne, Latonia, Welshman.*

APPENDIX IV

NEWSPAPER COVERAGE OF THE MEMORIAL CAMPAIGN

'Old sea-dog in navy showdown', John McGurk, *Sunday World*, 15/6/97

'Man kicked out of navy club after he backs Catholic VC,' John McGurk, *Sunday World*, 8/6/97

'VC Honoured,' *The Times*, 10/2/97

'VC hero snubbed claims nonsense,' W.J. Martin Cdr. RN (Rtd), Chairman, Newcastle Branch, Royal British Legion, *News Letter*, 5/2/97

'Victory at last in tribute over Catholic VC,' George Fleming, *Sunday World*, 5/2/97

'Sweet victory,' John Breslin, *Belfast Telegraph*, 5/2/97

'Old shipmates plan to honour Port's solo VC,' Michael Brooks, *Sunday World*, 13/1/97

'Two Honours for Belfast born hero,' Joe Oliver, *Sunday Life*, 26/1/97

'Memorial for hero,' Jim McDowell, *Sunday World*, 26/1/97

'City honours snubbed war hero at last,' Conor Hanna, *The Mirror*, 25/1/97

'Council backing for VC memorial,' Editorial, *News Letter*, 25/1/97

'A belated medal for bravery and friendship,' Jimmy Webb, *Irish News*, 20/1/97

'Letter from the heart,' Editor, *Sunday World*, 19/1/97

'Laoch nach bhfuair a cheart,' Pól Ó Muirí, *The Irish Times*, 8/1/97

'Old sailor calls for Waterfront navy memorial,' Jim McDowell, *Sunday World*, 5/1/97

'Campaign that led to victory for a VC,' George Fleming, *Irish News*, 26/12/96

'Honour hero, pleads veteran,' Editorial, *News Letter*, 21/12/96

'Belfast VC holder honoured in Sub. Museum,' John Monan, *Belfast Telegraph*, 19/12/96

'Cross-party support for monument to VC hero,' Phelim McAleer, *Irish News*, 17/12/96

'Waterfront VC memorial bid,' John Breslin, *Belfast Telegraph*, 16/12/96

'New twist in Ulster naval hero furore,' John Cassidy, *Sunday Life*, 16/12/96

'Castlereagh to honour its forgotten war hero,' Neil Greenless, *The Ulster Star*, 15/12/96

'Riverside site appeal for VC hero memorial,' John Cassidy, *Sunday Life*, 15/12/96

'For what King and country?' Squinter, *Andersonstown News*, 23/11/96

'Cross-party support for monument to VC hero,' Phelim McAleer, *Irish News*, 17/12/96

'Alliance welcomes VC memorial,' Brendan Anderson, *Irish News*, 11/12/96

'Form of memorial to VC heroes not decided,' Councillor Nelson McCausland, *Belfast Telegraph*, 6/12/96

'No sectarianism in the treatment of city's VCs,' Councillor Nelson McCausland, *Irish News*, 3/12/96

'Forgotten hero,' Deputy Editor, *Sunday Life*, 1/12/96

'Belfast finally honours Catholic VC winner,' John Harnden, *The Daily Telegraph*, 28/11/96

'Campaign for Magennis memorial gains pace.' Damian McArdle, *Herald And Post*, 21/11/96

'Navy veteran's bid to honour Catholic VC,' Editorial, *Irish News*, 22/11/96

'Memorial at last to VC holder,' George Fleming, *Belfast Telegraph*, 18/11/96

'City may honour the VC hero it shunned,' Joe Brady, *The People*, 17/11/96

'Shunned Catholic VC to be honoured,' Joe Oliver, *Irish News*, 18/11/96

'Old comrade backs Magennis memorial,' Damian McArdle, *Herald And Post*, 13/11/96

'There are no poppies on this sailor's grave,' George Fleming, *Andersonstown News*, 12/11/96

'VC winner set to be honoured,' Chris Hagan, *Irish News*, 11/11/96

'Tribute overdue for navy man's World War II bravery,' Greg Harkin, *Sunday World*, 10/11/96

'The Lost VC hero,' John Breslin, *Belfast Telegraph*, 9/11/96

'Memorial plea for city's forgotten hero,' Damian McArdle, *Herald And Post*, 6/11/96